# The Book of Deeds of Arms and of Chivalry

# The Book of
# Deeds of Arms
# and of Chivalry

## Christine de Pizan

*Translated by*
Sumner Willard (Brig. Gen., USA, Ret.)

*Edited by*
Charity Cannon Willard

The Pennsylvania State University Press
University Park, Pennsylvania

Library of Congress Cataloging-in-Publication Data


Christine, de Pisan, ca. 1364–ca. 1431.
    [Livre des faits d'armes et de chevalerie. English]
    The book of deeds of arms and of chivalry / Christine de
  Pizan : translated by Sumner Willard : edited by Charity Cannon
  Willard.
        p.    cm.
    Includes bibliographical references and indexes.
    ISBN 0-271-01880-1 (cloth : alk. paper)
    ISBN 0-271-01881-X (pbk. : alk. paper)
    1. Military art and science—Early works to 1800.
  2. English language—Middle English, 1100–1500—Texts.
  3. Military art and science—History—Medieval, 500–1500—
  Sources.    4. Military art and science—History—Medieval,
  500–1500—Sources.    I. Willard, Sumner.    II. Willard,
  Charity Cannon.    III. Title.
  U101.C47413    1999
  355.02—dc21                                    98-41056
                                                    CIP

It is the policy of The Pennsylvania State University Press to use acid-
free paper for the first printing of all clothbound books. Publications
on uncoated stock satisfy the minimum requirements of American
National Standard for Information Sciences—Permanence of Paper
for Printed Library Materials, ANSI Z39.48-1992.

# Contents

# Introduction

I t is unexpected in any era to find a woman writing a book on the art of
warfare, but in the fifteenth century it was altogether unbelievable, so
it is scarcely surprising that until recently Christine de Pizan's *Fais
d'armes et de chevalerie* should have been regarded with a certain disdain,
frequently with the complaint that she was freely pilfering the *De re militari* by the fourth-century roman writer Vegetius, which had already been
translated into French several times during the Middle Ages. A similar
accusation has been made concerning her use of the late-fourteenth-
century *Arbre des batailles* (Tree of battles) by Honoré Bouvet. Although
it is quite true that these are her most important sources, that is far from
the whole story. What she actually wrote is, in any case, not well known,
for since the end of the fifteenth century her book has been available primarily through Antoine Vérard's imprint of 1488 and William Caxton's
translation, entitled *The Book of Fayttes of Armes and of Chyvalrye*,[1] published the following year, a half century after Christine's disappearance
from the scene. Vérard even suggests that the work is his own translation
of Vegetius, making no mention of Christine. Caxton attributes the work
to Christine, but it has never been possible to identify the manuscript he

1. *The Book of Faytes and Armes and of Chyvalerye: Translated and Printed by William Caxton
from the French Original by Christine de Pisan*, ed. A.T.P. Byles, EETS (London: Oxford University
Press, 1932; 1937).

used as the basis for his translation. Both he and Vérard adapted the original text to their own purposes. Even the title was modified in the 1527 imprint made by Phillipe LeNoir, who chose to call it *L'Arbre des batailles et fleur de chevalerie* (The tree of battles and flower of chivalry).

Fortunately three manuscripts exist that are more or less contemporary with the composition of the work, notably Brussels, Bibl. Roy. MS 10476, which is the basis for this translation. This manuscript can be identified as having belonged to the library of the dukes of Burgundy from the period of John the Fearless. Paris, Bibl. Nat. MS fr. 603 also dates from the lifetime of Christine de Pizan, but as it omits all reference to the victory of John the Fearless over the rebellious citizens of Liège, it seems probable that it was copied after 1413, when the duke's political rivals had terminated his leadership in Paris, forcing him to leave. Another manuscript that appeared in a sale recently is also an early copy but bears no indication of its original owner.

Part of the disregard for the book undoubtedly arises from the mistaken expectation that Christine should have produced an entirely original work on chivalry, or perhaps a valid translation of Vegetius in accordance with evolving Renaissance concepts of the art. Little matter that either would have been unlikely to have been her intention. There had, of course, been an astonishing number of translations of Vegetius over the centuries, six in France during the thirteenth and fourteenth centuries. Some 150 manuscripts still exist in a variety of languages, dating from the tenth to the fifteenth centuries. It was first printed in Utrecht in 1473, with imprints soon following from Cologne, Rome, and Paris. It is assumed that Christine used the fourteenth-century translation of Jean de Vignai.[2]

A twentieth-century translation of Vegetius was made in 1944 and published until 1965 in several editions in a series entitled Military Classics. This has recently been superseded by a new translation in a series of Translated Texts for Historians. Why, then, if there were so many translations of Vegetius available even at the beginning of the fifteenth century, would Christine not have used it as the basis for the book she wrote around 1410?

In the first place, it would probably have been quite out of the question to write on the art of warfare without reference to Vegetius, and

2. Paul Meyer, "Les Anciens Traducteurs français de Végèce, en particulier Jean de Vignai," *Romania* 25 (1896): 401–23; Josette A. Wisman, "*L'Epitoma rei militaris* de Végèce et sa fortune au Moyen Age," *Moyen Age* 85 (1979): 13–31.

Christine was not alone in undertaking to show how certain ideas from an earlier day were still applicable and useful. It should be remembered also that to the medieval mind the whole concept of chivalry was thought to have originated in Rome.

The primary explanation of Christine's book, however, must be sought in events in France around 1410. Although the country was nominally ruled by Charles VI, this king was incapacitated by ever more frequent spells of mental instability, a situation that encouraged a deadly struggle among his relatives to dominate the government, notably between his brother Louis, duke of Orleans, and his uncle and then his cousin, dukes of Burgundy. Since 1405 the country had been on the verge of civil war, and at the end of 1407 John the Fearless, the second duke of Burgundy, had contrived to bring about the murder of his Orleans cousin. Although he fled from Paris immediately after his complicity in this murder became known, he lost no time in preparing a return to power there. This he achieved after a spectacular victory over the rebellious citizens of Liège, on the frontier of Burgundian territories, at the Battle of Othée in September 1408, a military exploit that testifies to his skill as a military leader. A reference to this victory in Christine's original text is important for dating it.[3]

John the Fearless was one of the few noblemen of his day in French circles who possessed a good sense of military strategy. This was undoubtedly due in part to his early experiences in the Battle of Nicopolis, where the French met defeat from the Turks in 1396. He was one of the few survivors and was released only after a time as a prisoner of the victorious Turks and payment of an enormous ransom. He was also a determined diplomat, for by the end of 1409 not only had he returned to Paris and gained influence over the French queen, Isabeau of Bavaria, but he had been given charge of the twelve-year-old dauphin, Louis of Guyenne, who also happened to be his son-in-law, having been married to his daughter Marguerite in 1405.

From early childhood Louis of Guyenne had been the victim of political rivals who wanted to control him for their own purposes. He was, by all accounts, a spoiled and frivolous youth. On taking charge of his education, the duke of Burgundy immediately surrounded him with advisors

---

3. For this date, see S. Solente, "Christine de Pisan," in *L'Histoire littéraire de la France* (Paris: Imprimerie Nationale, 1969), XL:64. The earliest manuscripts are those mentioned at the beginning of the Introduction: Brussels, Bibl. Roy. MS 10476; Paris, Bibl. Nat. MS fr. 603; and that which has recently been acquired by the French Bibliothèque Nationale.

in whom he had confidence, favorable to Burgundian ambitions, and it was undoubtedly he who thought that Louis should have some education in military leadership. He was, however, by no means alone in his concern for the prince's future, for already in 1405 Jean de Gerson, chancellor of the University of Paris, had written a letter to the prince's tutor outlining a suitable program of reading for his education.[4] In this he lists not only Vegetius, but the Roman history of Valerius Maximus, the *Factorum et dictorum memorabilium libri ix*, which had recently been translated into French by Simon de Hesdin and Nicolas de Gonesse. He also mentions the *Strategemata* of Frontinus, a selection of which formed book VI of the Valerius Maximus translation. It seems scarcely accidental that these texts, along with Honoré Bouvet's *Tree of Battles*, should have been the principal sources of the *Deeds of Arms and of Chivalry*.

Although there is evidence that Christine could read Latin, her usual sources were medieval French translations of Latin texts, all of which would have been available in the Royal Library in the Louvre. Christine's connection with the French court would have given her access to this admirable collection of manuscripts.

It should also be noted that she was not entirely without qualifications for writing such a book. In the *Epître d'Othéa* she had already proposed a moral education for a young knight, and the second part of her biography of Charles V is devoted to a discussion of chivalry. There she develops the idea that Charles V, not noted for his physical prowess, could nevertheless qualify as a military leader, for intelligence in directing military operations is more important than physical prowess in battle. She speaks of four qualities that characterize true chivalry: good fortune, good judgment, diligence, and strength, a standard attributed to Romulus, a concept inspired by Honoré Bouvet. Elsewhere she speaks of the opinion of various authors that it is necessary for military men to have some instruction before undertaking the profession, an idea not widely held in the France of her day.

It has been convincingly suggested that one of the objectives of Philip the Bold, the former duke of Burgundy, in commissioning Christine to write the biography of his brother Charles V, had been to provide the dauphin with a model of kingship, which his father was quite incapable

---

4. A. Thomas, *Jean de Gerson et l'éducation des dauphins de France* (Paris, 1930); Jean Gerson, *Oeuvres complètes*, ed. R. Glorieux (Paris: Desclée, 1962).

of doing. This would appear to be related also to Christine's lifelong interest in educating the young, from her own son to the royal children.

Such an objective is to be seen even more clearly in the *Livre du corps de policie*, addressed to the duke of Guyenne in 1407. Vegetius is an important source here, as he had been already in her long poem the *Chemin de long estude*, written at the end of 1402. In a chapter entitled "Les condiciones que bon chevalier doit avoir selon les dis des auctores" (The qualities a good knight should have according to the words of authorities) she quotes him as well as Valerius Maximus. Several examples cited there reappear in the *Fais d'armes*.

In the *Corps de policie* several chapters of the first part are devoted to the duties of kings or princes as military leaders, but the second part discusses in detail the role in society of the military class, the arms and the hands of the body politic.

In spite of these earlier works, however, it is evident at the beginning of the *Fais d'armes* that Christine was somewhat embarrassed by such an undertaking, so she takes refuge behind the figure of Minerva, who, according to mythology, as she had already explained in the *Cité des dames*, had invented the art of forging metal armor. After this beginning, however, the book devotes itself more to reality than to mythology. Along with citing examples from the Roman past, it addresses contemporary problems. There is special emphasis on Roman organization and discipline, qualities all too often overlooked in the Middle Ages, when knights were striving above all for personal glory. Christine's advice, however, is not intended exclusively for knights, for she makes it clear that she is speaking to all military men, some of whom are quite incapable of reading Vegetius or Bouvet for themselves but who will perhaps hear her text read aloud.

All things considered, the duke of Burgundy would surely have been the person most likely to commission such a text, and it could well have been he, the most powerful person in the French government at the time, who saw to it that Christine received a payment of 200 livres from the royal treasury on 11 May 1411.[5] It was probably his military men who were the advisors referred to by Christine. He also had the dauphin appointed captain of the royal château of Creil to provide him with experi-

---

5. Bibl. Nat. Coll. Dupuy, vol. 755, fol. 97v°, cited by S. Solente in the introduction to *Livre des fais et bonnes meurs du sage roy Charles V* (Paris: Champion, 1936–40), I:xxii–xxiii.

ence in command and to encourage him to engage in physical exercise, for which he had little enthusiasm. By 1412 Louis had developed sufficient skill to accompany the duke on two successful military missions. He was indeed beginning to show promise as a leader when his career was cut short by his unexpected death at the end of 1415.[6]

What was the nature of the advice Christine had to offer? The first pages of her text are devoted to a discussion of the concept of the Just War. This owes nothing to Vegetius, but was rather a matter that had occupied many, especially churchmen, from at least the time of Saint Augustine. In Christine's day the topic was engaging the attention of legal experts, but it was unusual for a layperson to express views on the subject. Christine upheld the current opinion that a Just War could be waged only by a king or legitimate ruler, not as an individual, but as a head of state responsible for the welfare of his subjects. A lawful war could be waged only to obtain justice, or against oppression or usurpation; wars of aggression or vengeance were in no way legitimate.

In this concept of just war, surprisingly modern in tone, Christine was undoubtedly influenced by the *Tractatus de bello* of John of Legnano. This important Italian jurist and Christine's father would have been contemporaries at the University of Bologna. Legnano had married into the family of another Bolognese legist, Giovanni Andrea, whose daughter, Novella, is praised by Christine in the *Cité des dames*. Christine was also aware of the civil strife in Bologna around 1350, which had inspired the *Tractatus*. Although her immediate source was probably Bouvet's *Arbre des batailles*, between them they did much to make Legnano's ideas known in France.[7]

Christine next discusses the qualities needed for a good military leader, qualities derived in large measure from Vegetius but common to all ages. She repeats here the point she made in the biography of Charles V: that the ideal commander need not be a king or prince. It is also here that she calls to the attention of her contemporaries certain differences between Roman armies and those of her day, in which discipline and good leadership were regrettably lacking. She makes a particular point of the necessity of training young boys, who should become accustomed to

6. C. C. Willard, *Christine de Pizan: Her Life and Works* (New York: Persea, 1984), 173–93.

7. *Tractatus de bello, de reprisaliis et de duello*, ed. T. E. Holland, trans. J. L. Brierly (Oxford, 1017); N.A.R. Wright, "The *Tree of Battles* of Honoré Bouvet and the Laws of War," in *War, Literature, and Politics in the Late Middle Ages*, ed. C. T. Allmand (Liverpool: Liverpool University Press, 1976), 25–26.

austerity and sobriety. One suspects here a discreet criticism of the up-
bringing of the overindulged Louis of Guyenne.

In speaking of marshalling troops in the field, she recalls the Battle of
Roosebeke (1382), where the youthful Charles VI had been present as
the French army defeated rebellious Flemings under Philip van
Artevelde, as well as the recent victory of John the Fearless near Liège. It
is noteworthy that, following Vegetius, she warns against the employment
of an army too large for the available space on the battlefield. This was, of
course, a major cause of the French defeat at Agincourt some five years
later. French military men would have done well to take Christine's advice seriously.

An especially interesting aspect of Part II is the series of chapters devoted to siege warfare, comparing Roman and contemporary practices.
These are exceptional in actually providing lists of arms, ordinance, provisions, tools, and workmen needed to protect a town or castle against
siege, as well as comparable information for those who would mount the
siege. All this is most unusual and provides significant information concerning old weapons and new missiles at an important moment in the
development of artillery, which would play an increasingly important
role in warfare. Part of this list of material was repeated in detail by the
eminent military leader Jean de Bueil in *Le Jouvencel*, written between
1465 and 1470.[8]

The third and fourth books of the *Fais d'armes* are concerned with
legal questions involving the so-called Laws of War. It is here that Christine makes extensive use of Bouvet's *Arbre des batailles*. She refers to her
source repeatedly, although without actually naming Bouvet, but it is evident that he is the wise old man who appears to her in a dream and with
whom she discusses such matters as capital punishment, the payment of
troops, the treatment of noncombatants and prisoners of war. She is unal-
terably opposed to the slaying of prisoners taken in battle, so she must
have been dismayed by the slaughter of French captives at Agincourt, especially as several of her friends were among the victims.

The final pages of the book are devoted to discussions of safe-
conducts, letters of marque, and judicial combats, to which Christine
was firmly opposed. These dialogues between Christine and her advisor
undoubtedly represented a clever way of presenting rather dry legal problems to men of action, some of whom might have been barely literate.

---

8. C. W. Coopland, "*Le Jouvencel* (Re-visited)," *Symposium* 5 (1951): 143–81.

The intention, obviously, was to promote the idea that in war all combatants should be bound by certain accepted and known rules of combat—the ultimate basis for international law.

The evidence of the success of this book is in some respects quite curious, for in addition to some early, rather handsome manuscripts, there are others that omit all reference to Christine as author. One may ask whether this is to be regarded as a slight, or whether it suggests that the manual was considered too good to have been written by a woman. Some copies in the second group, mostly paper manuscripts, appear to have been annotated and given hard use. All this rather confuses the problem of the significance of gender in medieval writing.

Probably accounting in part for the continued popularity of the text was the reform of the French army under Charles VII around 1445. The group of later manuscripts, notably the paper ones, appears to date from this period of reform. One of the king's principal advisors during this period was Arthur de Richmont, an important leader in the campaign that finally expelled the English from France.[9] Richmont would surely have been acquainted with Christine's book, for he was one of Louis de Guyenne's companions at the French court at the time the *Fais d'armes* was presented to him. Furthermore, he later married the dauphin's widow, Marguerite de Guyenne, the princess to whom Christine had dedicated the *Livre des trois vertus*. Richmont made an important contribution to the reorganization of the French army by bringing into hand the undisciplined freebooters and by insisting on adequate leadership, discipline, and regular pay, all qualities insisted upon by both Vegetius and Christine. The continued popularity of the text even beyond this time is shown by the three printed versions in French and English, the last in France appearing in 1527.

A modern military historian, in speaking of the end of the Middle Ages, makes a particular point of Richmont's contribution to the reappearance of professionalism in Western warfare after more than a millennium, but he also praises Christine de Pizan's contribution, observing that one indication of this development was the resumption of theoretical studies of warfare, almost unknown since Vegetius, of which the *Fais d'armes* was an early and outstanding example.[10]

When one considers the intellectual sophistication represented by this

9. E. Cosneau, *Le Connétable de Richmont* (Paris: Hachette, 1886), 355–76.

10. R. E. Dupuy and T. N. Dupuy, *The Encyclopedia of Military History from 1500 B.C. to the Present* (New York: Harper & Row, 1986), 400.

book, not to mention some of Christine's other writings, one is convinced that it is not enough to consider her merely a defender of women's place in society, or even an early feminist. Her observations on the art of warfare have been remembered far longer than those of most of her contemporaries.

This translation was undertaken by my husband, Brig. Gen. (ret.) Sumner Willard, during a stay in Brussels. I am responsible for the editing, not only because of a long interest in the writings of Christine de Pizan, beginning with my edition of her *Livre de la paix* (1958), but because of my belief that the great variety of her writings must be taken into account before she can be judged as a writer. Her depiction of the varied aspects of French society, which she knew and on which she expressed her views, is undoubtedly the most impressive accomplishment of her work.

An effort has been made in this translation to give an accurate idea of what she said but to simplify slightly her rather involved style, typical of the early humanistic intellectuals of her day. An attempt has also been made to give some idea of the sources of her ideas and of their significance at the time she was writing. An edition of the original French text is also in preparation.

# PART 1

## I.

### HERE BEGINS THE BOOK OF DEEDS OF ARMS AND OF CHIVALRY. THE FIRST CHAPTER IS THE PROLOGUE, IN WHICH CHRISTINE EXCUSES HERSELF FOR BEING SO BOLD AS TO DISCUSS SUCH A HIGH MATTER AS IS CONTAINED IN THE BOOK.[1]

As boldness is essential for great undertakings, and without it nothing should be risked, I think it is proper in this present work to set forth my unworthiness to treat such exalted matter. I should not have dared even

---

1. Prologue to Antoine Vérard's edition of 1488:

HEREAFTER FOLLOWS THE BOOK OF DEEDS AND CHIVALRY, WHICH IS DIVIDED INTO FOUR PARTS. THE FIRST OF THESE SPEAKS OF THE MANNER PRINCES SHOULD OBSERVE IN THEIR WARS AND BATTLES ACCORDING TO THE ORDER OF BOOKS, WORDS, AND WRITINGS OF THE NOBLE CON-QUERORS OF THE WORLD.

And first begins the prologue of the author, which is the first chapter.

As boldness is so essential for great undertakings that without it nothing would be risked, that applies to the understanding of this present work. Otherwise, in view of the unworthiness of my person, I should not be able to treat such exalted matter; I should not have dared even to think about it. But Seneca says: "As long as the words are good, it does not matter who speaks them." Wherefore, although boldness is blameworthy when it is foolhardy, I, not moved by arrogance or foolish presumption, but rather by true affection and a genuine desire for the welfare of noble men engaged in the profession of arms, am encouraged in the light of my previous writings as someone who has already built several strongholds is emboldened to

to think about it, but although boldness is blameworthy when it is fool-hardy, I should state that I have not been inspired by arrogance or foolish presumption, but rather by true affection and a genuine desire for the welfare of noble men engaging in the profession of arms. I am encour-aged, in the light of my other writings, to undertake to speak in this book of the most honorable office of arms and chivalry, not only detailing those things that belong with it, but also treating the rights pertaining to it, as set forth in divers laws and by several authors, just as the builder who has already put up several strongholds is bold enough to construct a cas-tle or fortress when he feels he has the materials to accomplish the work. So to this end I have gathered together facts and subject matter from var-ious books to produce this present volume. But inasmuch as it is fitting for this matter to be discussed factually, diligently, and sensibly, rather than with subtlety or polished words, and also in consideration of the fact that military and lay experts in the aforesaid art of chivalry are not usually clerks or writers who are expert in language, I intend to treat the matter in the plainest possible language so that, with God's help, I may make clear and comprehensible to all readers the doctrine set forth by the sev-eral authors whose works I have consulted.

As this is unusual for women, who generally are occupied in weav-ing, spinning, and household duties, I humbly invoke, in speaking of this very high office and noble chivalry, the wise lady Minerva, born in the land of Greece, whom the ancients esteemed highly for her great wis-dom. Likewise the poet Boccaccio praises her in his *Book of Famous Women*, as do other writers praise her art and manner of making trap-pings of iron and steel, so let it not be held against me if I, as a woman, take it upon myself to treat of military matters. Rather, follow the teach-ing of Seneca, who said, "Let the works be good." So it is both appropri-ate and poetic that I am pleased to address my entreaty to the lady mentioned above.

---

build a castle or some fortress when he has the necessary materials to accomplish the task. Thus I shall undertake to speak in this present work of the most honorable office of arms and of chivalry, of those things necessary to it as well as the rights pertaining to it, as set forth by laws and various authors. To this end I have gathered together and selected from several books material for my purposes in this present volume. But inasmuch as it is fitting for this material to be presented with diligence and sense rather than with the subtlety of polished language, and also considering that experts in the art of chivalry are not usually clerks accom-plished in their knowledge of language, I intend to treat the matter in the plainest and most understandable language that I can, so that the doctrine set forth by the several authors whom, with God's help, I propose to discuss in this present book may be clear and compre-hensible to all.

O Minerva![2] goddess of arms and of chivalry, who, by understanding beyond that of other women, did find and initiate among the other noble arts and sciences the custom of forging iron and steel armaments and harness both proper and suitable for covering and protecting men's bodies against arrows slung in battle—helmets, shields, and protective covering having come first from you—you instituted and gave directions for drawing up a battle order, how to begin an assault and to engage in proper combat. Lady and high goddess, may it not displease you that I, a simple little woman, should undertake at the present time to speak of such an elevated office as that of arms. In the aforementioned country of Greece, you provided the usage of this office, and insofar as it may please you to be favorably disposed, and I in no way appear to be against the nation from which you came, the country beyond the Alps that is now called Apulia and Calabria in Italy, where you were born, let me say that like you I am an Italian woman.

## II.

### HOW WARS AND BATTLES UNDERTAKEN BECAUSE OF A JUST DISPUTE AND BROUGHT TO A PROPER CONCLUSION ARE A MATTER OF JUSTICE AND PERMITTED BY GOD.

Cato,[3] the valiant warrior, by whose force of arms the Romans enjoyed many a fair victory and who never knew defeat in battle, said that it was more profitable for the public good to make use of the writings, rules, doctrine, and discipline of arms that he had composed and bound into a book than anything he had ever accomplished personally; for he said that whatever a man may do will endure only for an age, but what is written lasts for the common profit forever, and from it innumerable men may derive ben-

---

2. Minerva was obviously one of Christine's favorite icons. In the *Letter of Othea* (I, 13) she wrote: "Minerva was a lady of very great knowledge, and she discovered the art of making armor . . . and because of the great wisdom that existed in that lady, they called her a goddess." Minerva also figures in *The Long Road to Learning*, *The Mutation of Fortune*, and *The City of Ladies*. In the *Long Road to Learning* Christine refers to the *Moralized Ovid* as the source for what she says of Minerva, but here she cites Boccaccio, who was also one of her principal sources for *The City of Ladies*. Ovid was the source for Boccaccio's Minerva. Elsewhere Christine includes details found in the medieval historical compilation known as *Ancient History up to Caesar*. This is an excellent example of the complexity of Christine's sources.

3. Cato the Censor (234–149 B.C.), in addition to having a military and diplomatic career, wrote extensively, including a *De disciplina militari*. The text is lost, except for fragments, and although it is quoted by Vegetius, there is no reason to think that he had access to the original.

efit. Thus it is a matter of no small consequence to compose and create a book. But in order that this present work may not be accused by some envious people of being the product of idleness and a waste of time, as if it dealt with illicit matters, it is of primary concern to learn whether wars and battles, deeds of arms and of chivalry, of which we hope to speak, are to be considered just matters or not, for in the exercise of arms many great wrongs, extortions, and grievous deeds are committed, as well as rapine, killings, forced executions, and arson; all of these may well seem to some detestable and improper. For this reason, in answer to this question, it seems manifest that wars undertaken for a just cause are permitted by God.[4] We have proof of this in several places in Holy Writ, how our Lord even told the leaders of armies what they should do against their enemies, as is written of one who was called Jesus, whom He ordered to fight against his enemies and to make an ambush in order better to overcome them, and other such cases are duly recounted. Holy Writ also says of God that He is the Lord and Governor of Hosts and battles, and that wars and battles waged for a just cause are but the proper execution of justice, to bestow right where it belongs. Divine law grants this as do laws drawn up by people to repress the arrogant and evildoers. As for the evils committed outside what is right in war, as the authorities say, these are not the result of what is right in war, but of the evil will of people who misuse war. I hope, with God's help, to touch on matters that are limited by civil law and also canon law in the exercise of arms.[5]

III.

HOW IT IS NOT LAWFUL EXCEPT FOR KINGS
AND SOVEREIGN PRINCES, BY VIRTUE OF THEIR EXCEPTIONAL
AUTHORITY, TO UNDERTAKE WARS AND BATTLES.

In the first chapter we have touched briefly upon how wars and battles undertaken for the right are just, but as wars are often right and just, it is

4. Compare with Honoré Bouvet's *Arbre des batailles* IV, i: "Thus we must understand that war comes from God, and not merely that He permits war, but that He has ordained it; for God commanded a man called Joshua that he should do battle against his enemies, and advised him how he should set an ambush for the discomfiture of his enemies. Further, we say that our Lord God Himself is lord and governor of battles" (trans. G. W. Coopland, *The Tree of Battles of Honoré Bonet: An English Version with Introduction by G. W. Coopland* [Liverpool: Liverpool University Press, 1949]).

5. See Maurice H. Keen, *The Laws of War in the Late Middle Ages* (London: Routledge & Kegan Paul, 1965), 9: "The authorities were all agreed: Scripture, the Fathers, the Decretum,

suitable to return to the subject, to remind every man to do what is right. If it is lawful for each person to engage in war to preserve his own right, then it would seem reasonable that any man could start a war; but to point out the truth to those who might err on this point, it should be understood that there is no doubt in law, or in laws, that the undertaking of war or battle for whatever reason belongs to no one except to sovereign princes, which is to say, emperors, kings, dukes, and other landed lords who are duly and rightfully heads of temporal jurisdictions.[6] No baron, or any other person, however great he may be, may undertake war without the express permission and will of his sovereign lord. That this law is right is demonstrated by plain reason, for if it were otherwise, of what use would sovereign princes be, who were not set up except to do right for and on behalf of any of their subjects who might be oppressed by some extortion, to defend them and keep them as the good shepherd risks his life for his flock?[7] For this reason, the subject must turn to his lord as to his refuge whenever he is harmed in some way, and the good lord will take up arms for him, if need be. This is to say that he will help him, by virtue of his power, to maintain his rights, either by justice or by recourse to arms.

---

Aquinas himself. 'The lord appointed new wars,' wrote John of Legnano, quoting Judges V, and he had even instructed Joshua in the means of laying an ambush for his enemies. Taking up this point, which a wealth of Old Testament references bore out, Bonet, and Christine de Pisan after him, remind us of its implication; we must not conclude from the evil consequences of war that war is evil . . . as Augustine had written 'war is waged that peace may be had.' " Christine refers to this remark of Saint Augustine in her *Chemin de long estude* (vv. 4421–30). See Püschel ed., p. 189.

6. As Keen points out (*Laws of War*, 77), Christine's definition of a "sovereign prince" is more inclusive than the traditional one. Dukes and other secular lords were not usually without a superior. Keen suggests that Christine's definition was intended to fit the facts of the day, but it might also have been a gesture to favor the duke of Burgundy, who, in fact, had two sovereign lords: the king of France and the emperor. This definition would seem to be evidence of the Burgundian influence on the composition of this text.

7. The ruler as a good shepherd was a comparison favored by Christine. It had already figured in *Le Chemin de long estude* (p. 234):

As Aristotle in *Ethics* does say
That authentic princes in this way
Should be and so appear
As a father to his children dear
And like the shepherd with his sheep
Who from all damage would them keep.

The same comparison is developed in the *Livre du corps de policie* (I, 9 and 10), where she says: "As Vegetius tells it, the emperor Tiberius, in reply to those who asked him why he didn't tax his people more heavily when he could do so, said it is the duty of the good shepherd to sheer his sheep during one season of the year and not to fleece them perpetually or pluck the skin so much it bleeds."

Christine also showed her interest in the life of shepherds and shepherdesses in the "Dit de la

IV.

CONCERNING THE PRIME CAUSES OF WARS AND BATTLES.[8]

As it belongs to sovereign princes to undertake and carry on wars and battles, we must now consider the causes by which, according to lawful
means, they may be initiated and pursued. In this regard one is well advised, it seems to me, to remember that five grounds are commonly held
to be the basis of wars, three of which rest on law and the remaining two
on will. The first lawful ground on which wars may be undertaken or
pursued is to maintain law and justice; the second is to counteract evildoers who befoul, injure, and oppress the land and the people; and the
third is to recover lands, lordships, and other things stolen or usurped for
an unjust cause by others who are under the jurisdiction of the prince,
the country, or its subjects. As for the two of will, one is to avenge any loss
or damage incurred, the other to conquer and take over foreign lands or
lordships.

Returning to the first of these points, which concerns justice, it should
be remembered that there are three chief causes under which a king
or prince is empowered to undertake and carry out wars and battles.
The first is to uphold and defend the Church and its patrimony
against anyone who would defile it; this is expected of all Christian
princes. The second is to act on behalf of a vassal, if he should require it, in cases where the prince must settle a quarrel and is
duly obliged to bring about an agreement among various parties, but
then only if the adversary proves to be intractable. And third, the
prince, if it pleases him, may justly go to the aid of any other prince,
baron, or other ally and friend of his, or to help any country or land, if
the need arises and if the quarrel is just. In this point are included wid-

---

pastoure," composed in 1403, and in instructions given to the lady called upon to manage her estate
in the *Livre des trois vertus* (II, 10). One suspects that she had read de Brie's *Vray Régime et Gou-
vernement des bergers et bergères*, composed for Charles V's library in 1379.

8. The concept of the Just War occupied men, especially churchmen, at least from the time of
Saint Augustine. At the time that Christine was writing, the concept was engaging the attention of
legal experts, in particular, but it was unusual for a layperson to express views on the subject. Christine's concept of the just war was probably inspired by John of Legnano's *Tractatus de bello*. This important Italian jurist and Christine's father had been contemporaries at the University of Bologna
and would undoubtedly have known each other. Christine speaks elsewhere of the civil strife in
Bologna around 1350 that inspired Legnano's treatise. Her more immediate source would have been
Honoré Bouvet's *Arbre des batailles,* and together with him she contributed to making Legnano's
views known in France. Neither writer mentions him by name, probably because he was an
outspoken supporter of the Roman pope at a time when the French monarchy supported the Avi-
gnon rival.

ows, orphans, and all who are unjustly trampled under foot by another power.

For this purpose, and likewise for the other two aforementioned purposes, that is, to counteract evildoers and to recover lost property, it is not only permissible for the prince to start a war or to maintain it, indeed he is obliged to do so, through the obligation incurred by his title to lordship and jurisdiction in accordance with his proper duty.

As for the other two points, the one regarding revenge for some damage or loss inflicted by another prince, the other regarding acquisition of foreign lands without title to them—even though conquerors in the past, such as Alexander, the Romans, and others have done so, and have been praised and accorded chivalric titles, as have those who wreaked vengeance upon their enemies, for better or for worse—despite the fact that such actions are commonly undertaken, I do not find in divine law or in any other text, for causes such as these without any other ground, that it is acceptable to start any kind of war or battle upon any Christian land, but rather the contrary.

For according to God's law it is not proper for man either to seize or to usurp anything belonging to another, or even to covet it. Likewise, vengeance is reserved for God alone, and in no way does any man have the right to carry it out.

Thus, to set forth our ideas on this subject more clearly, and to answer any questions that might arise, it is true that it is lawful for any prince to keep for himself the same right that is granted to others. As for what the just prince would do if he considered himself wronged by some other power, should he simply depart, in order to obey divine law, without taking any further actions? In God's name, no, for divine law does not deny justice, but rather mandates that it should be carried out and requires punishment for misdeeds. In order that a prince may go about this matter justly, he will follow this course: he will gather together a great council of wise men in his parliament, or in that of his sovereign if he is a subject, and not only will he assemble those of his own realm, but in order that there be no suspicion of favor, he will also call upon some from foreign countries that are known not to take sides, elder statesmen as well as legal advisors and others; he will propose or have proposed the whole matter in full without holding anything back, for God cannot be deceived, everything according to what may be right or wrong, and he will conclude by saying that he wishes to recount everything and hold to the determination of doing right. In short, by these points the affair will be put to order, clearly seen and discussed, and if through such a process it appears that his cause is just, he will summon his adversary to demand of him restitution and amends for his injuries and the wrong done him. Now if it comes about that the adversary in question puts up a defense and tries to contradict what has been said, let him be heard fully without special favor, but also without willfulness or spite. If these things are duly carried out, as the law requires, then the just prince may surely undertake war, which on no account should be called vengeance, but rather the complete carrying out of due justice.

## V.

### CONSIDERATIONS A KING OR PRINCE SHOULD ENTERTAIN IN INITIATING WAR AND THE POINTS HE SHOULD KEEP IN MIND WHILE DELIBERATING THE MATTER.

As it is licit for a prince to engage in wars and battles, pursuing them for the reasons mentioned above, and as these are great and weighty matters that touch the lives, the blood, and the honor and the fortunes of an infinite number of people, it is necessary to look closely into the matter, for without such a look no such thing should be undertaken, nor should it be undertaken lightly by anyone without experience. That one should hesitate to undertake war even on someone weaker there are numerous demonstrations. What great blows the African power dreamed of, or the proud city of Carthage, its capital, and the Spaniards, not to mention the very powerful King Antiochus,[9] lord of a great part of the East, who led so many men into battle that with their frightful elephants the affair was quickly finished. Then there was also the mighty King Mithradates,[10] who was sovereign of twenty-four powerful countries and even of the whole world, but even these could not and did not subdue the very slight power of the Romans. For this reason, nothing that is in the power of For-

9. Antiochus (242–187 B.C.): Christine had already recounted his adventure in her *Mutacion de fortune* (IV, xxi and xxiii; Solente ed., III, pp. 235–41). He inherited the Seleucid lands and in a certain dispute, regained Parthia and Bactria, and also acquired Armenia; further victories in India and Arabia earned for him the epithet "the Great." He later invaded Europe to recover Thrace, but was defeated by the Romans at Thermopylae and Magnesia.

10. Mithradates VI: king of Pontus who eventually occupied most of Asia Minor. After various victories, however, he was expelled by Roman generals, notably Lucullus and Pompey (see *La Mutacion de fortune* IV, xxviii–xli; Solente ed., IV, pp. 9–20). According to Solente, her source here is the *Histoire ancienne jusqu'à César*.

tune should be risked lightly, for no one can know which side will be favored.

Therefore, it is necessary for the prince to be wise, or at the very least be disposed to use wise counsel, for as Plato said, fortunate is the country where the wise govern, for otherwise it is cursed, as Holy Scripture also testifies. There is absolutely nothing that so needs to be conducted with good judgment as war and battle, as will be seen later. No mistake made in any other circumstances is less possible to repair than one committed by force of arms and by a battle badly conducted.

What then will the wise prince upon whom it is incumbent do when, for any of the reasons mentioned, he must undertake wars and fight battles? First of all, he will consider how much strength he has or can obtain, how many men are available and how much money. For unless he is well supplied with these two basic elements, it is folly to wage war, for they are necessary to have above all else, especially money. Whoever has enough and wishes to use it can always find plenty of help from others, even more than he wants; witness the wars of Italy,[11] especially Florence and Venice, that are commonly fought more with their money than with their citizens. For this reason they can scarcely be defeated. So it would be much better for the prince, if he does not consider that he is supported by money from the treasury, or by rich subjects full of goodwill, not to conclude any treaty with his enemies if he feels threatened with invasion, or to undertake to begin a war if he lacks the means to carry it on. For it is quite certain that if he begins it in the hope of extracting more from his subjects than they are able to bear, and without their consent, he will merely increase the number of his enemies. It will profit him little to destroy enemies from the outside in order to acquire them nearby and in his domain. It should be remembered that the prince must not underestimate the power of any enemy, however slight it may appear to him, for he cannot know what fortune another will have in his favor. It is written of a shepherd named Briacus,[12] that Fortune was so favorable to him that she sustained him in power with a great number of thieves and

11. The wars of Italy: a reference to war waged with condottieri, or hired soldiers, who were a major feature of the military scene after the middle of the fourteenth century. The ruling class, which would normally have provided the majority of men-at-arms, had become progressively more absorbed in its professional activities and preferred to hire mercenaries. Cities had fairly easy access to cash to pay mercenaries, and such men were readily available.

12. Briacus (Viriathus): a shepherd who led a Lusitanian revolt against the Romans in 150 B.C. He was the first to make use of guerrilla tactics in the mountains, a form of warfare for which the Romans were quite unprepared. Though he was successful in his military campaign, he was eventually

pillagers he had assembled to fight Rome, powerful as it was, for a period of more than fourteen years. Much grief he brought to them, and he defeated them several times in battle, nor were they able to destroy him. His life was ended by one of his own men, who killed him.

Therefore, in order that such things may not come about, the prince will assemble in council the four estates of his realm, which should be summoned for such a purpose. That is to say, the elder nobles experienced in arms, who know how to organize and attack; also the law clerks, for in the laws are set forth the cases in which a just war can be undertaken, along with several examples of these; also the burghers, for it is necessary for them to participate in the organization, since they would need to take charge of fortifying towns and cities, and also to persuade the common people to help their lord. Additionally, there should be some representatives of the craftsmen, the more to honor these people. They must be carefully approached so that they will be the more inclined to help the lord financially.

O! how profitable it is for a land, realm, or city to have loyal subjects of great affection, for they lack neither able bodies nor worldly goods. This was evident many times in Rome when the city treasury depended on them for support in wars at the point where there was no other source of revenue. In order to help, the ladies willingly brought their jewels and rich ornaments, lending them to help the city in its dire need. These precious objects were later restored to them, as was only right and reasonable.

In this tradition, to set a good example, the good and wise King Charles, fifth of the name, father of the one who at present reigns, soon after he had been crowned at the age of twenty-five, saw that the English were keeping badly the agreements of the peace treaty he had concluded with them out of necessity and their good fortune, which treaty was so damaging to him. In spite of the agreement that allowed them to keep possession of a great part of the duchy of Guyenne and several other lands and lordships elsewhere in the kingdom of France, this treaty was not good enough for them. Rather, because of their overweening pride they also trampled under foot neighboring territories that did not belong to them. Therefore this king, before he did anything else, peacefully sent

---

undone because his political ability was inferior to his military skill. After some fourteen years of his leadership, his friends accepted a bribe from the Romans to murder him. Christine had already referred to his story in the *Mutacion de fortune* (Solente ed., III, pp. 253–59).

envoys to the duke of Lancaster, son of King Edward of England, by whom this outrage was carried out, inquiring if they wished to allow amends to be made for the suffering and damage inflicted since the treaty; whereupon it resulted that although the reply was gracious, the ambassadors themselves were killed. So the aforesaid king, in view of the fact that he had been obliged to agree to a dishonorable treaty, one that even the English did not keep, and for other reasons too long to explain, assembled in his parliament in Paris the aforementioned four estates, and with them wise jurists from Bologna and from other places. To these, in a very wise manner, he made his points against the English, asking their opinion whether he had reason to begin war again, for without just cause, their due consideration of the matter, and the conscience and goodwill of his subjects, he did not wish to undertake it. This council, after long deliberation, concluded that there was due and just cause to begin the war again. So with his own great prudence, all the lost lands were reconquered by the sword, as is well known.[13]

## VI.

### REASONS CONCERNING THE PERILS OF ADVERSE FORTUNE ARE SET FORTH EXPLAINING WHY IT IS NOT EXPEDIENT FOR A KING OR SOVEREIGN TO GO INTO BATTLE.

By the means already detailed, therefore, the wise king or prince will determine whether to undertake wars or battles. It is well known that in beginning, carrying on, and maintaining warfare, four principal things are necessary, namely, resources, boldness, strength, and constancy, without which everything would degenerate into confusion. Indeed, this would happen if even one of these ingredients were lacking. Now we must consider whether it is a good thing for a king or sovereign prince to go to war in person and take part in battle, inasmuch as the deed must touch him more deeply than any other person, so that his presence can represent the aforementioned four points. Along with this there is no doubt that knights and men-at-arms and the whole army would have greater courage in fighting, seeing their lord in his place, ready to live and die with them. Nevertheless, to answer this question, in spite of all that might be said on

---

13. Christine had already made this point about King Charles V in her biography of him, *Livre des fais et bonnes meurs du sage roy Charles V* (Solente ed., I, pp. 126–28).

this matter and the good that might come of it, the fact is that one finds many examples of kings and princes who have been present at their battles: King Alexander in his conquests, many kings of France, such as King Clovis and Charlemagne, as well as a number of others. Even Charles, who now reigns, when he was a youth of fourteen, newly crowned, was present at the Battle of Roosebeke against the Flemings, where his forces won a notable victory.[14] It is not, however, to be considered lightly if a king or sovereign prince should go there in person. It is better to avoid battle than to be present, except in certain cases, notably against his own subjects in case they should rebel against him. The reason for this is that a subject naturally fears to offend the majesty of his sovereign lord, especially in his presence. Thus they could not avoid the knowledge that some perverse will on their part would rob them of their courage on seeing themselves arrayed against the one they ought to help against everyone. The confusion is especially great on their part and the advantage the prince's when he is good to them and not a cruel tyrant. But notwithstanding whatever motive compels him to go, he should take such heed of his safety in the battle that the peril of evil Fortune may not fall on his head. But the general reason why it is not a good thing for him to go into battle is that no one can foresee to which side God will give the good fortune of victory. For if Fortune should go against the prince who was there in person, and if he were thereby killed, taken prisoner, or should flee, this would be a loss or dishonor not merely to his person, but to those of his blood and, in general, to all his subjects, and loss and disruption to his land and country, as can be known well enough by experience of such cases in this country, and those that have happened elsewhere.[15] Because of this, except for some particularly compelling reason, a prince who is too headstrong and eager to take a chance that might result in infinite troubles and disruption should not be believed, but should rather be dissuaded with causes and reasons, and with examples, which should dissuade him, considering the very great danger not only to himself, as is said, but to all his people. Apropos of this, the good sense and govern-

14. Battle of Roosebeke (1382): an episode in the struggle between the count of Flanders and the city of Ghent for control of Flanders. The count, Louis de Mâle, appealed to France for help, and the Flemish leader, Philip van Artevelde, to England. It was the king of France who responded, and on 26 November, led by Charles VI in person, even though he was barely fourteen years old, the forces backing Louis de Mâle won a resounding victory. See *Fais et bonnes meurs* (Solente ed., I, pp. 131–32).

15. Christine is, of course, referring to the capture of John II by the English and the misfortunes France suffered because of it.

ment of the aforementioned wise King Charles could indeed serve as an example,[16] for without moving from his royal throne in his palace, he reconquered all the lands lost by his most chivalrous predecessors, as is well known.

That good sense and diligence are more useful in warfare than the presence of the prince is evident in the case of the first duke of Milan, father of the current duke.[17] Without leaving his palace, he conquered by his good judgment so many lands and lordships in Lombardy and in the Marches, added so many cities to the one in his possession, that he created a very large and important duchy.

## VII.

### A CONSIDERATION OF WHAT SORT OF CONSTABLE SHOULD BE CHOSEN TO SERVE AS MASTER OF THE KING'S CAVALRY, AND THE CONDITIONS OF HIS SERVICE.

As it has now been explained how a king or sovereign prince must not, in the interest of public safety and welfare, decide to go personally into battle, it should therefore be considered to what persons, as one individual is not enough, can be entrusted the duties of such important offices as those of leader and master of his cavalry, who are to carry out his wars for him and in his name. This matter must be carefully considered, for nothing has greater importance than the selection of military leaders. As the exercise of their office, both in peace and in war, takes precedence over all others, the best possible persons should be selected. Especially great regard, thought, and deliberation should go into the selection of the one who will be put in charge of them all. The ancients used to call this person the duke of battles, or sovereign master of the cavalry, whom we in France at present call constable. Then, according to French custom, there are two marshals under whom are placed a certain number of men-at-arms.

In the selection of the sovereign master of the prince's cavalry, it is especially advisable to chose someone who is outstanding in all things that

16. In *Fais et bonnes meurs* (Solente ed., I, pp. 242–44), Christine acclaims Charles V truly chivalrous without his going personally to battle.

17. Duke of Milan: a reference to Jean-Galeas Visconti, whom Christine obviously admired, for she referred to him in the *Chemin de long estude* (vv. 5043ff., p. 215), deplored his death in *L'Avision* (Towner ed., p. 166), and spoke of his accomplishments in the *Mutacion de fortune* (Solente ed., IV, pp. 71–75).

the bearing of arms requires, which is to say that through long experience they should be so accustomed to the conduct of warfare that it should seem a natural calling. The continual exercise of arms provides all the necessary skills, as is the case with anyone who has on many occasions experienced a variety of military adventures in various countries and nations. For as Vegetius says, age of itself does not give any guarantee of skill and manner of combat, but rather experience.[18] So he should not be a novice in the routine and manner of dealing with men-at-arms, whom both in time of peace and during the demands of war he should know how to maintain, lead, and equip in the best possible manner.

It should also be noted that in this selection greater attention should be given to perfection of skill in arms, along with the virtues and the character and good bearing that should accompany this, than to exalted lineage or noble blood, although if both were to be found in the same person it would be very useful, for the simple reason that the nobler the blood, the greater the esteem in which he would be held in exercising his office, a quality necessary to every leader. Apropos of this, Valerius Maximus points out that the ancients who achieved great conquests, in order to be the more feared in their armies, pretended to be of such exalted lineage that they claimed to be related to the gods.[19] But this simple pretension is not sufficient without other qualities, so for this reason the electors should consider carefully the office rather than the man. For it would be a matter for reproach, however distinguished the blood, to give the charge to an ignorant person, especially where subtlety, good sense, and experience are more needed than even the number of troops or any other kind of force.

As Cato says, all other sorts of mistakes can be corrected, but those made in battle are immediately followed by the consequences, for those who know only how to defend themselves badly will perish, and those who take to flight seldom have sufficient courage to continue fighting.[20]

For this reason likewise, along with those already mentioned, it is necessary for the leader to be wise, with good common sense, as is true of anyone who needs to have knowledge of many things, like a chief justice,

18. Vegetius III, xxvi: "Few men are born naturally brave; hard work and good training makes many so" (Milner trans., p. 117).

19. Cited by Christine in the *Corps de policie* (II, 9).

20. Vegetius I, xiii: "[I]n other matters, as Cato says, mistakes can be corrected afterwards; errors in war do not admit of amendment, because the penalty follows immediately upon the slip" (Milner trans., p. 14). There is also mention of this in the *Corps de policie* (III, 9).

the prince's representative who must judge everyone fairly in all the cases that may arise through arms and deeds of chivalry, not only in the case of those under his command, but even of strangers, as happens in a number of situations.

It should also be remembered that according to the customs of gentility and true nobility a leader must observe in the conduct of arms in any circumstance that may arise all that good breeding requires, if he wishes to gain due honor and praise, meaning that even to his enemies he must be upright and truthful in act and judgment wherever required. Along with this, he will honor those who are good and meritorious as he would wish to be honored by them. This custom was observed by the valiant King Pyrrhus of Macedonia,[21] who gained great praise because, having observed so many brave deeds among the Romans, he honored them greatly when they came to him as envoys, even though they were his bitter enemies, and he even gave those killed in battle an honorable burial. Concerning the nobility of that king and his great openheartedness it is further written that he held the Romans in such great respect that he did not even wish to retain the prisoners captured in battle, but rather released them freely.

Thus the qualities and conditions that should be found in a good constable are these: he should not be stubborn, short-tempered, cruel, or malevolent, but rather moderate and temperate, firm in justice, kindly in conversation, of upright bearing and few words, with a composed face, not given to light talk, truthful in word and promise, brave, sure of himself, diligent, not covetous, proud before his enemies, magnanimous to the vanquished and to his inferiors, not easily angered or given to impulsive acts, not readily impressed by appearances or by words that do not seem truthful, not tempted to vanity, ornaments, or jewels. He should be well provided with equipment and saddle, and should present himself proudly. He should not be lazy, slow, or sleepy, too easily tempted by food and drink or a dissipated life. He should rather inform himself everyday regarding his adversaries state of readiness, be subtle, farseeing, and cautious in defending himself against them, assailing them wisely, and remain well-informed of their traps. He should know how to govern his own people, keeping them in order and commanding due respect, carrying out the right, disdaining games, honoring those who merit it and

---

21. King Pyrrhus (319–272 B.C.), famous king of Epirus, was a brilliant tactician and an adroit opportunist, although he never achieved a lasting victory. Christine had already described his exploits in the *Mutacion de fortune* (VII, xxxiv; Solente ed., III, pp. 201–8).

keeping them near him, rewarding those who are deserving, and showing generosity where the situation requires it. His ordinary talk should be of arms and deeds of chivalry, and of the valiant accomplishments of good men. He should avoid boastfulness, be reasonable, love his prince and be true to him, be helpful to widows, orphans, and the poor, refrain from exaggerating small slights to his person or minor disagreements, but readily pardon those who repent. Above all, he should love God and the Church and uphold what is right. All these conditions are suitable to a good constable, and likewise to marshals and all those who hold similar offices.

### VIII.
### HEREIN, WITH REGARD TO THE EXERCISE OF ARMS, SOME AUTHORS ARE CITED WHO HAVE SPOKEN OF THIS MATTER AND OF THE WAYS OF VALIANT CONQUERORS.

Having discussed what sort of officers should be chosen, at least the ones whose abilities most resemble those that have been discussed above, who should be commissioned captains and chivalric leaders of a king or prince, we must now discuss to what sort of deeds the exercise of arms ought to pertain. As many authors who have treated this matter have helped me to speak of this, I shall cite their works as witness, especially Vegetius,[22] who in the age of the emperor Valentinian wrote a notable work concerning the discipline and art of warfare possessed by the great conquerors, those who carried out through good judgment and skill in arms deeds that today would seem impossible. This was confirmed by the aforementioned King Pyrrhus, when he had experienced the valor of the Romans, a rather small number of whom had opposed his army, which was so large that mountains and valleys were filled with his men, for he said: "O god Jupiter, if I had such knights, I could conquer the whole world." For this reason it is to be supposed that by dint of hard work and great enterprise they were able to achieve such great accomplishments as conquering the world, which indeed the Romans did. Likewise did other conquerors, whose manner of fighting has been recorded by various wise men. Such things as these are useful to hear about as examples.

For Vegetius says that whoever wants peace should learn war; he who

---

22. The date of Vegetius's treatise, which Christine bases on a note by a late copyist, is less certain than she suggests. A more modern theory is that it was dedicated to Theodosius I (379–95). (Milner trans., introduction, pp. xxxvii–xli.)

likes victory must be adept with arms. The knight who seeks a good adventure should fight with competence, which is to say, using good judgment and not "from the hip." Nobody dares to injure or anger another who would be expected to come out on top if he were attacked.[23] So it appears by the great conquests achieved by the ancients in the past that men are not always as valiant as they ought to be, and the aforementioned Vegetius explains this by saying that long periods of peace make those who were once skilled in arms through long and repeated practice no longer attentive to this occupation.[24] Pleasure, laziness, and greed, which their noble predecessors, who valued only honor in arms, did not consider worthy of their time, caused knighthood to decline through negligence, forgetfulness, and indifference. He further says that even the Romans, who had conquered many lands, let themselves go to the point where they were conquered by Hannibal, prince of Africa, in the second battle, before Cannae in Apulia,[25] where they lost all their leaders. This was so horrible in that all the Romans were killed and their high command captured and put to death along with so many of their cavalry that after the great rout, as the stories go, Hannibal, who had the battlefield searched, recovered three hogsheads full of gold rings from their fingers, which he transported to his country as a sign of his glorious victory.

When they took up training again, they were always victorious. For this reason the author already mentioned concludes, while praising the practice of arms, that it is always more profitable for a king or prince to have men well instructed and experienced in this art, however small their

23. Vegetius III, prologue: "Therefore, he who desires peace, let him prepare for war. He who wants victory, let him train soldiers diligently. He who wishes a successful outcome, let him fight with strategy, not at random. No one dares challenge or harm one who he realizes will win if he fights" (Milner trans., p. 63).

24. Vegetius I, xxviii:

ON ENCOURAGING MILITARY SCIENCE AND ROMAN VALOUR.

. . .

However, a sense of security born of long peace has diverted mankind partly to the enjoyment of private leisure, partly to civilian careers. Thus attention to military training obviously was at first discharged rather neglectfully, then omitted, until finally consigned long since to oblivion. Neither let anyone wonder that this happened in the preceding age, because after the first Punic war twenty and more years of peace so enervated those all-conquering Romans as a result of private leisure and neglect of arms, that in the second Punic war they could not stand up to Hannibal. So it was that after so many consuls, so many generals, so many armies lost, they only finally achieved victory, when they had been able to learn military science and training. Therefore recruits should constantly be levied and trained. For it costs less to train one's own men in arms than to hire foreign mercenaries. (Milner trans., pp. 27–28)

25. Cannae in Apulia: site of Hannibal's victory over the Romans in 216 B.C. See the *Mutacion de fortune* VI, ii (Solente ed., III, pp. 215–20).

number may be, than to hire a large number of foreign mercenaries whom he does not know. Nothing, he says, is stronger or more fortunate or more praiseworthy than a country that has a large number of men-at-arms, well trained and hardened in what is required of them, for neither gold nor silver nor precious stones overcome the enemy, nor do they make the inhabitants live in peace. Only a valiant and powerful fighting force can do this. Such men should not be judged according to the fool-ish opinion of King Bituitus of Gaul,[26] who, when he had advanced against the Romans with four hundred thousand men and saw coming to-ward him such a small number of soldiers, scorned them and said that there were not enough men to satisfy the dogs of his army. But, as history tells us, there were nonetheless enough to destroy him and his large army soon afterward. To confirm these matters, according to this author, let us speak first of the doctrine noblemen prescribed for their children during their youth; then we will return to the matter of the captain or the cap-tains of the cavalry.

Vegetius speaks of this matter in the first chapter of his first book:[27] there is no other explanation for the way in which the city of Rome could have conquered the lands of this world except by skill at arms and by the instruction of their troops and cavalry. For it can readily be assumed that such a small force of men as they were in the beginning would be of little value against the hordes of Gauls, the knowledge of the Greeks, and the malice and strength of the Africans if they had not exercised great good judgment and ruse. So we must once more conclude, with what has al-ready been said, that it is better to have a small number of men well in-structed and skilled in arms through continuous training in all things that may happen in the dubious fortunes of battle than a very large number of rude and ignorant men. For, as he says, the science of what is important in matters of war and battle increases, nourishes, and gives the courage necessary for combat. Thus it is that nobody is at a loss in knowing what

---

26. King Bituitus: king of Arvernes (modern Auvergne) in Gaul. See the *Mutacion de fortune* VI, xxxii (Solente ed., III, pp. 264–66).

27. Vegetius I, 1:

THAT THE ROMANS CONQUERED ALL PEOPLES SOLELY BECAUSE OF THEIR MILITARY TRAINING.
    In every battle it is not numbers and untaught bravery so much as skill and training that generally produce the victory. For we see no other explanation of the conquest of the world by the Roman People than their drill-at-arms, camp-discipline and military expertise. How else could small Roman forces have availed against hordes of Gaules? . . . Scientific knowl-edge of warfare nurtures courage in battle. No one is afraid to do what he is confident of hav-ing learned well. A small force which is highly trained in the conflicts of war is more apt to victory: a raw and untrained horde is always exposed to slaughter. (Milner trans., pp. 2–3)

to do, for he feels instructed, experienced, and well informed. All arts and skills are refined through constant practice. If this is true, as Vegetius says, in small matters, how much more important it is to observe them in greater affairs.

O! how men experienced in war and clever in the exercise of arms can scarcely be overcome by strange and unexpected happenings, as was evident when the Romans found a way to kill the great number of elephants the Carthaginians from various parts of the Orient led against them in battle.[28] They are such strange and frightening animals that men and horses were frightened merely at seeing them. The clever Romans devised machines by which sharp spikes could be hurled against them and hot bars of iron, and with these they destroyed them. So, says our author, of all the arts the most to be praised in any country is in knowing how to fight, for it is in this way that the freedom of the land is preserved and the dignity of the region enhanced.[29] For this reason the knights of antiquity, as is said, protected these rigorously: first the Greeks, then the Spartans, valiant conquerors mighty in battle, and later the Romans strove to learn and know all this, as is evident from what happened to them afterward.

IX.

HOW THE NOBLE KNIGHTS OF ANTIQUITY INSTRUCTED THEIR
CHILDREN, TEACHING THEM THE DOCTRINE OF ARMS.[30]

The noblemen of ancient times, because of their great courage, wished that the practice of arms should be continued in order that the public welfare of their estates and cities might be increased and better defended. They did not have their children brought up at the courts of noblemen in order to learn pride, lechery, or vanity in dress, but rather arranged matters so that at a suitable age they might better serve their prince or their

28. Vegetius III, xxiv: "Elephants in battle cause men and horses to panic because of the size of their bodies, the horror of their trumpeting and the novelty of their very form . . . Various methods of resistance have been worked out against them . . . [C]ataphract cavalrymen who aimed *sarisae*, that is, very long pikes, at the elephants. Being covered in iron they were not harmed by the archers riding on the beasts, and avoided their charges thanks to the speed of their horses" (Milner trans., pp. 112–13).

[29. Vegetius III, x: "Who can doubt that the art of war comes before everything else, when it preserves our liberty and prestige, extends the provinces and saves the Empire? The Spartans long ago abandoned all other fields of learning to cultivate this, and later so did the Romans" (Milner trans., p. 86).

30. See the *Livre du corps de policie* II, 2: "HOW THE ANCIENT NOBLES TRAINED THEIR CHILDREN."

country in a manner worthy of the calling of a nobleman. Therefore, it was their custom to have their sons, from the age of fourteen onward, taught and indoctrinated in all things concerning arms and chivalry. There were proper schools in certain places where they were taught to wear armor and take care of themselves in combat.

Wherefore, Vegetius says, when he speaks of this matter in the fourth chapter of his first book, nobles should strive to imbue their children from an early age with a love of arms, for a young child learns readily what is shown him, and children are by nature easily and happily excited by such things, as can be observed from the way they wrestle, jump, and play with each other so actively.[31] So it is then that they should be taught the tricks of agility in striking with their arms and learning to sidestep blows, which may come from either side, leap over ditches, throw darts and spears, protect themselves with a shield, and other such things. They should be shown how, in throwing a spear or dart, one puts the left foot forward, so that, in balancing what one wants to throw, the body is steadied and the thrust of the weapon is thus greater; but when it comes to hand-to-hand combat with swords, then the right foot should be forward, because the thrust comes from the left.[32] In order to instruct them better in all sorts of attacks and fights, the masters would put them in mock battles, so that they would learn the order of battle and the use of weapons through experience, and make them march a certain number of paces in close order without falling into confusion. Using light staves at first so that they would do no harm, they would attack each other. And in order to discourage any sort of bad feeling, those who were victors would the next time be put as companions to these they had conquered. Then they would be ordered to defend certain places against each other, as if these were castles.

31. Vegetius I, iv: "Next let us examine at what age it is appropriate to levy soldiers. Indeed if ancient custom is to be retained, everyone knows that those entering puberty should be brought to the levy. For those things are taught not only more quickly but even more completely which are learned from boyhood. Secondly military alacrity, jumping and running should be attempted before the body stiffens with age. For it is speed which, with training, makes a brave warrior. Adolescents are the ones to recruit, just as Sallust says: 'Directly as soon as youth was able to endure war, it learned military practice in camp through labour.' For it is better that a trained young man should complain that he has not yet reached fighting age, than that he should regret that it has passed" (Milner trans., p. 5).

32. Vegetius I, xx: "It should be noted, also, that when missiles are being exchanged, soldiers should have the left foot forward; this way the throw is stronger, for hurling darts. But when it comes to what they call 'to javelins,' and the fighting is hand-to-hand with swords, soldiers should have the right foot forward, so as to draw the flank away from the enemy lest they be wounded, and to have the right hand closer so it can land a blow" (Milner trans., p. 22).

.

Later, as their strength increased, in order to continue the practice of moving their arms in striking, and also to be able to stand up under sustained effort, they would be made to attack with swords, axes, and other weapons stakes fixed in the ground for that purpose. Against these stakes, as if they were the real enemy, the apprentices at arms would try their skill, assailing and smiting first the head, then the left and right sides, then practice dodging blows.[33] In this sort of assault they would develop strength and breath as well as skill in attacking and fighting. As their age and strength developed, they would be given increasingly heavy loads to carry, and even heavier arms than those used in battle, so that those they would use later would seem light in comparison. Then they would learn to strike with a rapier. The Romans were the first to put this weapon to use, for they mocked those who struck with the edge of a sword, saying that one could scarcely kill that way, because the hardness of bones breaks the force of the blow, but the rapier makes a mortal wound if it enters the head or the body even as much as the span of two fingers. Also, when one fights with a sword, he uncovers his left side when he raises his arms, as one who strikes with a rapier is not obliged to do.[34] Moreover, the man striking with a rapier can keep the arms close to the body, so that he can wound before the opponent has had time to raise his arm.

33. Vegetius I, xi: "The ancients, as one finds in books, trained recruits in this manner. They wove shields from withies, of hurdle-like construction, and circular, such that the hurdle had twice the weight that a government shield normally has. They also gave recruits wooden foils likewise of double weight, instead of swords. So equipped, they were trained not only in the morning but even after noon against posts. Indeed, the use of posts is of very great benefit to gladiators as well as soldiers. Neither the arena nor the battle-field ever proved a man invincible in armed combat, unless he was judged to have been trained at the post. Each recruit would plant a single post in the ground so that it could not move and protruded six feet. Against the post as if against an adversary the recruit trained himself using the foil and hurdle like a sword and shield, so that now he aimed at it as if it were the head and face, now threatened the flanks, then tried to cut the hamstrings and legs, backed off, came on, sprang, and aimed at the post with every method of attack and art of combat, as though it were an actual opponent. In this training care was taken that the recruit drew himself up to inflict wounds without exposing any part of himself to a blow" (Milner trans., p. 12).

34. Vegetius I, xii: "Further, they learned to strike not with the edge, but with the point. For the Romans not only easily beat those fighting with the edge, but even made mock of them, as a cut, whatever its force, seldom kills, because the vitals are protected by both armour and bones. But a stab driven two inches in is fatal; for necessarily whatever goes in penetrates the vitals. Secondly while a cut is being delivered the right arm and flank are exposed; whereas a stab is inflicted with the body remaining covered, and the enemy is wounded before he realizes it. That is why, it is agreed, the Romans used chiefly this method for fighting. The hurdle and foil of double weight they gave out so that when the recruit took up real, and lighter arms, he fought with more confidence and agility, as being liberated from the heavier weight" (Milner trans., p. 13). Roman preference for this method of fighting has already been mentioned in the *Fais et bonnes meurs* (Solente ed., I, p. 223). Solente attributes the quotation to Henri de Gauchi's translation of Gilles de Rome, Bibl. Nat. MS fr. 1203, fols. 136v°–138v°.

The masters trained them to carry packs, in addition to all their arms, to accustom them to carrying heavy loads, so that in case of necessity they could carry their supplies with them. In confirmation of this practice, Vegetius says that nothing learned by long practice is difficult. Virgil likewise confirms this practice when he says that the valiant Romans often carried with them their necessities in addition to their arms.[35]

Besides all these things, the youths learned to leap completely armed, spears raised high, onto wooden horses, and they learned to climb walls swiftly with ropes, and even to make light ladders from knotted ropes in order to scale walls.

X.

### MORE OF THE SAME, AND ALSO THE SKILLS TAUGHT TO THE CHILDREN OF THE COMMON PEOPLE.

People of classical times introduced their offspring to all these usages mentioned and others as well, with the good doctrine of honorable words instilling in them courage, so that when they came to engage in actual battle, they were as if already trained in everything necessary and were so sharp that they could scarcely be restrained. Such doctrine was necessary in the times of the great conquests, and would still be useful in France or in any country where it is sometimes necessary to take up arms. Sallust says that the knight and the man-at-arms should learn the skills of arms from early youth, and through practice should know the art of chivalry. It is better, he says, that young men should be excused for not having entirely mastered the martial art than that they should be reproached in old

---

35. Vegetius I, xix:

Recruits should very frequently be made to carry a burden of up to 60 lb. and route-march at the military step, since on arduous campaigns they have necessarily to carry their rations together with their arms. This should not be thought hard, once the habit has been gained, for there is nothing that continual practice does not render very easy. We know that the ancient soldiers used to do this exercise from the evidence of Vergil himself, who says:

"Just as the bold Roman in his national arms
Cruelly laden takes the road, and before
The enemy expects it stands in formation, having pitched camp."

Virgil, *Georgics* vv. 3.346–48
(Milner trans., pp. 18–19)

age for never having known it.[36] For this reason the ancients valued so little the nobles who knew nothing of it that they made no distinction between them and peasants. But concerning the fact that they greatly
valued valiant men, Vegetius says in praises of them:[37] "O! men worthy of
such marvels through having wished to exercise the noble art of chivalry,
you performed so well that fighting seemed to come to you naturally. It
should be recognized that you are the ones without whom other men
could not live in peace or be defended."

It is therefore greatly to the advantage of a young man of goodwill, if
he has time and place, to learn the art and science of warfare, a task no
one should consider easy or without pain. One, he says, who is well
versed in such a discipline has no fear of fighting against an adversary,
but rather finds it true pleasure and delight. Along with this the authors
add that the skill in which the common people were versed, which was
knowing how to use a sling effectively, is very useful for those who know
how to do it well. It was much used by the ancients, of whom Vegetius
says that as carrying a sling is very light, it is a very useful thing. It sometimes happens that a battle takes place on stony ground, or that it is necessary to defend a mountain. Even in the assault or defense of a fortress a
sling can be very useful. It was formerly held in such high esteem that in
some of the Greek islands mothers would not give food to their children
until they had struck their meat with a slingshot blow.[38] Along with this
they taught them how to shoot with a bow or crossbow. Their teachers instructed them to hold the bow on their right side with the left hand, and
then the cord was drawn by the right hand with great force and skill, the
arrow near the ear, the heart and eye fixed steadily on the mark and at-
tentively aimed. In this art young Englishmen are still instructed from
early youth, and for this reason they commonly surpass other archers.
They can hit a barge aimed at from a distance of six hundred feet. Vegetius says that this art must be practiced constantly even by skilled mas-

36. Sallust is quoted here by way of Vegetius I, iv: " 'Directly as soon as youth was able to endure
war, it learned military practice in camp through labour.' For it is better that a trained young man
should complain that he has not yet reached fighting age, than that he should regret that it has
passed" (Milner trans., p. 5).

37. Christine here gives a free translation of all of Vegetius I, viii.

38. Vegetius I, xvi: "It is advisable that recruits be thoroughly trained at casting stones by hand or
with slings. The inhabitants of the Balearic Isles are said to have been first to discover the use of slings
and to have practised with such expertise that mothers did not allow their small sons to touch any
food unless they had hit it with a stone shot from a sling" (Milner trans., p. 16).

ters, for practice is necessary. Cato says in his book of arms that good archers are very useful in battle. Claudius testifies to this when he says that archers and those trained in throwing darts overcame their enemies with relatively few men;[39] so does the valiant fighter Scipio the African. Along with this they were trained to throw stones, to bear shields and cover themselves with these, to throw lances and other such weapons. It is said that well-trained and experienced masters were there to take note of the physiognomy and the bodies of the youths. They noted those who were the most agile and suitable for the discipline and instruction in arms: those whose eyes were alert and spirits flexible, heads high and broad of chest, with large shoulders, long arms that were muscular and well-shaped bony hands, lean bellies and trim lower backs, large thighs and well-formed sinewy legs, broad straight feet. As for the height of the body, that was immaterial. Attention was paid above all to bodily strength and litheness.[40] They instructed such well-formed young men carefully and diligently in the art of warfare. When, along with physical aptitude, they were seen to have a good grasp of what they were doing, they were held in high esteem and instructed in the things a military leader should know.

Along with all this they were taught to swim in rivers and in the sea. Vegetius explains that this skill is useful for all military men to know, as it may sometimes be put to the test. It can happen, and often does, that they are forced to cross rivers and streams to escape danger, or to take a shortcut, or for some other need such as to get where they are going on time and in this way surprise an unsuspecting enemy.[41]

Through the water the ancients very cleverly dragged after them their baggage and equipment on slabs of wood and on dried thornbush, which they guided as they swam. In this way a man-at-arms could escape from mortal peril, as is written of the brave Julius Caesar, who, in order to safe-

39. Vegetius I, xv (Archers): "This art needs to be learned thoroughly and maintained by daily use and exercise. How much utility good archers have in battle was clearly shown by Cato in his books On Military Science, and by Claudius, who overcame an enemy to whom he had previously been unequal by establishing and training numerous darters" (Milner trans., p. 15).

40. Vegetius I, vi: "So let the adolescent who is to be selected for martial activity have alert eyes, straight neck, broad chest, muscular shoulders, strong arms, long fingers, let him be small in the stomach, slender in the buttocks, and have calves and feet that are not swollen by surplus fat but firm with hard muscle. When you see these points in a recruit, you need not greatly regret the absence of tall stature. It is more useful that soldiers be strong than big" (Milner trans., p. 7).

41. Vegetius I, x: "Every recruit without exception should in the summer months learn the art of swimming, for rivers are not always crossed by bridges, and armies both when advancing and retreating are frequently forced to swim" (Milner trans., p. 11).

guard his life, swam three hundred feet in the sea. Likewise, Cena, that most valiant Roman knight, although severely wounded, escaped alone from a great multitude of his enemies by swimming across a great river. In this same way some people besieged in a castle were helped with food at night by their friends swimming without the knowledge of their enemies. Similarly the ancients taught their cattle and their horses this skill.

In answer to those who might say that these things are easy to speak of but hard to learn, our author says that, although all things may seem difficult to the pupil before he knows them, if the teacher is diligent and intent upon demonstration, there is no skill so difficult to learn that by long usage it does not become easy.[42] Another custom observed by the Romans, among others, was that the nobles should wear a different costume from that worn by those who were not noble, and they also had robes for joyful occasions and others for mourning, which they wore according to the fortunes of the moment. If they had lost some important battle, or if a country had rebelled against them, or a great injury had been done them that cried out for vengeance, then they donned the mourning robe, not wearing any other until they were avenged and had come out on top; then they again wore their joyful clothes.

XI.

### HERE ARE DISCUSSED THE PRACTICAL MILITARY SKILLS MEN-AT-ARMS SHOULD POSSESS AND IN WHICH THEY SHOULD BE INSTRUCTED.

We have already discussed at some length the sorts of instruction in feats of arms that the ancients provided for their children, which are good to remember as examples. We must now return to what has been said before, which is what things the good and wise leader of knights or his lieutenants will make use of. First of all, he will attach to his command, as has been said, the best and most outstanding men-at-arms possible, and he will cherish them. Speaking of a good man-at-arms, Vegetius outlines the qualities that become him, saying that with boldness, without which nothing is of any value, he must be taught to use his equipment properly and be comfortable in its use, so that he may assail his enemy rapidly,

---

42. Vegetius I, xix: "[T]here is nothing that continual practice does not render very easy" (Milner trans., p. 18).

leap a ditch lightly, scramble up a high embankment if it stands in his way, assault the lodgings of his adversaries over hedges or pavilions if the situation requires it, dodge blows with suppleness, or invade by leaping over the enemy, if the nature of the battle requires it. He says that this sort of expertise startles the enemy and frightens him, and the advantage is often given to the skillful man over one who is stronger than he, so he wounds him before he is able to defend himself.[43] The great Pompey,[44] he says, used such tricks when he fought.

If I should be asked where the best men-at-arms are to be found, I would reply that it is said that in hot lands, near the sun, men, although wise, wily, and malicious, are not very brave, because due to the excessive heat they do not have a great deal of blood. On the other hand, it is said that those from the cold lands are hardy but not wise, so that neither the one nor the other should be chosen, but rather those from temperate lands should be taken.[45] As for myself, I would insist that no other rule should be followed except to choose those who have had the greatest experience and who are most pleased in the pursuit of arms, in which labor their greatest pleasure is centered, without their desiring other happiness or honor beyond that which comes to them from chivalrous deeds. And these, from whatever nation they may come, are to be received and chosen. It is true that it is prudent to agree with the authorities that if the leader needs common men, he should choose them above all from certain trades, such as butchers, who are accustomed to shed blood and strike with an axe, carpenters, smiths, and all others who exercise the body in their work and make use of their arms,[46] and also villagers, to

43. Vegetius I, ix: "The soldier should also be trained at jumping, whereby ditches are vaulted and hurdles of a certain height surmounted, so that when obstacles of this kind are encountered he can cross them without effort. Furthermore, in the actual conflict and clash of arms the soldier coming on by a running jump makes the adversary's eyes flinch, frightens his mind and plants a blow before the other can properly prepare himself for evasive or offensive action" (Milner trans., p. 11).

44. Pompey the Great: Roman general and statesman, he was a member of the first triumvirate and was married to Caesar's daughter, Julia.

45. Vegetius I, ii: "They tell us that all peoples that are near the sun, being parched by great heat, are more intelligent but have less blood, and therefore lack steadiness and confidence to fight at close quarters, because those who are conscious of having less blood are afraid of wounds. On the other hand the peoples of the north, remote from the sun's heat, are less intelligent, not having a superabundance of blood are readiest for wars. Recruits should therefore be raised from the more temperate climes. The plenteousness of their blood supplies a contempt for wounds and death, and intelligence cannot be lacking either which preserves discipline in camp and is of no little assistance with counsel in battle" (Milner trans., pp. 3–4).

46. Vegetius I, vii: "Masons, blacksmiths, wainwrights, butchers and stag- and boar-hunters may usefully be joined to the military" (Milner trans., pp. 7–8).

whom hard beds and the pain of labor are not foreign, and who are nour-
ished on coarse food. These are suitable to suffer pain and travail, without which no war can be long sustained.[47]

## XII.

### A DISCUSSION OF THE QUALITIES A GOOD CONSTABLE OR COMMANDER SHOULD DEMONSTRATE IN THE CONDUCT OF HIS OFFICE.

In the event that war is set in motion, after the prince's deliberation and
with the usual hindrances encountered, the wise leader will, to begin
with, order that the frontiers be well garrisoned, with both good men-at-
arms and artillerymen, as well as with other necessary things and provisions, depending on the skill of the enemy. Cities and fortresses should
be prepared so that nothing further will be needed. The leader will then
determine what number of men will be necessary, according to the nature of the undertaking. He will then select the best among his men-at-
arms, archers, gunners, and others, according to the number considered
necessary.

With regard to the fact that nowadays it is held that victory in battle
can reasonably be expected to fall to the side that has the most men, Vegetius says that, on the contrary, in ordinary battle it is sufficient to lead
one legion of men-at-arms with their aides. A legion numbers 6,666 of
what we should call spears or helmets. All authors who have written on
this matter agree with Vegetius that too great a number of men encourages confusion, so that the most needed against an even greater number
of enemies would be no more than two legions of good men-at-arms, but
they must be led by an excellent commander.[48] This would amount to no
more than thirteen thousand helmets. One finds that many armies have

47. Vegetius I, iii: "The next question is to consider whether a recruit from the country or from
the city is more useful. On this subject I think it could never have been doubted that the rural populace is better suited for arms. They are nurtured under the open sky in a life of work, enduring the
sun, careless of shade, unacquainted with bathhouses, ignorant of luxury, simple-souled, content
with a little, with limbs toughened to endure every kind of toil, and for whom wielding iron, digging
a fosse and carrying a burden is what they are used to from the country" (Milner trans., p. 4).

48. Vegetius II, iv: "In all the authorities it is found that individual consuls led against the most
numerous hostile forces no more than two legions each, with *auxilia* of the Allies added" (Milner
trans., p. 34).

been thrown into disarray by their own great number rather than by enemy forces.[49] And why is this so? Certainly there are good reasons, for a great multitude is more difficult to maintain in good order and is often in trouble because it requires more provisions, is more quarrelsome, and is subject to more delays on the roads. Thus it can easily happen that the enemy, though fewer in number, will surprise-attack at narrow passages or rivers. Therein lies the difficulty, for the large army cannot move forward, but so many men will rather get in the way of each other, and in battle formation they lunge forward so hastily that they mingle needlessly with the enemy and are exterminated. For this reason, as has been said, the ancients who had mastered such things useful in battle, knowing the perils from experience, placed a higher value on an army well taught and well led than a great multitude.[50]

The good commander must place over such men as he has assembled various captains and constables, to each of whom he will commit a certain number of men-at-arms, to some more than others according to their capabilities. He will also arrange for himself and his subordinates to observe his foot soldiers and archers in the field on various days. Care should be taken that none are included who are not acceptable, so that nothing will be at fault in the men or in the equipment or mounts, regardless of social status. There should also be wise clerks who see to it that there are no deceptions with regard to pay, so that those who are not accepted will not be rewarded. From the earliest times the leaders were under strict oath to serve their prince or country loyally, without fleeing or abandoning the battlefield because of fear of death or other peril. These clerks would likewise receive the oath of each man-at-arms when they accept them for pay.[51]

When these things have been well and duly accomplished, when there is good security and the pay of the men-at-arms has been set for whatever length of time they are expected to be needed—the leaders must have due regard for this matter, since it will mean the achievement

49. Vegetius III, i: "For when one reads the examples of Xerxes, Darius, Mithridates and other kings who armed countless populations, it is clearly apparent that over-large armies have been overcome more by their own size than the bravery of the enemy. For a greater multitude is subject to more mishaps. On marches it is always slower because of its size; a longer column often suffers ambush even by small numbers; in broken country and at river-crossings it is often caught in a trap as a result of delays caused by the baggage-train" (Milner trans., p. 64).

50. Vegetius III, xxvi: "Bravery is of more value than numbers" (Milner trans., p. 117).

51. This same advice from Vegetius had already been mentioned in the *Livre des fais et bonnes meurs* (Solente ed., I, pp. 200–201). Christine probably also had in mind the *lettres de retenue* devised by Charles V in 1374. (See Philippe Contamine, *War in the Middle Ages*, 153.)

or failure of their undertaking (nobody can expect to have good soldiers who are badly paid, because their courage will decline along with their pay)—then the leaders will take leave of the prince and in the field will put these men into such action as circumstances require.

XIII.

HERE IS DISCUSSED THE MANNER IN WHICH
A COMMANDER IS EXPECTED TO LODGE HIS ARMY,
ACCORDING TO BOOKS DEALING WITH ARMS.

If it happens that the aforementioned commander undertakes to draw up a battle formation against his enemies, whose arrival he expects, whereby he must have a piece of ground on which to lodge his men, he will consider the matter according to his expectations of the enemy's arrival. Accordingly, he will lodge his men as advantageously as possible, beginning by determining whether he can have a situation advantageous to him, and not to his enemy.[52]

Titus Livius[53] says that in the time when the armies of Gaul and of Germany marched against the Romans, these latter, warned of their coming, went ahead of them and by arriving first took advantage of the field and the situation. They decided to lodge themselves in such a way that they were between their enemies and a river, so that they conquered them more by thirst than by power of arms. But it is not sufficient just to take up a good situation in the field; it should be one where the enemy, if it approaches, cannot find a better one for itself. Shelter should be established on high ground, so that no mountain overshadows it, near a river if possible. It will be wise to choose some suitable situation in good air, if at all possible, where the space between lodgings is adequate.

52. Vegetius I, xxii: "Camps—especially when the enemy is near—should be built always in a safe place, where there are sufficient supplies of firewood, fodder and water, and if a long stay is in prospect choose a salubrious site. Care must be taken lest there be a nearby mountain or high ground which could be dangerous if captured by the enemy. Thought must be given that the site is not liable to flooding from torrents and the army to suffer harm in this event. The camp should be built according to the number of soldiers and baggage-train, lest too great a multitude be crammed in a small area, or a small force in too large a space be compelled to be spread out more than is appropriate" (Milner trans., pp. 23–24).

53. Titus Livius (Livy): It is impossible to identify the exact passage from Livy, although it is undoubtedly a reference to book IV, which describes the conquest of Rome. Christine would have known Livy through the translation by Pierre de Bersuire, commissioned by King Jean II, although she mistakenly refers to the sponsorship of Charles V in the biography of the king (Solente ed., II, p. 44). The handsome copy from Charles V's library is now in Paris, Bibl. Sainte-Geneviève MS 777.

According to Vegetius, this should be a place where there is good pasturage,[54] water, and wood, and where the field is not liable to retain rainwater, where there are no abundant swamps, and where the adversaries cannot cause water to flow abundantly on them by breaking the edges of ponds or sluices. It should also be borne in mind that in accordance with the number of men and the abundance of empty and loaded carts, the lodging spaces should be selected so that many of them will neither be too close together nor occupy more space than is necessary, for that would make the site less strong. The carts should be placed all around, joined together; the lodging is most satisfactory when the space occupied is a third longer than it is wide. In the middle should be the most heavily fortified section, constructed like a real fortress of timber, if possible, and, if necessary, with a gate facing the enemy and other gates through which supplies can be brought. Vegetius also says that several banners should be placed on the high points. If the commander expects to hold the enemy there for a long period, he will have the place surrounded by good ditches and fencing of stakes with wooden-beam enclosures like castles, in which will be placed the stores of supplies, which should be wisely provided before anything else is undertaken.

As Vegetius says, hunger wounds more than the sword, for many things can be suffered and borne in an army, but for the demands of battle there is no endurance or remedy except by meat, although, he says, it is above all fitting that in an army men should be satisfied with a small amount of meat. For this reason, the wise commander should see to it that food is not lacking before a siege is undertaken, for sometimes sieges last longer than is foreseen, and more men are added. When the enemy sees that the army is short of rations, it becomes more aggressive in its opposition, for because of hunger it expects to overcome more easily. Because of this, men in an army try to seize food from each other, especially those who are maintaining a siege before a fortress. Thus care should be taken that those who dispense food are not themselves thieves and do not steal from the army by their many crafty schemes, for in this way armies have some-

---

54. Vegetius III, iii:

The order of subjects demands that I speak next about the provisioning-system for fodder and grain. For armies are more often destroyed by starvation than battle, and hunger is more savage than the sword. Secondly, other misfortunes can in time be alleviated: fodder and grain supply have no remedy in a crisis except storage in advance . . .

. . . Faithful stewardship of granaries and controlled issue usually provides for a sufficiency, especially if taken in hand from the outset. But economy comes too late to save (grain) when there is a deficiency. (Milner trans., pp. 67–68)

times suffered hunger, grief, discomfort, and many dangers. So one must look after this matter with care.

## XIV.
### MORE OF THE SAME.

In addition to all the things already said, the good commander, if he wishes to lead men in war according to his duty and justly toward God and the approval of the world, must pay his men so well that they have no need to resort to pillage in friendly territory. In this way the army should not be wanting, for all goods and foodstuffs would arrive in timely fashion. So that merchants can travel unharmed, let him decree upon penalty of death that nothing be taken without payment nor merchants in any way be wronged. Would to God that it were done this way everywhere, for it would be of great benefit. I believe that all things would come to a better end. It is dangerous in time of war for an army to be more driven by greed for pillage than by the intention to preserve the rightness of their cause or the honor of chivalry or to gain praise. Such men as these could better be called thieves or robbers than men-at-arms or knights. The Gauls provide a good example of this right intention. They, having conquered the Romans with a great army and in a great battle on the Rhône River, had acquired great booty. But in order to show that they gave no importance to this, such not being their intention, they took all the booty, including rich harnesses, plate, gold, silver, and threw it all into the river, which astonished the Romans, who had never seen any such thing done before.

Therefore, the wise commander, who is well provided with the things mentioned above, will not wait for foragers, who all too often cannot find anything to take, but will have provided for everything before his departure, not only all the supplies needed for war, but all sorts of victuals that he will have sent before him in carts and bundles: wheat, wines, salted meat, dried beans, salt, vinegar, which is quite refreshing with water when wine is lacking in summertime, as well as all the other useful things that he will distribute wisely.

The book of arms says further that if the army must remain for long in one place to await a great enemy host, the spot must be fortified with very good ditches, twelve feet wide and nine feet deep, or thirteen if the earth taken from the ditches is nearby, and they should be rigid and strong on the sides to be protected from the enemy, with stakes and other encumbering objects placed there. But, he says, if the army does not need to remain there for a long time, or if no great force is expected, there is no need for such fortifications, but rather it is sufficient, if ditches are desired, to have them eight or nine feet in width and seven in depth.[55] In order to do this, the good commander should assign experienced men-at-arms with weapons to guard the workers while the fortifications are in progress. To accomplish all this the wise commander will have provided the proper tools: iron shovels, rakes, pickaxes, saws, axes with augers, and the sort of metal tools needed to build lodgings and set up the tents and pavilions required, and also workmen who know how to do these things.

Nevertheless, says Vegetius, men-at-arms should themselves be skilled in cutting wood, making roads through thickets, building lodgings, making fences of timber and branches, gathering together planks for bridges, if necessary, filling ditches with branches in order to cross, making ladders, and other such things.

According to the aforesaid author, the ancient conquerors took with them in their armies forges to make helmets and all sorts of armor, tools to make bows, arrows, spears, and all other sorts of armaments, with workmen skilled in all these things. Their primary concern was that whatever the army might need could be provided as it would be in a city, for they would not soon be returning to their homes. There were even sappers who knew how to dig underground in order to take the enemy by surprise.[56]

Along with this, Vegetius describes what must be considered to keep

---

55. Vegetius I, xxiv:

THE SORTS OF FORTIFICATION OF A CAMP.

There are three different sorts of fortification of a camp. When there is no pressing danger, turves are cut from the earth and from them a kind of wall is built, 3 ft. high above the ground, with the fosse from which the turves are lifted in front. Then there is a temporary fosse 9 ft. wide and 7 ft. deep. But when more serious forces of the enemy threaten it is advisable to fortify the perimeter of the camp with a proper fosse, 12 ft. wide and 9 ft. deep below the "line," as it is called. Above it revetments are built on either side and filled with earth that has been raised from the fosse, rising to a height of 4 ft. The result is that (the fosse) is 13 ft. deep and 12 ft. wide. Above are fixed stakes of very strong wood, which the soldiers are accustomed to carry with them. For this work it is advisable always to have in readiness mattocks, rakes, baskets and other kinds of tools. (Milner trans., p. 24–25)

56. Vegetius II, xi:

THE DUTIES OF THE PREFECT OF ENGINEERS.

Moreover, the legion has engineers, carpenters, masons, wagon-makers, blacksmiths, painters and other artificers, ready-prepared to construct buildings for a winter camp, or siege-the army in good health if it stays for a long time in one place. For this he outlines four conditions, which is to say, location, water, weather, and exercise: a place that is not subject to swamps or hazy marshes; water that is not contaminated, dirty, or stagnant in ditches full of vermin; weather that in the heat of summer is tempered by trees to shade the lodgings. Nor should good water be lacking for men or horses, and medicine should be provided by practitioners and doctors, along with all things needed by the sick, as would be available in a city, for although these men are accustomed to suffer pain, fatigue, and hard beds, they are done in when they are ill, to which they are unaccustomed.[57] Such as these are ready for battle, are prepared to endure cold, heat, hard beds, and a rigorous life, for nothing can happen to them that they have not already experienced. So in this way, according to Vegetius, the wise commander will have his lodgings built where, in due order, he will establish his captains with their men under various standards and banners,[58] so that they can go

---

engines, wooden towers and other devices for storming enemy cities or defending our own, to fabricate new arms, wagons and the other kinds of torsion-engines, or repair them when damaged. They used to have workshops, too, for shields, cuirasses and bows, in which arrows, missiles, helmets and arms of every type were made. For the main aim was to ensure that nothing which the army was thought to require should be lacking in camp, to the extent that they even had sappers who, in the fashion of the Bessi, sank mines underground, and dug through the foundations of walls to emerge unexpectedly and capture hostile cities. The particular officer responsible for these matters was the Prefect of engineers. (Milner trans., p. 43)

57. Vegetius III, 2:

HOW THE ARMY'S HEALTH IS CONTROLLED.

Next I shall explain a subject to which special thought must be devoted—how the army's health is preserved—that is, by means of site, water-supply, season, medicine and exercise. By "site" I mean that soldiers should not camp in pestilential areas near unhealthy marshes, nor in arid plains and hills, lacking tree-cover, nor without tents in summer. They should not move out too late in the day and fall sick from sunstroke and marching-fatigue, but rather start a march before dawn, reaching the destination in the heat of the day. They should not in severe winter weather march by night through snow and ice, or suffer from shortage of firewood or an inadequate supply of clothes. For a soldier who is forced to be cold is not likely to be healthy or fit for an expedition. Neither should the army use bad or marsh water, for bad drinking-water, like poison, causes disease in the drinkers. Besides, it requires constant vigilance on the part of the officers and tribunes and of the "count" who holds the senior command to see that ordinary soldiers who fall sick from this cause be nursed back to health with suitable food and tended by the doctors' art. It is hard for those who are fighting both a war and disease.

But military experts considered that daily exercises in arms were more conducive to soldiers' health than doctors. (Milner trans., pp. 65–66)

58. Vegetius III, viii: "So first the standards are set up in their places inside the camp, because nothing is more revered by the soldiers than their majesty, the headquarters is prepared for the general and his staff-officers and the pavilions are erected for the tribunes, who are served with water, firewood and fodder by privates assigned to services" (Milner trans., p. 81).

directly into battle in the formations that have been assigned to them. The commander will be placed in the middle, with his own men and with his own standard raised above them.

XV.

HERE IS DISCUSSED THE CARE THE COMMANDER
SHOULD TAKE OF HIS FORCES.

Among other qualities to be especially recommended to a duke or military commander is this: that he be a gentleman of great loyalty, as is written of the good Fabricius, commander of the Roman army. For his great valor and goodness King Pyrrhus, his enemy, offered to give him a quarter of his realm and his treasury if only he would surrender and join his forces. To this he replied that he despised too greatly riches gained by treason and malice, and that though he might be conquered by force of arms, he would not be by disloyalty. In this regard Vegetius says that the commander, to whom is entrusted so great a thing as the responsibility and direction of knighthood's honor, the affairs of the prince, the commonweal, the safety of cities, and the fortunes of battles, should not merely be responsible for the army in general, but for each and every member; for if something should go wrong, it is seen to be his fault.[59] For this reason, the valiant commander and duke, commissioned by the prince, as it is said, will make a great point of seeing to it that his men behave themselves in their lodgings, as indeed they should. For the book says that these young squires, when they are at leisure, should amuse themselves by hand-to-hand combat, demonstrating that exercise pleases them more than idleness, for it often happens among young people together that noise and unruly behavior result if they are not held in check, and the wise leader should be aware of this. The master says that noisy and quarrelsome men are a danger in an army, and for this reason, when such there are, a way must be found to get rid of them, though not merely by dismissing them, so that they can go elsewhere, if they are foreign recruits or if they are capable of stirring up trouble, but by sending

---

59. Vegetius III, x: "So the general who has bestowed on him the insignia of great power, and to whose loyalty and strength are entrusted the wealth of landowners, the protection of cities, the lives of soldiers and the glory of the State, should be anxious for the welfare not just of his entire army, but for each and every common soldier also. For if anything happens to them in war, it is seen as his fault and the nation's loss" (Milner trans., p. 87).

them elsewhere on some invented mission.[60] It is further said that if the necessity arises to give such as these strong medicine, they should not be spared, for the most useful thing is for others to profit by their example; they should not be allowed to offend and outrage other people.[61] Moreover, he says, captains are more to be praised when their men are disciplined by rule and good doctrine than when they are restrained merely by fear of punishment. In this regard, the authority says that men gathered from various places and nations in an army are readily moved to noise and tumult, and it also sometimes happens that there are some who have a cowardly fear of battle and so pretend to be angry so that they will not be sent into combat. This arises from one of two causes, or perhaps from both. Either they have more sympathy for the other side, or they are accustomed to leading a lazy and undisciplined life; for this reason the burden of unaccustomed effort annoys them and does not bring out the best in them.[62] The books say that it is greatly to the credit of a leader when his men conduct themselves properly in the army, and in this connection it is said that when Cymas, the messenger of King Pyrrhus, was dispatched to deal with the Roman army, he found there knights of such high and noble bearing that he reported back that he had seen an army made up entirely of kings.

60. Vegetius III, iv:

Soldiers who have been so trained and exercised at their base, whether they are legionaries, *auxilia* or cavalry, when they come together for a campaign from their various units inevitably prefer warfare to leisure in the rivalry for valour. No one thinks of mutiny, when he carries confidence in his skill and strength.

But the general should be careful to learn from tribunes, "vicars" and officers in all legions . . . if there are any disorderly or mutinous soldiers. The more prudent policy is then to segregate them from camp to do some work which might seem to them almost desirable or else to allocate them to fortifying and guarding forts and cities, with such subtlety that they seem to have been specially selected although they are being cast off. (Milner trans., p. 70)

61. Vegetius III, x: "Let him assume maximum authority and severity, punish all military crimes according to the laws, have a reputation for forgiving no errors and make trial of everyone in different places in diverse situations" (Milner trans., p. 87).

62. Vegetius III, iv:

An army gathered together from different places occasionally raises a riot and, when in fact it is unwilling to fight, it pretends to be angry at not being led out to battle. This is chiefly the action of those who have lived at their home base in idleness and luxury. Taking offence at the harshness of the unaccustomed effort which it is necessary to endure on campaign, fearing battle besides, having shirked exercises in arms, they plunge headlong into a rash enterprise of this sort.

A compound treatment is usually applied to this wound. While they are still separate and in their base, (soldiers) should be held to every article of discipline by the strictest severity of tribunes, "vicars" and officers. (Milner trans., p. 69)

Thus the wise commander, who will be provided with all his needs, will take great care that nothing will be left undone through his own fault without his being aware of it. He will scarcely sleep and will take little rest, for a courageous heart is the result of great effort in all things. Thus he will be inspired to send surreptitiously spies and scouts here and there to seek out and learn the situation of his enemies, so that he can decide according to their reports how many men he has with reference to how many they have; what sort of people he has and what sort they; how strong they are and how well armed; which side has better horses, the more archers and foot soldiers, and from what nation; what reinforcements and from where they might come for both his adversaries and himself; what situation and what advantage either side might have. On these matters he will wish to have the opinion of several wise knights, good leaders who will be on his staff, experienced and honorable men expert in arms.[63] He will not wish to act entirely on his own, but rather on the advice of several others, and with them he will consider the best course to follow, if he will undertake battle or not, sooner or later, or if he will wait to be attacked, always watchful to deceive the enemy by some trap. If he discovers that the others are awaiting reinforcements, he will hasten to attack them at once, or if he himself is expecting relief, he will delay if he considers himself weaker, so he will make his preparations and remain on alert. He will take care that a good watch is maintained, so that nothing happens inopportunely during meals and they cannot be surprised, for the master says that in greater security there is greater peril.[64] For this reason the commander should, if he sees the opportunity, attack his enemy when they are eating, or when they are sleeping, or fatigued from marching, or their horses are feeding, when they think they are safe, because for those surprised in such a way neither skill nor strength will help them, nor are numbers of any use.[65] One who is conquered in full battle

63. Vegetius III, ix: "An important art useful to a general is to call in persons from the entire army who are knowledgeable about war and aware of their own and the enemy's forces, and to hold frequent discussions with them in an atmosphere from which all flattery, which does so much harm, has been banished, to decide whether he or the enemy has the greater number of fighters, whether his own men or the enemy's are better armed and armoured and which side is the more highly trained or the braver in warfare" (Milner trans., p. 84).

64. Vegetius III, xxii: "Necessarily, more freedom from fear generally brings with it graver danger" (Milner trans., p. 109).

65. Vegetius III, x: "Let him so regulate his march that, fully prepared, he attacks the enemy when they are suspecting nothing, when they are eating meals, sleeping or at any rate resting, when they are relaxed, unarmed, unshod and their horses unsaddled, to the end that his men may acquire self-confidence in battles of this kind" (Milner trans., p. 88).

because his knowledge and experience of arms have been of little use to him can, nevertheless, in his anger complain to fortune, but the one who is overcome or damaged by a deceitful trap can blame only himself, for he could have avoided it if he had been as careful to protect himself as his enemy had been to take him by surprise. How well this was demonstrated by that wise master of the art of warfare, the valiant Scipio the African, when he found a way to have a fire break out at night in the tents of his enemy, and then jumped on them with such force that they did not know what was happening. In this way they were conquered more by astonishment than by arms.

With respect to spying on one's enemies, Vegetius says that it is very profitable to have wise spies who know well how to discover the strategy of the adversaries.[66] For such as these know how by gifts and promises to intervene and by ruse to attract one or several, even from the council of the other side, if possible, so that they can learn the whole plan of action, and in this way their commander can decide the best thing to do.

With all this, Vegetius says that it is very profitable to find ways of sowing dissension in the enemy ranks,[67] so that they do not deign to obey their commander, of whom it should undertaken to learn the situation, and if one can in any way catch him in his own traces. For the wise commander should be well aware that no nation, however small, can be completely wiped out by an adversary if it is not disrupted by discord within itself. But just as the commander will take care to send his spies, he will make sure that his own situation is not discovered by spies, that this cannot be revealed, or even that the ordering of his army or the number of men be known by his enemy, so that they could take advantage of these things. Nevertheless, another method is useful to some: if they feel themselves so strong and well equipped with so many men-at-arms, they may be pleased for their enemy to see and know their strength in order that they might fear it all the more, as happened when King Pyrrhus of Macedonia sent his spies to learn the state and quality of his enemies. These

---

66. Vegetius III, vi: "Just as it is to our advantage to avoid these things by being prudent, so we ought not to let slip any opportunity which the enemy's inexperience or negligence offers to us. We should reconnoitre assiduously, solicit traitors and deserters so we can find out the enemy's present and future plans and, with our cavalry and light armament in prepared positions, catch them in unforeseen ambushes while marching or seeking fodder and food" (Milner trans., p. 77).

67. Vegetius III, x: "It is (also) the mark of a skilled general to sow seeds of discord among the enemy. For no nation, however small, can be completely destroyed by its enemies, unless it devours itself by its own feuding. Civil strife is quick to compass the destruction of political enemies, but careless about the readiness of (the nation's) own defence" (Milner trans., p. 88).

spies were captured and led before the leader of the Roman host, who did not wish for them to suffer injury but rather commanded that they should be led everywhere so that they would report his great strength. As a result Pyrrhus was greatly impressed by the Romans and feared them all the more. Likewise, it is said that the great Alexander, at the time of his conquests, did this. But where it is possible to learn whether the adversary has more foot soldiers, or more men-at-arms, or more bowmen, the commander can accordingly make plans best to serve his own purposes, to the disadvantage of the enemy.

The authorities who have spoken of this matter say that in former times army commanders had distinctive insignia on their helmets in order to be recognized by their men, and banners with certain devices where their men could assemble. One hundred knights, or men-at-arms, were under one captain, and these were called centurions. Others had a greater number and some fewer. The banners and standards of the leader were carried by the most valiant knights, the most faithful and most dependable—an order that is still observed today because by looking at the banner the host and the battle are directed. It is written how, through the fault of a traitor who once held the standard in Greece, a great army was defeated in battle by a smaller number of men.

## XVI.

### HEREIN IS DESCRIBED THE PROCEDURE THE COMMANDER SHOULD FOLLOW IN MOVING FROM ONE PLACE TO ANOTHER AND THE ROUTES BY WHICH HE SHOULD LEAD HIS ARMY.

If it should come about that the army must depart and change place, the wise commander will consider how to accomplish this. Vegetius says that before the leader moves, he should know the situation of the enemy well enough that he can decide if it is better to leave by day or by night.[68] But he must already have taken into account the condition of the roads, so as to be prepared to protect his army from being surprised, as for example in too narrow passes where it can be cornered, or in the marshes or swamps where others know better the details of the terrain. Therefore, as is the case for those who travel by sea and do not know its perils, the routes or narrows which they must take should have been painted on a map in

---

68. Vegetius III, vi: "We ought also to know the habits of the enemy—whether they usually attack by night, at daybreak or during the rest-hour when men are tired—and avoid that which we think they will do from routine" (Milner trans., p. 77).

order to know how to avoid the perils. The commander and other leaders should know the routes and passes, mountains, woods, bodies of water, streams, and narrows that they will encounter. And yet, in addition to being well informed, the wise commander, for fear of failure, will take along, if need be, guides chosen from those who know the way. These people used as guides should be so well guarded that they cannot escape and will not have an opportunity to betray the army or do any sort of harm. He will give them money and promise them great rewards if they lead loyally, but will also threaten them with great harm if they do otherwise.[69] The commander will also have forbidden, under oath, those in his council to reveal the road chosen, or where the army is being led, for there is scarcely any army without traitors, and it is quite unlikely that among such a large group of people, where there are numerous foreigners, all should be of good courage. But the commander should know that nothing is less acceptable to princes, lords, or commanders of armies than those who turn out to be undependable. They deserve punishment, even though through falsehood they may appear to be obedient. The Romans demonstrated this to those who had treacherously killed Sertorius, their lord, because they thought this would please the Romans. Although he was Roman, he had conducted a great war against those of Rome because of the spite and envy he bore against other Roman princes. When the traitors came for their reward, however, they were repaid with death, and were told that such pay befitted treason. Likewise, it is written that Alexander did the same to those who, thinking to please him, had killed their lord, King Darius.

Along with this, the wise commander will have ordered several of his good and faithful men, mounted on good horses, to search everywhere to make sure that the army is not being spied upon. Vegetius recommends that spies be sent ahead as if they were pilgrims or laborers, to search day and night for ambushes.[70] If these spies do not return, the commander should follow another route if possible, for this is an indication that they have been captured. Such people are apt to tell under torture all they

69. Vegetius III, vi: "Furthermore he should collect at the risk of those responsible for choosing them able guides, knowledgeable of the roads, and keep them under guard having given them a demonstration of punishment and reward, they will be useful when they understand that there is no longer any chance of escape for them, and that there is ready reward for loyalty and retribution for treachery" (Milner trans., p. 74).

70. Vegetius III, vi: "When a general intends to set out with his army in column, he should send ahead very reliable and quick-witted men on excellent mounts to reconnoitre those places through which the army is due to march, both in advance and in the rear, and to right and left, to prevent the enemy laying ambush. Scouts operate more safely at night than in daytime. In some measure a general betrays himself if his scout is captured by the enemy" (Milner trans., p. 75).

know. Thus he will not show lack of experience in putting his army in
good form before departure, which is to say, placing the best of his men
with abundant ammunition on the side from which he thinks the greatest
peril may come. He will also command the weakest to obey the strongest.
He will order and command that the vanguard should proceed in good
order, closely serrated, ready to encounter the enemy if need be, the
main part of the battle formation coming afterward, close together like a
wall, standards, banners, and pennants held high, fluttering in the wind,
then followed by the rear guard in similar array. As sometimes an attack
or an ambush may come from the side, there should be men-at-arms and
archers available, and if the enemy is on all sides, protection should be
everywhere available.[71] Depending on the men at his disposal, he would
be well advised to take advantage of the road, whether through a flat
field, through woods, or over mountains, if he can. For horsemen defend
themselves better in woods; in mountains those on foot are better off.
Such men are used a great deal in Lombardy and in certain other countries, where they are called brigands or *fantassins*. Vegetius points out that
they can be very useful if they are good, as they can be used in fields or
cities, on mountains and in valleys, for they can throw themselves into
more places than horsemen if they are skilled and light-footed. Those
who are experienced are usually hearty, and one can have a large number at fairly low cost. The book of arms says that the captain should take
particular care of the way his men proceed; this should be in good order
and at the same pace. A badly organized host in which one company hur-
ries forward while another lags behind is in grave peril; nothing is more
harmful in case of battle than disarray. He says that the progress of the
army should be ten thousand paces in five hours in summer, which can
amount to five leagues. If need be they can go an additional two thousand paces, but no more.[72] The good commander should be further advised that on a long march he should not force his men, because the

71. Vegetius III, vi: "So let the cavalry take the road in front, then the infantry, with the baggage,
pack-horses, servants and vehicles placed in the middle, and the light-armed portion of the infantry
and cavalry bringing up the rear. For attacks on a marching army are sometimes made at the front,
but more usually in the rear. The baggage-train should also be enclosed on the flanks with equal
strengths of soldiers, for ambushers frequently attack the sides" (Milner trans., p. 75).

72. Vegetius I, ix: "So, at the very start of the training recruits should be taught the military step.
For nothing should be maintained more on the march or in battle, than that all soldiers should keep
ranks as they move. The only way that this can be done is by learning through constant training to
manoeuvre quickly and evenly. For a divided and disordered army experiences danger from the
enemy which is always most serious. So at the military step 20 miles should be covered in five hours,
at least in summer time. At the full step, which is faster, 24 miles should be covered in the same
time" (Milner trans., p. 10–11).

need of rest can make them ill. For this reason he should start out at a good hour so that they can be lodged before nightfall. During the short days of winter they should not start out so late that because of rain, snow, or frost they are obliged to march during a part of the night. They should be provided with firewood, for nothing is more necessary to an army than fire. They should not be allowed to drink polluted water that can make them ill, for in such an assemblage there is no place for illness. It is a great misfortune when the necessity of battle drives away those who, because of illness, are already unable to do what is needed.

## XVII.

### HEREIN IS DISCUSSED THE CROSSING OF RIVERS AND STREAMS.[73]

It sometimes comes to pass that it is necessary for an army to cross rivers or streams. To do this is cumbersome and filled with danger. The way to accomplish such crossings is explained by Vegetius. He says that first of all the commander should be well informed of where the ford might be less deep. In that spot he should put a line of men who are well mounted

---

73. Vegetius III, vii:

HOW TO CROSS LARGE RIVERS.

When crossing rivers careless armies often get into serious difficulties. For if the current is too strong or the river-bed too wide it is likely to drown baggage-animals, grooms and sometimes even the weaker warriors. So when a ford has been reconnoitred two lines of horsemen on picked mounts are lined up in parallel with sufficient space between them for infantry and baggage-train to pass through the middle. The upper line breaks the force of the waters, while the lower line collects up any who may be snatched away or swept under, and brings them safely across. But where the water is too deep to allow either infantry or cavalry to cross, if the river flows through flat country, it may be dispersed by digging multiple channels and easily crossed when divided. Navigable rivers, however, are made passable by driving in piles and boarding over the top, or else, for a temporary work, empty barrels may be tied together and timbers placed upon them to provide a passage. Also the cavalry are accustomed to take off their accoutrements and make fascines from dry weeds and sedge and place upon them cuirasses and arms, so as not to get them wet. They and their horses swim across, drawing [on reins] the fascines that they have tied to themselves.

But it has been found better for an army to carry around with it on carts "single timbers," which are rather wide canoes, hollowed out of single trunks, very light because of the type and thinness of the wood. Planks and iron nails are also kept in readiness. The bridge thus speedily constructed, tied together by ropes which should be kept for the purpose, provides the solidity of a masonry arch in quick time.

The enemy often launch rapid ambushes or raids at river crossings. Armed guards are stationed against this danger on both banks, lest the troops be beaten by the enemy because they are divided by the intervening river-bed . . . But if a bridge is needed not just for one crossing, but for returning and for supply-lines, broad fosses are dug around each bridgehead and a rampart constructed to receive soldiers to defend and hold it for as long as strategic needs require. (Milner trans., pp. 78–79)

and below them another line, so that the great body of the army will pass between them. Those upstream will hold back the force of the water, and those downstream can sustain those turned aside by the water's force. If the crossing is so wide that this plan will not serve, but the river must be crossed, or being on the other side is of great benefit, the commander will have good portable bridges made. He will have them brought on carts. Some of these can be made of empty barrels tied and attached to each other, with solid planks well hooked together placed upon them. Like a drawbridge, these can be placed in the water at once by the skill of clever artisans, with whom he will be well provided. Others can be made with stakes planted in the water to which heavy ropes are attached with planks laid on top of them. Still others can be made by attaching boats to each other and then covering them with planks and also with manure. These last are the most dependable bridges possible, for anyone who has enough boats. If he does not, he should have long planks of wood well fastened together, with planks and reeds on top of them, covered with manure and firmly anchored in the water. By such means one can easily cross over. Cyrus, the king of Persia, devised various solutions when he was going to take the city of Babylon. He found himself by the great River Euphrates, so wide and deep that it seemed impossible to cross. He ordered men to dig ditches, excavating the earth so that the river was divided into three hundred and sixty-six streams, and in that way he crossed over. There is nothing that cannot be accomplished by man's ingenuity when judgment and willpower are involved.

Along with this, ancient histories tell us that in the past conquerors were so skilled and well trained in swimming that they thought nothing of swimming across broad rivers, and they had pieces of wood hollowed out in which they could put their equipment; others made bundles of dry branches, which they held above themselves, and so crossed over. If there is to be a bridge for crossing and recrossing, it should be fortified with ditches and a barrier on the enemy's side, this guarded by good men-at-arms with a good supply of arrows.

Although such devices may seem easy when heard about, those who have not learned how to do them, who might say that such things are merely imagined, would find them difficult. It is no joking matter. The great Roman armies, in a space of thirty years, which often went from Rome into Africa, as far as the city of Carthage, and even to more distant lands, were obliged to cross a number of wide and deep rivers, and likewise in all the regions they conquered there were no bridges or boats on the banks by which they could cross over, so they were obliged to use

such devices as these. If it happens that it is possible to cross by moon-
light, or so stealthily that the enemy is unaware of it, they should immediately rearm themselves in good order, and continue on their way
normally, so that if the enemy should appear, they will be prepared to
sustain a greater threat than the enemy is prepared to offer. But if they
can escape through mountains, putting the others below them, this can
be a great protection and advantage. If they should find the paths narrow
because barred by woods or hedges, it is better, Vegetius says, to make an
effort to open and broaden them, cutting a way through them by hand,
rather than to risk danger in broad and open roads.[74]

## XVIII.

### HEREIN IS DISCUSSED THE ACTION A COMMANDER MUST TAKE WHEN IT APPEARS THAT BATTLE IS IMMINENT.

After what has been said, it is time to speak of certain points, opinions,
and rules that a commander can usefully consider when he expects to
engage in battle soon, according to the book of arms and those of other
authors who have written of this matter. This is to say that when one
thinks that an enemy wants to attack, one should not wait for him to
enter the country in order to do so, but rather go out to meet him with a
large army, for it is better to trample another country than to allow one's
own to be trampled under foot. The commander then, when he has
reached the spot where he expects soon to have a day of battle, sensing
the enemy at hand, will be on his guard, but will not hasten to attack him
in full-scale battle if it is not to his advantage. For this reason he will take
great care to inform himself, as is said, of the enemy's situation, what sort
of commander there is, if he is foolish or wise, valiant or not, what sort of
advisors he has, if his subordinates are experienced in war or not, how
faithful and loyal his troops are, their view of the conflict, and how great
their will to fight,[75] and if they have adequate food or not, for hunger

---

74. Vegetius III, vi: "But if there are routes which are narrow but safe, it is better for soldiers to go
ahead with axes and picks, opening a road with their toil, than to suffer peril on the best route" (Milner trans., p. 77).

75. Vegetius III, ix: See note 62 above. "It is also relevant to find out the character of the adversary himself, his senior staff-officers and chieftains. Are they rash or cautious, bold or timid, skilled in
the art of war or fighting from experience or haphazardly? Which tribes on their side are brave or
cowardly? What is the loyalty and courage of our *auxilia*? What is the morale of the enemy forces?
What is that of our own army? Which side promises itself victory more? By such considerations is the
army's courage bolstered or undermined" (Milner trans., p. 85).

fights from within and can conquer without the use of arms. So he will take counsel with his advisors to decide if it is better to have the battle sooner or later, or if he should wait until attacked. For if he should discover that the enemy is suffering from hunger, or that it is badly paid, whereby the men are falling away little by little and abandoning their commander because they are malcontent, or that there are men present who are spoiled by the ease of courtly life with its luxuries, or even that there are men who can no longer endure the rigors of the field and the hard military life, but rather long for repose, men who will not be in a hurry to engage in battle—then he will remain quiet as if he were not paying attention, and as quietly as he can he will set out to bar the ways of escape. Thus he will surprise the enemy if it is at all possible.[76] It can be of great profit to a commander to know how to place ambushes wisely and surprise his enemies, as was shown when Hasdrubal came to the rescue of Hannibal, prince of Carthage, his brother, with a marvelous army against the Romans, who, when they became aware of this, ambushed the army at the foot of the mountains and overran them with such force that they killed more than a thousand men and took a great amount of booty, in spite of the many elephants the Carthaginians had with them, which they knew very well how to make use of in battle. Vegetius affirms that this is the way to proceed, saying that one should spy on his adversaries in case their army is intending to cross rivers, or they are tired from marching, or caught in swamps or any narrow passages, so that they are occupied with problems and may be killed before they can arrange themselves in battle formation. But if the commander is aware that his enemies are strong and very courageous and eager to engage in battle against him, he should likewise make a great effort to avoid them, and if it happens that the enemy army comes up to the encampments to attack at some hour when they are not expected, the troops must go out to defend themselves without appearing not to want to take them on. But if he concludes that they are somewhat in disorder, or entertaining themselves by hunting, then he should go forth in fine array and attack them vigorously, inflicting as much damage as possible.

However, he should take care not to encourage his men to undertake a sortie when they are tired from a long march or a difficult day, for men

76. Vegetius III, x: "When he has seen to these things properly, let him choose a moment when the enemy are roving carelessly about, scattered for ravaging, to send in his well-tried cavalry or infantry . . . Routing the enemy at a favourable opportunity . . . raises the morale of the rest" (Milner trans., pp. 87–88).

who are tired are already half conquered. In this way the usually astute Antiochus, the powerful king of Syria, of Asia and of Europe, attacked at night when his enemy was tired and in need of rest. The men did not take any precautions, with the result that the Romans, although small in number, killed more than sixty thousand, as history tells us.

Vegetius tells us that as a battle is finished in two or three hours, after which the weaker side has lost all hope, and because the fortune of victory can never be known in advance, the wise commander should never willingly or lightly enter into battle if he does not see that it is to his advantage.[77]

That a day of battle is redoubtable because it is so uncertain was experienced by the Romans when they sent a large army to Spain, which had rebelled against them. From the battle they engaged in nobody was left to carry the news back to Rome, where their destruction became known only sometime later through foreigners. For this reason the commander should undertake to harass his enemy often through watches and ambushes, and in this way diminish its strength as best he can from day to day.

Likewise, Vegetius says that when prisoners are taken during the conflict, either in skirmishes or otherwise, they should not be treated so severely that their lives are despaired of by those on their side, for in case a battle were expected, those others would have less hope of finding pity if they should be conquered, and so they would defend themselves more fiercely. For it has often been noted that a small number of desperate men will conquer a large and powerful army because they would rather die fighting than fall into the cruel hands of the enemy, so there is great peril in fighting such people as these, as their strength is doubled. The commander should, as he says, be like a righteous judge, knowing how to judge both the strength and the advantage of his adversary, with what means and what methods he can damage him, as this is his responsibility. Thus he can give advice on how to undertake a surprise attack wisely, for in such a way a small number of men with good leaders have often conquered a great multitude, as has already been said.

But if it should come about, as Vegetius says, that your enemy presses you hard to choose a day of battle, and if he presses you to combat, note

---

77. Vegetius III, ix: "[A] pitched battle is defined by a struggle lasting two or three hours, after which all hopes of the defeated party fall away. That being so, every expedient must be thought of previously, tried out in advance and implemented before matters come to this final pass. For good generals do not attack in open battle where the danger is mutual, but do it always from a hidden position, so as to kill or at least terrorize the enemy while their own men are unharmed as far as possible" (Milner trans., pp. 83–84).

carefully if this is to your advantage or to your regret, and do nothing unless you see your advantage.

XIX.

THE KINDS OF ACTION A COMMANDER SHOULD TAKE
IF HE SHOULD WISH TO ABANDON THE FIELD
WITHOUT WAITING FOR, OR ENGAGING IN, BATTLE.[78]

Let us suppose that the prince orders the commander to return without engaging in battle, or to remain facing the enemy, or that the commander himself for some reason should wish to abandon the field: it must be considered what plan he will follow in order not to frighten his men or make his enemy aware of his decision. Vegetius says that there is no greater villainy than to leave the field where the enemy is present, without making contact, if there has not been some sort of agreement between them. In this regard there are two dishonorable aspects: one, that he is frightened and so is moved by cowardice; the other, that he has little confidence in his men, and thus gives courage to his enemies. As it sometimes happens that two armies are drawn up without making contact, it is a good thing to discuss the best way out of this situation. If it is desirable to depart, as Vegetius teaches, take great care that your men do not know that you are leaving to avoid a battle, but rather spread word secretly among them that it is better because of some secret trap to cause damage elsewhere and preferable to reach the enemy when he is off his guard and to capture him by ambush. For, as Vegetius says, if your men knew that you were leaving for no particular reason, they would hold it against you and would soon drift away little by little because they would consider that you were afraid to engage in battle; this could be very harmful to you. Beyond this, he says, you should be careful that your enemies do not notice your withdrawal, for they might straightway attack you. For this reason some in this situation have assembled a large number of horsemen to run here and there, covering foot soldiers who have meanwhile departed; others have left at night, the most shameful way because it appears that they have simply taken flight. Such manners of departure, he says, are not especially praiseworthy unless they are undertaken through

---

78. This chapter as a whole is inspired by Vegetius III, xxii: "HOW TO RETREAT FROM THE ENEMY IF THE PLAN TO FIGHT IS REJECTED" (Milner trans., pp. 108–10).

great need to save the army. The best way, he says, is for the infantry and the lightly armed men to leave all at once and go to occupy a certain field that will be advantageous for them, where the whole army should join them. If the enemy begins to pursue the first of them there, they will be the advance guard that holds them at bay until the entire army is assembled. Then from the point of advantage offered by the new location they can repulse the enemy and make it pay dearly for its pursuit, for nothing is more perilous for those in reckless pursuit than to be caught in a trap, or in a spot that has been chosen in advance by the adversaries. When they depart, a well-organized part of the army should go by the main road in case the enemy has any idea of following them, and another company should be sent secretly by another route. It commonly happens that those who pursue by the main road, because they can see around them, dally here and there and then depart. But when they think they are safe and that the pursuit has been abandoned they pay little attention to their battle formation, like those who think they are in safe territory. Then the others, who have been lying in wait, attack them with great energy, thus inflicting on them great damage. However it may be, one who departs from his enemy must make sure by all possible means that if he is pursued, the pursuers should suffer damage in return, whether by laying an ambush, or by reinforcements, or in some other fashion. If it turns out that the pursuers have to cross some river or stream, ambush should be set to attack those who cross first, and if possible, place another part of your men behind to attack those who are waiting to cross. If you yourself have to pass through any woods or narrow places, send before you wise soldiers in whom you have confidence, who could report on the route and whether there is any ambush. It would be less shameful to be damaged fighting openly with the enemy than to be caught through negligence in an ambush you did not know about.

## XX.

### HOW A COMMANDER, IF HE BECOMES INVOLVED IN A PEACE TREATY OR TRUCE WITH THE ENEMY, MUST GUARD AGAINST THE PERILS INTO WHICH HE MIGHT FALL THROUGH DECEPTION.

In order that nothing suitable or useful to be put into our book should be forgotten, dealing with situations that often arise or could arise, it is well to speak of a matter that can cause grave harm to an army and conquer more readily than steel or anything else. It must therefore be avoided above all, even though this is very difficult when an army becomes involved in it, as will now be explained.

We have discussed sufficiently how an army can most safely depart from the field whenever the best decision suggests that battle should be avoided. Now let us consider another situation: on a field of battle, where two armies are drawn up with great effort on both sides to engage in a day of battle, for certain reasons they instead enter into discussion of a treaty and peace. It thus becomes necessary to keep in mind what has already been said, that the commander must be wise enough that in all matters he can work to his best advantage. In order to pursue the way that wisdom teaches, he must first take into account two principles: one is that he will consider who are the people involved in the treaty and what their motives may be; the other, on what basis the treaty rests, what is being demanded of him, and what offered. The first of these must be considered if the aforesaid negotiators are his friends, or if they are ordinary people who are not taking sides, or if they are merely representatives of the other side. If they are merely representatives of the other side, it is a good sign if no fraud is involved, for either they have been inspired by God, or it would appear that they are afraid and have doubts about the battle. Nevertheless the commander should take into account the form of the demand, and also the offer, as this is a matter of great importance. He will take counsel with the wisest of his advisors and will consider all aspects, so that in his reply he will not appear to be ignorant; and in order that nothing is forgotten, he will make sure that the honor and advantage of his prince as well as his own are protected, and that nothing may impede the way to an agreement in its reasonable aspects, an agreement that should of course not be concluded without permission from the prince, to whom all offers and demands will have been sent in good order and in writing. Care should be taken to avoid agreeing to anything advantageous to his enemy without the prince's permission and that of his council. Here we recall the case of a leader of the Roman army who had been dispatched to the city of Mainz, where he and four thousand men were overcome. As after this he agreed to peace with the citizens of Mainz without permission from Rome, they did not keep to the agreement, but sent him captured and bound to Mainz, thus breaking their agreement. This is to be noted if you become aware that your enemies are speaking to you at great length. If they are finding trivial excuses to prolong the time, you can be certain that all is deception and a pretext for delaying the battle until help arrives, or until your supplies have been diminished and your men, bored by the long delay, have little by little left.

Likewise, if the treaty is brought about by some other means, if the pope has sent a representative to bring about peace, or another prince or lord inspired by goodwill (although he should have first approached the prince) has intervened, or in the event that you yourself are the prince, you should in such circumstances explain thoroughly the action, case, right, or just quarrel that you have for making war against the opponent, so that the arbitrator in question, who would like to end this conflict without bloodshed, may be well advised to have presented to you sufficient amends and satisfaction, pointing out to the enemy their great wrong. Likewise, if the enemy insists on having the greater right, do not be so blind that this will prevent you from submitting to what is reasonable. If you believe that in certain matters you are right and in others not, you should be the more willing to consent to the treaty and allow a part of the demands of the others without dishonoring yourself, if you can do better by giving up something that is really your right.

Let us suppose further that the enemy army is smaller, and that yours is increased in numbers and strength and the other diminished through some misfortune, so that they fear battle and thus wish to negotiate and achieve peace, making you good offers in order better to establish their rights and to avoid bloodshed; what would you do then? Or even if they were inspired to want peace, though their strength was more or less the equal of yours, should you be so proud as to make them think that as they would be at a disadvantage if it came to battle, you would by no means wish to come to an agreement? Even so that the more offers that were made, the more difficult you would be? No, indeed, for you would scarcely find that in refusing just offers, however right they might be, however large the number of men with reference to fewer, that misfortune might not overcome them in the end; for it seems that in such a case God would have it in for those who refuse, and so punish them. But you must look at this carefully, for there is the danger that you may be deceived treacherously by dishonest means, under the pretense of discussing peace. How can you recognize this? In God's name, by conjecture, you can have the appearance of suspecting this and being on your guard, whereby, if it should happen that the idea of entering into a treaty should come from one of your own men, by his condition you can consider what might be the cause that has moved him to wish for a treaty; for if he is wise, prudent, and with a just conscience, and you know him to be thus, you should not be surprised that such a man would willingly look for a way to avoid bloodshed by a good and honorable treaty and that there should be peace. But if it is a man not usually to be found in such a situation, lacking in courage although he may be clever and speak well, you may conclude that this could come from cowardliness, but even so you should not entirely discard his arguments, but rather consider if these are good and whether they resound to your honor and profit.

Another matter to consider is that in listening to the one who suggests the treaty and a mode of agreement, you should take notice if peace can be more to his advantage than war, and if in speaking he goes to some lengths to put you in the way of making a peace that, because of the great wish he has for it, may not be very honorable for you.

Or if he is a greedy person, who through gifts or promises can be made to speak, if such an exchange can be ascertained, no credence should be given to such as this; he should rather be dismissed, if you are sufficiently informed, for such a disloyal counselor is interested only in his own advantage. The loyal one is more concerned with the public good than his own. Now it is necessary for you, during the negotiations in question, as the ambassadors of the opposition arrive, to send back your own. In this matter you should be very well informed so that you may not be misled, for if these are not honorable men, the danger may be great. By such means and envoys many cities, lands, and kingdoms, Troy in ancient times as well as others, have been deceived by such disloyal ambassadors pretending to be loyal and good. There is no danger equal to this. So much is hidden that scarcely anybody, however wise he may be, can protect himself against a traitor who has undertaken to cause injury through treachery. For this reason there is no better precaution than to send those most closely related by blood, if you have such as these with you, who would suffer great loss from your death and who are also your best friends, rather than those in whom quite by chance you place this great trust. Many have been deceived by such men. Rather choose those you have put in high places, who would stand to lose much if you were not there, and others in whom you sense the life and conscience to be good, honest, and loyal. The value of using loyalty in all cases of war and battle, so that treason can be rejected according to the sayings of good men, was well demonstrated by the good Fabricius, of whom we have already spoken, when he was leading an army against King Pyrrhus, who did enormous harm to the Romans in battle.[79] The physician of that king came to Fabricius and offered to poison his master, but only if Fabricius would be willing to reward him. The valiant man replied that it was contrary to the customs of the Romans to conquer by treachery. So he had the physician sent back to his master, who, when he learned of the matter, said in a loud voice: "O! the sun would deviate from its course before Fabricius would abandon loyalty." So King Pyrrhus departed, and for that act of kindness would not give battle at that time.

XXI.

THE WAY A COMMANDER SHOULD SPEND THE DAY
BEFORE HE EXPECTS TO HAVE A BATTLE.

Continuing what has been said, to come to the point where war leads, that is to say, the formation for battle, as this is the essential fact, we should say the following: if it happens that finally the necessity of combat has obliged the army to assemble on a certain day in the face of the enemy, then the wise commander must not fail in any of the things he should do, and must advise for the best; for there are certain things that should not be overlooked. What, then, will he do? He will have much to think about, because a greater event cannot take place among men than one wherein lies the fortunes of all the land, the state of the prince and the life of an infinite number of persons, the honor or dishonor of the overlord, the knights, and all the nobility.

Therefore, he will summon all the commanders of the army to his presence and will address them as a group, as many as possible being present, more or less as follows:

"Very dear brothers, companions and friends, we are gathered together here, as you may know, by order of our good prince, to protect and hold his interests here as his lieutenants, to sustain by the sword the just quarrel, his by right, which his noble predecessors long maintained, or which for a good reason he has undertaken against such a king or nobleman from whom he has suffered many wrongs. This is the truth as we are informed of it and know it to be so; therefore we are obligated to him as his loyal subjects, or those sworn to support him, taking from him pay and

---

79. Fabricius and King Pyrrhus were referred to in *La Mutacion de fortune*, Solente ed., III, pp. 206–7, where the episode is said to have been inspired by *L'Histoire ancienne*. The chapter as a whole is based on contemporary practice rather than on Vegetius.

recompense to uphold his good cause, exposing life and limb as we have loyally promised by our oaths, without deserting for fear of death. Let us now do as much, this I beg and require of you as dear brothers, friends and companions, so that by us and the effort of our bodies and the strength of our stout hearts we will bring victory to our good prince in this battle, so that he may have honor and profit from it, and we along with him will be forever honored and praised and shall merit his gratitude. So we have indeed good cause, fair lords, to attack with great courage and invade with strong will the land of these people, I can assure you, for they are wrong and we are right, so God is with us. Therefore we shall win without fail if we have it in us, which gives me strength. Now, my dear friends, may each of you in his own way do so well that I may have reason to give such a good report of you that you will henceforth always be honored. As for myself, I swear to you that whoever does this task well, I will reward him greatly, so that he will evermore feel the honor and advantage. Now let us go forth bravely and without fear, my dear friends, children and brothers, against these people, commending ourselves to God, that He may give us the honor we desire."

Such words as these will the wise commander say to his men. That this should be done is in accord with all the authors who have spoken of this matter.[80] They say that this custom was observed by Scipio, Julius Caesar, Pompey, and other conquerors. Along with this, they agree that the commander must be generous and affectionate. That is to say that the books of chivalry do not recommend any greed in a commander, but only that he have merit and honor in arms. Certainly the good duke Fabricius demonstrated this well, whom we have remembered for his good qualities so many times in this book.

When King Pyrrhus, his enemy, who very much wished to draw him to his side because of his great courage, sent him a great quantity of gold and silver vessels because he had heard that he was so poor that he was served at his table only from wooden bowls, and sent word to him that it was proper for such an important man to be richly served, Fabricius refused all this and replied that he preferred to eat honorably from wooden bowls than with shame and reproach from golden dishes. It is also the duty of the good commander to treat his men kindly, for otherwise he is

---

80.  This custom of addressing troops before battle persisted up to fairly modern times and is still practiced by some generals. See Vegetius III, ix: "When the men despair, their courage is raised by an address from the general, and if he appears fearless himself, their spirits are raised" (Milner trans., p. 85).

not worthy of his office. For it is said that by means of his generosity and kindness he can better engage the hearts of his men to expose with him body and life than in any other way. His benevolence should embolden even those of humble estate to dare to point out to him and say what seems important to them concerning deeds of arms, as it can happen that some humble soldiers can have good opinions, as God sometimes gives them His grace, and such as these should not be turned away because of their simple and poor status. It is written that valiant conquerors of the past shared generously their conquests and booty with their men-at-arms, and that for themselves the honor of battles was sufficient, and that in this way they did with their men what they wished.

Vegetius says that pleasing words are useful for this purpose, and that the good admonition of the valiant leader increases determination, courage, and strength. For this reason he should often and firmly show his men the rightness of their cause and the enemy's error, and how they are obligated to the prince and the country, admonishing them to do well, to be valiant—promising offices and great gifts to those who do so—and, in fact, to give an example to the others. He should honor those who have distinguished themselves and show them favor, so that they have greater courage because of it. With such words he can also increase the anger and ill will of his own men against their enemies and their love and good-will towards the prince.[81]

## XXII.
### THE WAY TO TAKE ADVANTAGE OF THE FIELD, ACCORDING TO VEGETIUS.

Vegetius says that on the day the commander wishes to engage in battle, he should take notice of how his men feel about it, for he can perceive from their faces if they are afraid, as from their words and the movements of their bodies. He says that fear will not be understood by those who are inexperienced in arms, but it would be a wonder if they were not affected. But if those experienced in arms are doubtful, the commander

---

81. Vegetius III, xii: "An army gains courage and fighting spirit from advice and encouragement from their general, especially if they are given such an account of the coming battle as leads them to believe they will easily win a victory. This is the time to point out to them the cowardice and mistakes of their opponents, and remind them of any occasion on which they have been beaten by us in the past. Also say anything by which the soldiers' minds may be provoked to hatred of their adversaries by arousing their anger and indignation" (Milner trans., p. 92).

should try to put off the decision to another day.[82] If there are men from
some other land, who are young and inexperienced, whose loyalty he
doubts, he should put them in the charge of good, loyal captains who
know well how to deal with the situation, and place them in a position
where they cannot run away, for by the flight of such people the battle
can be put at risk. He should train them well to be obedient, for nothing
is more useful in an army than to obey the captains. For this reason he
says that by a single voice those who are far from their captain cannot
know sudden changing needs that might occur in battle, so the ancients
found a way to make use of certain signs by which they quickly told the
army what it should do,[83] either by the sound of trumpets, by different
calls, or by the horns they called bugles, or otherwise. But because the
enemy, on hearing the same sort of sound several times, would understand, they changed these from time to time, the troops being notified in
advance. From childhood on they would be taught the use of arms, such
habits being acquired by them so that in the heat of battle they would understand quite well. For this purpose trumpets were invented that could
diversify their sounds according to need.

Now comes the point of drawing up battle formations, according to
Vegetius. The wise commander will decide, as has been said, to be the
first to take advantage of the terrain. There are therefore three points to
consider: the first is to take the high place; the second is to make sure
that at the hour of combat the sun will be in the enemy's eyes; the third,
that the wind should be against them.[84] If these three things can be

82. Vegetius III, xxii: "Explore carefully how soldiers are feeling on the actual day they are going
to fight. For confidence or fear may be discerned from their facial expression, language, gait and ges-
tures. Do not be fully confident if it is the recruits who want battle, for war is sweet to the inexperienced. You will know to postpone it if the experienced warriors are afraid of fighting" (Milner trans.,
p. 92).

83. Vegetius III, v: "Many indeed are the orders to be given and obeyed in battle, since no remis-
sion is given to negligence when men are fighting for their lives. But of all the rest there is nothing so
conducive to victory as heeding the warnings of signals. Since an army in the confusion of battle cannot be governed by a single voice, and many orders have to be given and carried out on the spur of
the moment in view of the urgency of events, ancient practice of all nations devised a means
whereby the whole army might recognize by signals and follow up what the general alone had
judged useful" (Milner trans., p. 71).

84. Vegetius III, xiv: "When the general is ready to draw up his line, he should attend first to
three things, sun, dust and wind. When the sun is in front of your face, it deprives you of sight. Head-
winds deflect and depress your missiles, while aiding the enemy's. Dust thrown up in front of you
fills and closes your eyes. Even inexperienced generals usually avoid these things at the time of ordering the lines, but the provident general should take care of the future lest, a little while later as
the day wears on, the changed position of the sun may be harmful or a head-wind may habitually
arise at a regular time, during the fighting. Therefore let the lines be ranged with these problems behind our backs, and if possible so that they may strike the faces of the enemy" (Milner trans., p. 93).

arranged, he will profit, as there is no doubt that the one in the highest place has an advantage of strength over the one below.

Item, sun in the eyes dazzles and is a great trial, and likewise the wind that blows dust in their faces, and the arrow carried by the wind has greater force, weakening and deflecting the strength of the opposition. One should know that by two such ruses the Romans vanquished those of Cicambria and the Tyos,[85] invading them from a direction that made them have the sun in front of them, and also pressing them at such close range that they did not have time to organize themselves.

XXIII.

A BRIEF CONSIDERATION OF HOW TO DRAW UP AN ARMY
FOR COMBAT ACCORDING TO PRESENT-DAY USAGE.

Vegetius provides several ways of drawing up a battle formation, as will be explained later, but these are perhaps different in some respects from present-day battle order. The reason is perhaps that then troops fought more commonly on horseback than on foot. Likewise, as there is nothing in the order of human nature that in the course of time does not alter and change, it seems to me a good idea to speak briefly and in understand-able terms of orders common in these times, as they are well enough known to those who bear arms: that is to say, making the advance guard of considerable length, with men-at-arms arranged close together, so that one should not pass another, the best and most select being in the fore-front, the marshals with them, following their standards and banners, and in wing formation at their sides the firepower, cannoneers along with crossbowmen and archers similarly arranged. After this first formation, called the vanguard, comes the principal battle formation, where the great mass of men-at-arms is ordered by their captains, who are in their midst, their banners and standards raised. These are in various ranks, arranged in order, for the constable will have announced that under pain of his displeasure none are to get out of order. Some say that if this in-cludes a considerable number of common people, these should be used to reinforce the wings in well-ordered ranks behind the firepower, and that they should be commanded by good captains, and also that they

---

85. The defeat of the Cimbri and Thiois (Gauls and Germans) by the Romans was described by Christine in *La Mutacion de fortune* IV, i–iv, where it is based on the *Histoire ancienne*.

should be put in front of the major part of the formation, so that if they should be tempted to flee, the men-at-arms behind them would prevent it. In the middle of this great formation stands the commanding prince, the principal banner before him, on which the formation keeps its eyes. For this reason it is given into the care of one of the best and most important men in the army. Around him are the best and most experienced men-at-arms, for the safety of both the prince and the banner. Next, following this great formation, comes the third part, called the rear guard, arranged to support those in front. These are likewise well ordered, and behind them are the yeomen on horseback, who can aid the others if they have need of it. These are good men, holding the horses of their masters and forming an obstacle so that no one can attack the army from the rear. In this case, if there are enough men and it is supposed that the enemy will come from that direction, those who are most eager to fight, and are expert in their skill with arms, would form another battalion that has its back to the others, ready to receive those who come forward. With all these arrangements there is usually put in order a quantity of men-at-arms, skilled in their craft, mounted on good steeds or chargers, all ready on the sides to come racing to break up and throw into disarray the battle formations of the enemy when they have assembled. In this way the battle is won by those who best know how to be of assistance.

Even though this manner of organizing an army is the most customary, some experts on arms advise that when it happens that there are not too many common people, but more good men-at-arms, they should all be put in a single battalion without either advance guard or rear guard, except in the forward wings, as has been said. They claim that in this formation one fights more securely. This was used in the Battle of Roosebeke,[86] where the king of France, Charles VI of the name, who now reigns, was victorious against forty thousand Flemings. The same was the case, not long ago, at the Battle of Liège, where John, duke of Burgundy, who still lives, son of Philip, son of the king of France, with a rather small number of good men-at-arms, was victorious against twenty-five thousand Liégeois.[87]

It should be known that even in ancient times they used in their bat-

---

86. For the Battle of Roosebeke, see note 14.

87. The victory of John the Fearless over the rebellious citizens of Liège at Othée at the end of September 1408 greatly advanced his military prestige and his influence in the Netherlands, but it also strengthened his power and influence in France. See Richard Vaughan, *John the Fearless* (London: Longman Green, 1966), 49–66.

tles several sorts of machines and tricks to break up battle formations, as has been said before. Oxen with fire under their tails were chased toward the opponents, and they even used certain machines similar to those we now call ribaudequins.[88] These were set on wheels, a man within, in a little castlelike structure all of iron, and he would fire a cannon or crossbow. On each side there was a loophole and pointed irons. In front were lances of a sort, and through the force of men or horses, a number would go together to make a frontal attack on the enemy formation.

XXIV.

THE ORDER AND ARRANGEMENT OF BATTLES, ACCORDING
TO VEGETIUS AND THE ANCIENTS.

Even though drawing up an army and engaging in battle have been discussed elsewhere, the ancients who have spoken of this matter say that the best way of arranging troops is to do so in a circle, and that several groups should be put at the front, before, and at the sides. Where the enemy attack is expected, only the best and most experienced should be placed. If they keep to serrated ranks, they can scarcely be undone, supposing that the others will be more vulnerable. If it happens that the adversaries are fewer in number, the formation should be arranged like a horseshoe. Thus, he says, you will surround them if you maintain good order. If the others are numerous, the formation should be arranged like a wedge, with the front in a position to pierce. But Vegetius wisely points out that a commander who must organize the formation should not decide to alter the arrangement or lead any number of men elsewhere, making them leave the lineup, for this would upset everything and sow confusion in the ranks.[89] Nothing, he says, is more profitable in battle than to maintain the necessary order and distance and space that there should be between the ranks. For care should be taken that they do not squeeze or bunch together, but also that they do not fall apart, but remain properly serrated. For by pressing together they will lack space to

---

88. A ribaudequin was an early form of cannon much used in the fourteenth century. It fired stones, as did its Roman predecessor, before the development of gunpowder. In this respect, and in various others, early medieval artillery had improved little since Roman times.

89. Vegetius III, xix: "Beware also of deciding to change your ranks or transfer certain units from their stations to others at the moment when battle is being joined. Uproar and confusion instantly ensue, and the enemy more easily press upon unready and disorderly forces" (Milner trans., p. 103).

fight and will hinder each other. If there is too much light showing between them they will provide an opening for the enemy and will thus be in danger of being broken up and scattered, whereby the very fear at seeing the enemy among themselves might destroy them.

He also says that they should go onto the field in good order, where the commander has shown them ahead of time how, when the battle takes place, they should maintain themselves: the first rank extended as necessary, and then the second, and the others, so that order will be maintained among them. Certain knights, he says, had the custom of arranging their formations in squares, and then in triangles, which they called "wedges," and that formation served them very well in battle. And when a great enemy force breached the line, they reformed themselves into a circle, the best at front, thereby preventing their men from turning to run away and also avoiding too much harm.[90] The ancients customarily did not put all their men in one formation, but rather made several formations, so that those who were rested could come to the rescue of the fatigued.[91] In this way they could scarcely ever suffer defeat, for whatever one group lost, the next recovered. Nevertheless, the outcome of battles is uncertain, so that nobody should have too much confidence, but

---

90. Vegetius I, xxvi:

HOW RECRUITS ARE TRAINED TO KEEP RANKS AND INTERVALS IN THE LINE.
   It is agreed that nothing is more advantageous in battle, than that by dint of their constant exercises soldiers should keep their appointed ranks in the line, and not mass together or thin out the formation at any point inconveniently. For when densely packed they lose room to fight and impede one another, and when too thinly spread and showing the light between them they provide the enemy with an opening to breach. It is inevitable that everything should at once collapse in panic if the line is cut and the enemy reach the rear of the fighting men. Therefore recruits should be led out constantly to the exercise-field and drawn up in line following the order of the roll, in such a way that at first the line should be single and extended, having no bends or curvatures, and there should be an equal and regular space between soldier and soldier. Then the command should be given that they at once double the line, so that in an actual assault that arrangement to which they are used to conform may be preserved. Thirdly the command should be given suddenly to adopt a square formation, and after this the line itself should be changed to triangular formation, which they call a "wedge." This formation is usually of great advantage in battle. Next they are commanded to form circles, which is the formation commonly adopted by trained soldiers to resist a hostile force that has breached the line, to prevent the whole army being turned to flight and grave peril ensuing. If recruits learn these manoeuvers by continual practice they will observe them more easily in actual battle. (Milner trans., pp. 25–26)

   91. Vegetius III, xvii: "The best principle, and that which contributes most towards victory, is for the general to hold in readiness behind the line the pick of the infantry and cavalry, together with unattached 'vicars,' 'counts' and tribunes, some about the wings, and some about the middle" (Milner trans., p. 99).

should merely hope for the best for himself, because often the opposite of what is initially expected will occur. For example, who would have thought that such a great slaughter could occur in the battle between the Romans and the three great armies assembled by the Carthaginians that not a single man remained on either side.

He says that on the day a battle is to take place, it is wise to eat little, in order to have more breath and to be more agile and light-footed.[92] But whoever can should drink good wine, which gives mobility to the limbs and vigor to the mind of the one who drinks it properly and not too much of it. It happens, he says, that the courage of nearly all men is troubled when they must go into battle, but anger gives strength and courage, so that those who feel it ignore all peril. For this reason, the wise comman-der, in order to encourage his men to be more hearty, should several times before the principal battle have his men engage in several skir-mishes with the enemy, so that through receiving blows and injuries from them they become more hostile toward them.[93] He says that the least wise and the least brave often raise the battle cry before the battle begins, but this should not happen, because blows should accompany the battle cry.[94] The ancients took great care in arranging their battle lines, so that the men-at-arms should not be frightened by the cries raised by peasants when they see the army assemble, or made by those who are afraid, so they will warn them of these by a certain trumpet call. Also, those who are inexperienced often fear all this, and so, says the book, they should be engaged in other matters rather than arms. For those who have not yet seen men killed or blood shed are frightened by it, and in this case think more about fleeing than fighting;[95] they are thus more of a hindrance than they are worth, and at least they should not be put under the com-

---

92. Vegetius III, xi: "In ancient times it was customary to lead soldiers into battle after they had been treated to a light meal, so that the food ingested might give them strength" (Milner trans., p. 91).

93. Vegetius III, ix: "[T]hey should not even then be lightly led into a pitched battle, but on a carefully chosen opportunity, and only after being blooded in smaller-scale conflicts" (Milner trans., p. 86).

94. Vegetius III, xviii: "The war-cry, which they call *barritus*, should not be raised until both lines have engaged each other. It is a mark of inexperienced or cowardly men if they cry out from a distance. The enemy are more terrified if the shock of the war-cry is made to coincide with the blows of weapons" (Milner trans., p. 101).

95. Vegetius III, x: "For those who have not for a long time, or never at all, seen men being wounded or killed are greatly shocked when they first catch sight of it, and confused by panic start thinking of flight instead of fighting" (Milner trans., p. 88).

mand of good captains. Some say that they should be put all together, but others say no, they should rather be mingled with the good soldiers.

Once more, to recapitulate what is useful to keep in mind in drawing up troops according to the ancients, there are several points the commander should consider carefully: first, that he has in advance chosen an advantageous location if possible, where he has placed his troops in good formation; second, that they are protected on one side by a mountain that will present no danger to them, or by sea or a river, or something else that prevents the enemy from reaching them; third, that there is neither dust nor sun to injure their eyes; fourth, which can be very useful, that they are well informed of the condition of their enemies, knowing how many there are, from what direction they are advancing, and their battle array, for in this way they can draw themselves up, wait for them, and receive them advantageously; fifth, that they should not be overcome, overburdened, or weakened by hunger; sixth, that they are all of one mind to hold their place, and would rather do so than flee, for such as these are not easy to defeat; seventh, that their enemies are not aware of their intentions or what they have in mind to do and what means they have at hand. Nevertheless, as has been said before, the fortunes of battle are marvelous. Sometimes it would appear that God wished to help one side and not the other, as happened when the Romans were fighting two Oriental kings of great power, Jugurtha and Bottius.[96] When the heat of the sun was so great that the Romans nearly perished, suddenly there arose such a great wind that the trajectory of the arrows, of which the kings had a great abundance, was badly deflected. Then came a heavy rain, which greatly refreshed the Romans, but had the opposite effect on the others, for the cords of their bows were loosened, and their elephants, of which they had many (but it is an animal that cannot endure water), could not move, and the ropes that held the castles on their backs were loosened, and the castles filled with water, so that these were only a burden to them. In this way the Romans, now invigorated anew by the coolness, invaded the territory of the others so roughly that even though they were fewer in number, yet they gained the victory.

96. Jugurtha was a very clever and devious king of Numidia who, in 134 B.C., proved to be a powerful rival of the Romans, in large measure through a series of intrigues. He was eventually defeated militarily by an efficient Roman general, Q. Metellus and his successor, Marius, although only after Jugurtha had displayed his talent for guerrilla warfare. He was finally betrayed by his father-in-law, Bocchus, king of Mauretania. Christine had already made use of this example in the *Mutacion de fortune* (Solente ed., III, pp. 267–71).

## XXV.

### THE SEVEN WAYS OF DRAWING UP AN ARMY FOR
### COMBAT, ACCORDING TO VEGETIUS.[97]

Once more, according to Vegetius in his third book, twenty-first chapter, there are given seven ways to draw up battle formations and to combat the enemy, although he states them rather obscurely, and they are not intended for everyone, but only for those who are experienced in the exercise and office of arms. I set them forth as follows:

97. Vegetius III, xx (basis for the next two chapters):

HOW MANY MODES FOR ENGAGING IN A PITCHED BATTLE THERE ARE, AND HOW THE SIDE THAT IS INFERIOR IN NUMBERS AND STRENGTH MAY PREVAIL.

There are seven types or modes of general actions, when hostile standards engage from two sides. The first action has the army in rectangular formation with an extended front, just as even now it is usual to do battle almost always. However, experts in military science do not consider this type of action best, because when the line is extended over a wide area, it does not always meet with even ground. If there are any gaps in the middle, or a bend or curve, that is the point at which the line is often breached. Further, if the enemy has the advantage of numbers, he envelops your right or left wing from the sides. There is great danger in this unless you have reserves who can move up and hold back the enemy. Only he who has more numerous and strong forces should engage in this formation. He should envelop the enemy on both wings and enclose him as it were in the embrace of the army.

The second action is oblique, and better in very many respects. With this, if you draw up a small strong force in the proper position, you will be able to bring off a victory even though you are impeded by the numbers and strength of the foe. The method is as follows. When the drawn lines advance to the encounter, you will remove your left wing farther from the enemy's right, so that neither missiles not arrows can reach it. You should fasten your right wing to the enemy's left, and start the battle there first, while using your best cavalry and most reliable infantry to attack and surround the enemy's left flank, on which you have fastened, and by dislodging and outflanking them, reach the enemy's rear. If once you begin to rout the enemy from then on, with those of your men who are attacking you will undoubtedly gain a victory, while the part of your army which you moved away from the enemy will remain undisturbed. The lines in this mode of battle are joined in the shape of a letter A or a mason's plummet-level. If the enemy does this to you first, you should assemble on your left wing those cavalry and infantry we said should be placed behind the line as reserves, and then resist the adversary with maximum force to avoid defeat through tactics.

The third action is similar to the second, but inferior insofar as you begin by engaging his right from your left wing. For its attack is as it were maimed; the men fighting on the left wing are clearly in difficulties when attacking the enemy. I shall explain this more clearly. If you find that your left wing is far superior, reinforce it with your strongest cavalry and infantry, and in the encounter attach it first to the enemy right wing and make as much haste as you can to defeat and surround the right flank of the enemy. But the other part of your army, in which you know you have inferior warriors, remove as far as possible from the enemy left, so that it is not attacked with swords or reached by missiles. With this formation, care must be taken that your transverse line shall not be harmed by wedge-formations of the enemy. It will only be useful to fight in this mode in the case where your adversary has a weak right wing, and you have a far stronger left.

The fourth action is as follows. When you have ordered your line, at 400 or 500 paces before you reach the enemy, suddenly spur on both your wings when he is not expecting it, in

The first way of marshaling soldiers in the field, he says, is in a long front line, as is done now; but this formation, he says, is not very good, because the space has to be lengthy and the army very much extended. It does not always happen that a field suitable for this is available. Where there are ditches or hollows or a difficult terrain, the formation can easily be broken up. Along with this, if the adversary has a great number of men, he will take possession of the left or right wing and envelop the formation; so there is great danger in this. The authors say that in a case where you do not have large numbers of men who are organized and set against the enemy, take your best men and encircle the enemy, if you can, in the midst of your army.

The second way is better. If you can draw up a small number of brave and very experienced men in the proper position, you may be victorious even supposing that your adversary has more men. When the formations

---

order to turn the enemy to flight by catching him unprepared on both wings and win a quick victory. But although this type of battle may overcome quickly, provided you deploy highly experienced and brave men, it is nevertheless risky, because he who uses this formation is forced to denude the middle of his line and divide his army into two halves. Moreover if the enemy is not beaten at the first assault, he has opportunity to attack the divided wings and the undefended middle line.

The fifth action is like the fourth, but with the sole refinement of placing the light armament and archers before the front line, so it cannot be breached while they defend it. The general is then free to use his right wing to attack the enemy left and his left wing to attack the enemy right. If he can turn him to flight, he wins at once; if not, his middle line does not come under pressure, being defended by the light armament and archers.

The sixth action is the best, being very similar to the second. It is used by those generals who despair of the numbers and bravery of their men, and if they draw up their men well, they always win a victory even with fewer forces. For when the drawn line nears the enemy, apply your right wing to the enemy left, and start the battle there using very reliable cavalry and very swift light infantry. Remove the remaining part of your army as far as possible from the enemy line and extend it in a straight line like a spit. Once you begin cutting down the enemy left wing from the flank and rear, you will certainly put them to flight. But the enemy is prevented from assisting his men in trouble either from his right flank or from the middle of his line, because your line is extended and projects as a whole like a letter I, and recedes a very long distance from the enemy. This formation is often used in encounters on marches.

The seventh action aids the combatant by using the terrain. This also allows you to hold out against the enemy with fewer and less brave forces. For example, if you have on one side of you a mountain, sea, river, lake, city, marshes or broken country, so that the enemy cannot approach from that direction, draw up the main part of your army in a straight line, but on the side that does not have protection place all your cavalry and light infantry. You may then safely engage the enemy at your pleasure, because on one side the nature of the terrain protects you, and on the other there is roughly double cavalry posted.

But note this-nothing better has been found: if you intend to fight with your right wing alone, place your strongest men there. If with your left, station the most effective there. If you wish to form "wedges" in the middle to breach the enemy lines, draw up your most experienced soldiers in the "wedge." Victory is usually owing to a small number of men: so important it is for picked men to be ranged by a highly skilled general in those positions which judgement and utility demand. (Milner trans., pp. 104–7)

come to assemble, you will move your left wing from its position to another, so that you have a long view of the right wing of your enemy, and so that they can neither shoot nor throw missiles there. Your right wing joins their left, and there you begin a rough and strong battle with the best of your men, and the left wing with which you have made contact is so thoroughly invaded by cavalry and infantry that you can go about striking and outflanking in such a way that you can reach the enemy's rear. If you can once begin to divide the troops approaching yours, you will no doubt be victorious. The part of your army that you will have withdrawn from the rest will remain in safety. This battle formation is arranged like the letter X, and if your adversaries arrange theirs in this way, first send from yours a great number of men from the front, assembling them at your right wing in such a way that you will oppose your enemy with great force, so that he will not throw you back by his tactics.

The third manner is somewhat similar to the second, and differs from it only in that your left wing begins to fight the left wing of your adversary. If you have in your left wing better men than in the right, then add to them strong cavalry and infantry, and on assembling join first your left wing to the right wing of your enemy, and as best you can throw back this wing until you surround it. The other part of your army, where you know that there are those who are less strong, remove as far as you can from the left wing of the opponents, so that neither swords or missiles can reach them. Here you must take care that your enemies do not make a wedge-shaped formation to break through your own formation. In this way one fights with profit, especially if it happens that the left flank of your adversary is somewhat weaker than yours.

The fourth manner of fighting is this: when you have ordered your battle lines with four or five hundred men before the approach of your enemies, who know nothing of this plan, then you will move suddenly both your wings, so that both the unprepared wings of your enemy will be obliged to turn their backs. If you can do this quickly enough, the victory will be yours; but I consider this way dangerous unless you have very strong and experienced men-at-arms, for if half your formation is obliged to be uncovered and divided into two parts, and your enemy is not overcome at the first assault, it has the opportunity to invade your divided troops and the middle, which will be divided from its wings.

The fifth manner of combat is similar to the fourth, but if there are more than the archers and the lightly armed men placed in the front line, so that it cannot be easily breached, then you can also invade and attack with your right flank the left flank of your enemy, and with your left flank his right. You can thus put him to flight, but your middle is not placed in peril, because it is protected by the lightly armed men and the archers.

The sixth manner of combat is very good and almost like the second: good fighters are accustomed to use this in the expectation of victory. Let us suppose that a few men are organized in their formation. With regard to the enemy's formation join your right flank to their left and so initiate the battle with the best cavalry and infantry you have, and let the rest of your army follow from a distance your enemy's formation, and extend this part into a straight line. If you can reach your enemy's left wing, he will be obliged to turn his back, and cannot be rescued by his right wing or his center line, nor can he be of help to any of the others, for the tail of your army is extended like the longer part of the letter L and is far removed from your enemy.

## XXVI.
### MORE OF THE SAME.

The seventh way of combat is this: when the situation and area are favorable to the one who arrives there first, you take possession of a spot your enemies cannot easily reach, because of sea, mountains, or other obstacles. Let us suppose that you have few enough men, whom through very good tactics you have arranged in battle formation, and that on the side where there is no obstacle, you have put your cavalry. Then you will fight with assurance if attacked, for on one side you will have the protection of the site and on the other the strength of the cavalry. So it is always important to consider where you want to fight, and always and first of all to put forward the bravest you have. However few they may be, do not be dismayed, for victory is frequently achieved by a small number of combatants, if only the wise commander puts them where expediency and reason require.

## XXVII.
### THE ORDER AND MANNER THE GOOD COMMANDER SHOULD OBSERVE WHEN FORTUNE IS FAVORABLE TO HIM IN BATTLE.

Some who are not familiar with the deployment of arms may think that their situation in battle can be improved by enclosing their enemies in a limited space, or by encircling them to such an extent and by such a great number of men that they have no escape route; but this is very doubtful, for the enclosure increases the boldness of those who consider themselves condemned without hope of being able to withdraw or escape, so they sell themselves more dearly. For this reason the remark of Scipio was praised, that one should make a way for the enemies to escape, and lay an ambush where they must pass, for in that way they think they can save themselves by flight; that way they can more easily be killed than when they are defending themselves.[98] Some of them throw down their arms so that they can flee more easily. Thus they are killed by their pursuers like animals. The more numerous they are, the greater their confusion. One should not give importance to the number when courage is broken by fear. Those wise in arms say that when fortune is favorable to one side, so that it is victorious in battle, it should pursue that fortune to the end, however long it may last, while the enemies are fearful. They should not rejoice or take any undue pride in a little victory at the beginning, so that everything is left aside with the idea that it can easily be recovered later; for in this way a number have been deceived and never have achieved this end. Take, for example, Hannibal, who, after the Battle of Cannae,[99] had he gone directly to Rome, would have taken it without question, for the Romans were so overcome by fright and grief because of their great loss that they would not have known how to resist. But thinking to accomplish this at his pleasure and occupying himself

98. Vegetius III, xxi:

> Most people ignorant of military matters believe the victory will be more complete if they surround the enemy in a confined place or with large numbers of soldiers, so that they can find no way of escape. But trapped men draw extra courage from desperation, and when there is no hope, fear takes up arms. Men who know without a doubt that they are going to die will gladly die in good company.
> For this reason Scipio's axiom has won good praise, when he said that a way should be built for the enemy to flee by. For when an escape-route is revealed, the minds of all are united on turning their backs, and they are slaughtered unavenged, like cattle. Nor is there any danger for the pursuers once the defeated have turned round the arms with which they could have defended themselves. In this tactic, the greater the numbers, the more easily is a mass cut down. For there is no need of numbers in a case where the soldiers' minds, once terrified, wish to avoid not just the enemy's weapons but his face. Whereas trapped men, though few in number and weak in strength, for this very fact are a match for their enemies, because desperate men know they can have no other recourse. "The only hope of safety for the defeated is to expect no safety." (Milner trans., pp. 107–8)

99. Battle of Cannae: Hannibal was victorious over the Romans at Cannae in 216 B.C. and sent an impressive amount of booty back to Carthage, but the Romans reformed their army and surprised and defeated the Carthaginians. Hannibal's subsequent attack on Rome, years later, was a dismal failure. Christine discussed this event in the *Mutacion de fortune* (Solente ed. III, pp. 215–20).

only with his booty, he did not pay attention to this opportunity, which he
never again was given, however much he tried with all his strength to accomplish it.


## XXVIII.

### THE ORDER AND MANNER THE COMMANDER SHOULD ADHERE
### TO WHEN THE FORTUNES OF BATTLE TURN AGAINST HIM.[100]

Now there is another point, namely, that if one part of the army prevails
and the other flees, what remains, if it is the stronger, can still hope for
victory. It has turned out many times that those who were less favored
have won the battle. So these should rouse themselves with horn and
trumpet, thus frightening the enemy and comforting their own, as if they
had been victorious everywhere. If it should turn out that the damage has
involved the whole army, you should nevertheless seek a remedy, for fortune at the time of flight has rescued many. Men wise in the practice of
arms say that in the case of a full battle, the commander should be re-

---

100. Vegetius III, xxv:

WHAT TO DO, IF PART OR IF ALL OF THE ARMY IS ROUTED.

   Note that if part of the army is victorious and part is routed, one should be hopeful, because in a crisis of this type the steadfastness of the general can reclaim the whole victory for
himself. This has happened in countless battles, and those who have despaired the least have
been taken for the winners. Where their situations are similar, he is judged the stronger who
is not dismayed by his adversaries. Let him be first, therefore, to take spoils from the enemy
slain-as (the soldiers) themselves say, "collect the field." Let him be seen to be first to cele-
brate with shouts and bugles. By this show of confidence he will terrify the enemy and double
the confidence of his own men, as if he had come off victor in every part of the field.

   But if for some reason the whole army be routed in battle, the disaster can be mortal; yet
the chance to recover has existed for many, and a remedy should be sought. Let the provident
general therefore engage in pitched battle only if he has taken precaution that, should something go wrong owing to the variability of wars and the human condition, he may still get the
defeated away without great loss. For if there are hills nearby, if there are fortifications to the
rear, or if the bravest troops resist while the rest retreat, they will save themselves and their
comrades. Often a previously routed army has recovered its strength and destroyed those in
loose order and pursuing at random. Never does greater danger tend to arise for the side that
is celebrating, than when over-confidence is suddenly turned to panic.

   But in any event survivors should be collected up, stiffened for war by means of appropriate exhortations and restored with new arms. Then new levies of legionaries and new *auxilia*
should be sought and, what is more important, opportunities to attack the victors themselves
through concealed ambushes should be exploited, and morale regained in this way. There is
no lack of opportunity, since human minds are carried away by success to become so much
the more arrogant and careless. If anyone shall think this his last chance, let him reflect that
the results of all battles in the early stages (of a war) have been more against those destined to
ultimate victory. (Milner trans., pp. 114–15)

solved and advised to reassemble his own men, as the good shepherd does his sheep. In case they flee, he should make every effort to rescue the vanquished and bring them back to himself in some out-of-the-way place, or on a mountain, if there is one behind him, or in some other safe spot. If he can to some extent reorganize the brave ones in good order, he might still harm their enemies, for it frequently happens that those who are wildly chasing the defeated here and there, if their adversaries are wise, can be changed to flight, so that those who in the beginning were pursuers are killed. No greater confusion can overtake them than when their boldness is changed to fright. For this reason, whatever the adventure may be, one should comfort and regroup the defeated with suitable exhortation, and reassemble them, refurbishing them with fresh men and equipment if possible. Thus it is a good thing to consider in advance the unexpected adventure, which means thinking about how a trap might be laid, so that the enemies who have been pursuing them should suddenly encounter them in some unexpected place or in several places. So, by the good commander, the fear of those in flight might be transformed into enough courage to lie in wait and pursue, if need be. Nevertheless, the good commander, if he is wise, should not despair, however fortune may turn against him, for it sometimes comes about that through favorable chance and good fortune those who think that they have won everything may set themselves up arrogantly, and in this way, less wisely than they should, descend on their enemies, who, well-advised, receive them with great agility and overcome them. For this reason the wise commander should have thought of all the things that might happen, because they have often happened in the past. As it is said, the vanquished were in their turn conquerors, pursuing the others.

That this is so is demonstrated well enough by the case of the Romans in the adventure that befell them after the defeat of Cannae, when all despaired of ever being able to recover either happiness or prosperity. They wanted to abandon their city and go live elsewhere, but a valiant prince among them kept them from this by saying to them that he would fight them if they went away. So he gave them hope of better fortune and gathered them together once more, and among those gathered there he created knights, and with such strength as he could muster, he went to attack Hannibal, who did not expect it, so they took him by surprise. Thus it was that in such an hour he was overcome to the point that he never again gained a victory over them, and in the end the Romans destroyed him.

## XXIX.
### A BRIEF RECAPITULATION OF THE MATTERS DISCUSSED.

To summarize briefly the substance of what Vegetius undertakes to say in his book, he places an epilogue at the end where, in the manner of proverbs, he says this: You who wish to win honor in arms, put into practice what training in youth teaches you in order to be a master of the skills of chivalry in maturity, for it is better to be able to say "I know" than to say "Why did I not learn?"[101]

Insofar as you are able, always do what will injure your enemy and be

---

101. Vegetius I, iv: "Adolescents are the ones to recruit, just as Sallust says: 'Directly as soon as youth was able to endure war, it learned military practice in camp through labour.' For it is better that a trained young man should complain that he has not yet reached fighting age, than that he should regret that it has passed" (Milner trans., p. 5).

The remainder of this chapter follows Vegetius III, xxvi:

GENERAL RULES OF WAR.

In all battles the terms of campaign are such that what benefits you harms the enemy, and what helps him always hinders you. Therefore we ought never to do or omit to do anything at his pleasure, but carry out only that which we judge useful to ourselves. For you begin to be against yourself if you copy what he has done in his own interest, and likewise whatever you attempt for your side will be against him if he chooses to imitate it.

In war, he who spends more time watching in outposts and puts more effort into training soldiers, will be less subject to danger.

A soldier should never be led into battle unless you have made trial of him first.

It is preferable to subdue an enemy by famine, raids and terror, than in battle where fortune tends to have more influence than bravery.

No plans are better than those you carry out in advance without the enemy's knowledge.

Opportunity in war is usually of greater value than bravery.

In soliciting and taking in enemy soldiers, if they come in good faith, there is great security, because deserters harm the enemy more than casualties.

It is preferable to keep additional reserves behind the line than to spread the soldiers too widely.

It is difficult to beat someone who can form a true estimate of his own and the enemy's forces.

Bravery is of more value than numbers.

Terrain is often of more value than bravery.

Few men are born naturally brave; hard work and good training makes many so.

An army is improved by work, enfeebled by inactivity.

Never lead forth a soldier to a general engagement except when you see that he expects victory.

Surprises alarm the enemy, familiarity breeds contempt.

He who pursues rashly with his forces in loose order is willing to give the adversary the victory he had himself obtained.

He who does not prepare grain-supplies and provisions is conquered without a blow. . . .

When an enemy spy is wandering secretly in camp, let all personnel be ordered to their tents in daylight, and the spy is immediately caught.

When you discover that your plan has been betrayed to the enemy, you are advised to change your dispositions.

Discuss with many what you should do, but what you are going to do discuss with as few and as trustworthy as possible, or rather with yourself alone.

to your own advantage, for as soon as you stop pursuing him, you will injure yourself.

Be sure you know a knight before you lead him into battle, and if there is any doubt, do not trust him, for it is much better to doubt one's enemies by being on one's guard than to trust in battle people one does not know.

It requires great security to attract to oneself enemies in flight, for even those in flight can damage adversaries more than those killed. One is not completely vanquished if he can have control of his own men and also his adversaries.

In arranging for battle, it is better to leave behind some relief forces than to spread out soldiers too widely, for fresh troops can bring relief to the fatigued.

Bravery is more helpful than numbers, and the situation is often more valuable than force.

Man profits by effort and is enfeebled by inactivity.

Never lead a knight into battle if he does not expect victory, for if he has little hope, he is already half vanquished.

Surprises alarm the enemy. He who pursues his enemy unwisely is trying to give him the victory he himself has won.

The one who does not prepare supplies for the battle in advance is conquered without a blow.

Keeping to an order of battle properly gives victory to both the strong and the weak.

When you know that the enemy's spies are wandering around your army, make your men retire to their tents.

If you suspect that your plan has been revealed to the enemy, change your dispositions.

No plans are better than those of which the enemy has no knowledge until they are carried out.

Chance gives victory more often than does strength.

It is impossible to foresee the outcome of the battle, which is in Fortune's power.

---

Soldiers are corrected by fear and punishment in camp, on campaign hope and rewards make them behave better.

Good generals never engage in a general engagement except on some advantageous occasion, or under great necessity.

It is a powerful disposition to press the enemy more with famine than with the sword.

The mode in which you are going to give battle should not become known to the enemy, lest they make moves to resist with countermeasures. (Milner trans., pp. 116–17, 118–19)

# PART II

## I.

### THE FIRST CHAPTER SPEAKS OF SCIPIO THE AFRICAN.

In the second part, having discussed (according to Vegetius in particular) the ways that were formerly observed by the valiant conquerors of the world in deeds of arms during their conquests, men who knew how to take advantage of more than one way of waging war, it seems useful, in order to develop our subject further, always for the profit of the followers of chivalry, to add in this part the sorts of wiles and subtle chivalric devices that the authors who have discussed the matter have called military stratagems. On these stratagems a valiant man named Frontinus wrote a book in which he discussed the deeds of these same noble and chivalrous conquerors. Reading these can set a good example for similar action, if deemed desirable, by those who find themselves in similar situations through the fortunes of war. Hence it is from this book that we have

In this part Christine quotes extensively from the *Strategemata* of Sextus Julius Frontinus (c. A.D. 30–104). Although the complete work was not translated into French until the middle of the fifteenth century, she would have known it through the commentary accompanying the translation of the *Facta et dicta memorabiles* of Valerius Maximus made by Simon de Hesdin and Nicolas de Gonesse (1375–1401). Book VI of this translation was made up entirely of quotations from the *Strategemata*. Christine would have made use of a manuscript such as Paris, Bibl. Nat. f. fr. 282, which had already served as a principal source for the *Livre du corps de policie*.

made use of some cases. This author states at the outset that the valiant
conqueror, prince and leader of a great army of Romans, namely Scipio
the African, who conquered with his sword all of Spain, Africa, and
Carthage, on one occasion, when he was with a great host against King
Syphax, who likewise had assembled a great army against Scipio, sent to
this king, as if on a mission, one of his knights, named Laelius. With him
he sent some of his wisest captains disguised as slaves or minor servants,
so that they might observe carefully the order, the ways, and the size of
the army of the aforesaid King Syphax. When they arrived there, they executed their mission well, overlooking nothing. In order to observe the
army more freely, they pretended that one of their horses had run away,
and running after it here and there, they found what they were looking
for, being able in a short time to observe everything fully as experts.
When they returned and made their report to their commander, Scipio,
he learned that they had placed dry branches in the king's camp, so they
arranged to have fires set by night in several places. When this happened,
as Syphax's men rushed to save their horses and lodgings, they were overcome. In this way Scipio destroyed them completely.[1]

II.

CONCERNING DUKE MARIUS, SERTORIUS, DUILIUS,
AND PERICLES.

Marius, the gallant leader of the Roman army, when he was obliged to
fight against a proud people called the Cimbri and the Teutoni, had in
his ranks several soldiers from Gaul. So, in accordance with the teach-
ings of the wise man who said, "Try out a man before trusting him
greatly," he undertook to try out the loyalty and obedience of those
Gauls. Therefore he sent them letters in which, among other things, he
told them that he forbade them from opening, before a certain stated

1. Frontinus I, ii, 1: "Scipio Africanus, seizing the opportunity of sending an embassy to Syphax,
commanded specially chosen tribunes and centurions to go with Laelius, disguised as slaves and entrusted with the task of spying out the strength of the king. These men, in order to examine more
freely the situation of the camp, purposely let loose a horse and chased it around the greatest part of
the fortifications, pretending it was running away. After they had reported the results of their observations, the destruction of the camp by fire brought the war to a close" (Bennett trans., Loeb Classical
Library, pp. 17–19). See also Livy XXX, pp. 4ff.; Valerius Maximus, Paris, Bibl. Nat. MS 282, fol. 284.
Syphax was the chief of a Numidian tribe. Christine had already written of the exploits of Scipio in
the *Chemin de long estude*, vv. 3811–17 and 4359–74, and in the *Mutacion de fortune*, Solente ed.,
III, pp. 222–30. S. Solente identified her source as the *Histoire ancienne*.

day, some small letters enclosed in the larger ones he was sending them. But before that day had arrived, he sent for them, along with the opened letters, and as these showed that his orders had been disregarded, he knew that they were not very loyal to him, and so he did not put further trust in them.[2]

Likewise, a valiant knight named Sertorius, a commander of a large army, came to Spain, where he had to cross a river, and as his enemies were following him closely to destroy him when he crossed it, he thought of this strategy. He stopped on the river bank and made his camp in semi-circular form rather distant from the bank. It was made of branches and of wood, and he set fire to it. While it was burning, he had his army cross in safety in spite of his enemies, who could not reach him without passing through the fire.[3]

Likewise, Duilius, chief of the Roman army, once brashly got (his vessel) caught in the enemy city of Syracuse, where a chain was raised to entrap him. He was nevertheless able to escape. When he saw the trap, he had the bow, which is the forward part of the boat, drawn toward the chain, while the stern, the back part, was toward the land. Then he had all his men gather in the stern, so that the bow was light and rose up in the water. Then by vigorous rowing they carried the boat for the most part onto the chain, whereupon he had his men return to the bow, so that the stern rose up, and with strong rowing the boat passed over the chain, and they escaped from this peril.[4]

2. Frontinus I, ii, 6: "During the war with the Cimbrians and Tuetons, the consul Gaius Marius, wishing to test the loyalty of the Gauls and Ligurians, sent them a letter, commanding them in the first part of the letter not to open the inner part, which was specially sealed, before a certain date. Afterwards, before the appointed time had arrived, he demanded the same letter back, and finding all seals broken, he knew that acts of hostility were afoot" (Bennett trans., p. 21).

Gaius Marius (157–86 B.C.): The reputation he had gained in earlier battles made him the leader of choice against the Teutons and the Cimbri when they threatened northern Italy. He trained his army and finally defeated the Teutons in 102 B.C. and the Cimbri in 101, victories largely due to military reforms he had introduced.

The Cimbri were a Germanic tribe from North Jutland. Overpopulation drove them to migrate, in company with the Teutons and Ambrones, over a wide territory in Europe. In 105 they moved toward northern Italy. Marius defeated the Cimbri near Vercelli in the Po valley.

3. Frontinus I, v, 1: "When Quintus Sertorius (c.122–72 B.C.), in the Spanish campaign, desired to cross a river while the enemy were harassing him from the rear, he had his men construct a crescent-shaped rampart on the bank, piled it high with timber, and set fire to it. When the enemy were thus cut off, he crossed the stream without hindrance" (Bennett trans., pp. 35–37).

4. Frontinus I, v, 6: "When the consul Gaius Duilius was caught by a chain stretched across the entrance to the harbour of Syracuse, which he had rashly entered, he assembled all his soldiers in the sterns of the boats, and when the boats were thus tilted up, he propelled them forward with the full force of his oarsmen. Thus lifted up over the chain, the prows moved forward. When this part of the boats had been carried over, the soldiers, returning to the prows, depressed these, and the weight

Likewise, Pericles, who was an Athenian leader, was once driven by the Peloponnesians into a spot enclosed by formidable mountains and from which there were only two outlets. When he saw this, he immediately made at one of these outlets a wide and steep ditch as if he were arranging it to prevent his enemies from reaching him from that direction. Into the other outlet he led his men as if he would attempt to escape by force. When his enemies saw this, they, as they did not believe he could escape by way of the ditch, undertook to defend the other outlet, as in a siege, but Pericles had maliciously constructed good wooden bridges over the ditch, and in that way his men left freely, without the knowledge of their enemies.[5]

### III.

#### THIS SPEAKS OF THE CITY OF THE BOII,[6]
#### OF HANNIBAL, OF DENIS THE TYRANT.

At the time of the Roman conquests, it once happened that the Roman army had to pass through the Litana Forest to reach the city of Bologna. When the inhabitants learned this, they went into the forest and cut the trees where the Romans would have to pass, to the point where they were held up by only slight support. Then they hid themselves at the farther edge of the forest, and when the army had entered, those who were hidden came out and pushed the trees over onto the Roman army, so that a great part of it was crushed.[7] In this way they were delivered from their enemy. This was done in a similar fashion on another occasion.

---

thus transferred to them permitted the boats to pass over the chain" (Bennett trans., p. 39). Gaius Duilius, as commander of the Roman fleet, defeated the Carthaginian fleet near Sicily (260 B.C.), Rome's first naval triumph.

5. Frontinus I, v, 10: "Pericles the Athenian (c. 495–429 B.C.), being driven by the Peloponnesians into a place surrounded on all sides by precipitous cliffs and provided with only two outlets, dug a ditch of great breadth on one side, as if to shut out the enemy; on the other side he began to build a road, as if intending to make a sally by this. The besiegers, not supposing that Pericles' army would make its escape by the ditch which he had constructed, massed to oppose him on the side where the road was. But Pericles, spanning the ditch by bridges which he had made ready, extricated his men without interference" (Bennett trans., p. 41; MS fr. 1543, fol. 311).

6. The Boii were Gauls who entered Italy c. 400 B.C. They established themselves between the Po and the Apennines, where their chief city was Bononia (Bologna).

7. Frontinus I, vi, 4: "When our army was about to pass through the Litana Forest, the Boii cut into the trees at the base, leaving them only a slender support by which to stand, until they should be pushed over. Then the Boii hid at the further edge of the woods and by toppling over the nearest trees caused the fall of those more distant, as soon as our men entered the forest. In that way they spread general disaster among the Romans, and destroyed a large force" (Bennett trans., p. 55).

Likewise, Hannibal, prince and emperor of Carthage and Africa, was accustomed to leading elephants into battle. It once happened that he had to cross a wide river with his whole army, but there was not any way to make the elephants enter the water. He then devised this scheme. He had in his company a man who was an excellent swimmer and was also very courageous. He had this man injure and wound one of the elephants he had already led to the river. Then the elephant, cruel and furious, immediately went into the river after him to avenge himself, and the others also entered the water. So they all crossed to the other side.[8]

Likewise, Denis the Tyrant, prince of Syracuse, knew that the Carthaginians intended to come against him with a large army of many men. Thus he had his men protect towns and castles near and far by which they would pass, and he gave the order that when the enemy should approach, these men should leave the strongholds as if in fear, and should join him in Syracuse. When this had taken place, the Carthaginians, who thought they had won everything, took possession of these places and fortified them well with their own people, thus diminishing their army greatly, whereas the forces of Denis had grown to the point where they were virtually equal to the other army. So he engaged them in a battle where they were vanquished, and those in the strongholds were destroyed by starvation.[9]

## IV. OF SPANIARDS, ALEXANDER THE EPIROTE, LEPTINES, HANNIBAL, AND OTHERS.

On one occasion the Spaniards were to fight against Hamilcar, leader of the Carthaginian army, where there were many men in good array. They

---

8. Frontinus I, vii, 2: "When Hannibal on one occasion could not force his elephants to ford an especially deep stream, having neither boats nor material of which to construct them, he ordered one of his men to wound the most savage elephant under the ear, and then straightway to swim across the stream and take to his heels. The infuriated elephant, eager to pursue the author of his suffering, swam the stream, and thus set an example for the rest to make the same venture" (Bennett trans., pp. 55–57).

9. Frontinus I, viii, 11: "When the Africans were planning to cross over to Sicily in vast numbers in order to attack Dionysius, tyrant of Syracuse, the latter constructed strongholds in many places and commanded their defenders to surrender them at the coming of the enemy, and then, when they retired, to return secretly to Syracuse. The Africans were forced to occupy the captured strongholds with garrisons, whereupon Dionysius, having reduced the army of his opponents to the scanty number which he desired, and being now approximately on an equality, attacked and defeated them, since he had concentrated his own forces, and had separated those of his adversaries" (Bennett trans., pp. 63–65).

thought of this device to break up the battle formation of their enemies. They took several steers pulling carts and covered with oil and pitch pieces of wood that they attached under their tails. They further covered these with fronds dampened in oil, and put these steers in the front line of battle. Having set fire to the fronds, they drove the steers toward the enemy, who fled, breaking up all their formations; so Hamilcar was defeated.[10]

Likewise, Alexander, prince of Epirus, was making war against some people called Illyrians, who wore a distinctive costume. So Alexander selected a considerable number of men and gave them Illyrian clothes he had formerly captured in battle. When they were dressed, he gave them the order that when the Illyrians were near enough to see them, they should begin to set fire to their own lands, as if they were out to destroy everything. When this order was carried out, the enemy, who saw this, thought it was their own people and so followed those who were going before them until they came to a narrow pass, where Alexander had laid his trap, and there the Illyrians were all killed or captured.[11]

Likewise, Leptines, prince of Syracuse, did a similar thing to the Carthaginians who approached him for battle. He had had his own men set fires in his principal cities and castles, whereupon the Carthaginians, who thought it was their own people destroying everything in this fashion, wanted to rush there to help them. But Leptines had put men to wait in a place the Carthaginians had to pass, and there all were killed.[12]

Likewise, that wise old warrior Hannibal, prince of Carthage, of whom I have already spoken, once had to deal with Africans who had rebelled. He knew that these people were fond of wine, so he had a large amount of it mixed with mandragora, which intoxicates men and puts them to sleep. After this, he arranged for a small skirmish, from which he ordered

---

10. Frontinus II, iv, 17: "The Spaniards, when fighting against Hamilcar, hitched steers to carts and placed them in the front line. These carts they filled with pitch, tallow, and sulphur, and when the signal for battle was given, set them afire. Then, driving the steers against the enemy, they threw the line into panic and broke through" (Bennett trans., p. 131).

11. Frontinus II, v, 10: "Alexander, the Epirote, when waging war against the Illyrians, first placed a force in ambush, and then dressed up some of his own men in Illyrian garb, ordering them to lay waste his own, that is to say, Epirote territory. When the Illyrians saw what was being done, they themselves began to pillage right and left-the more confidently since they thought that those who led the way were scouts. But when they had been designedly brought by the latter into a disadvantageous position, they were routed and killed" (Bennett trans., pp. 137–39).

12. Frontinus II, v, 11: "Leptines, the Syracusan, also, when waging war against the Carthaginians, ordered his own lands to be laid waste and certain farm-houses and forts to be set on fire. The Carthaginians, thinking this was done by their own men, went out themselves also to help; whereupon they were set upon by men lying in wait, and were put to rout" (Bennett trans., p. 139).

his men to flee, as if in fear. When the rebels, who thought they had won completely, drew near and midnight arrived, Hannibal pretended that he did not dare to await them, so he fled, leaving his camp full of good things that he had treated. Then, in the morning, when the enemy did not see anyone, they came to the camp and joyfully sacked everything. Like starving people they ate ravenously, consuming the good food and wine arranged for them, so all were affected, made drowsy and drunk until they lay down as if dead, aware of nothing. Hannibal returned in due time and killed them all.[13]

Likewise, those who were fighting against a people called Erythraeans took their enemy's spies and made them point out their army's position. Then they took the Erythraeans' clothing and dressed their own people of a similar size in it, and had them go up onto a high mountain where they could be seen by the opposing army. As the enemy had directed their spies to indicate what they had found, the "spies" gave the signal that the army should advance. This they did, believing that these were their own spies, and so they found themselves caught in an ambush, where all were killed and cut to pieces.[14]

V.

OF MENOLE (MEMNON), COMMANDER OF RHODES, OF SCIPIO,<br>OF SERTORIUS, OF HANNIBAL, LENTULUS.

Menole (Memnon), commander of Rhodes,[15] was in army formation against his enemies. He had more and better horsemen than his enemies, who remained in the mountains so that Memnon was unable to make

---

13. Frontinus II, v, 12: "Maharbal, sent by the Carthaginians against the rebellious Africans, knowing that the tribe was passionately fond of wine, mixed a large quantity of wine with mandragora, which in potency is something between a poison and a soporific. Then after an insignificant skirmish he deliberately withdrew. At dead of night, leaving in the camp some of his baggage and all the drugged wine, he feigned flight. When the barbarians captured the camp and in a frenzy of delight greedily drank the drugged wine, Maharbal returned, and either took them prisoners or slaughtered them while they lay stretched out as if dead" (Bennett trans., p. 139). Maharbal was a Carthaginian officer under Hannibal, who was better known to the medieval reader.

14. Frontinus II, v, 15: "The Chians, when waging war against the Erythreans, caught an Erythrean spy on a lofty eminence and put him to death. They then gave his clothes to one of their own soldiers, who, by giving a signal from the same eminence, lured the Erythreans into an ambush" (Bennett trans., p. 141).

15. Memnon, a native of Rhodes in the fourth century B.C., became a Persian general in Asia Minor.

contact with them. He therefore devised a scheme to make them defend themselves. He chose one of his knights who was wise and brave and charged him to behave as if he were fleeing from the army, as if, being displeased with it and the pay, he was turning to the other side. He did this, and along with his other complaints about Memnon, he gave them to believe that because of Memnon's poor command qualities there was a great deal of dissension in the army, which in turn was causing many to leave. In order that they might believe this all the more, Memnon made many of his men leave so that those in the mountains would see them go, but he put them here and there in various ambushes. Because of this deceit the ones in the mountains came down, thinking the enemy army so diminished that they expected to get the better of them, but they were soon surrounded on all sides and trapped by the cavalry, which killed them all.[16]

Likewise, when Scipio was to go with a large army to Spain and Africa, King Syphax sent him a message expressing grave threats with many discouraging words, concerning both the difficulty of the terrain and the strength and number of the people. This did not greatly frighten the valiant man, but in order to prevent the messenger from spreading the word among the troops so that they might take fright, he immediately sent him back and instead spread the word that the king as a friend had sent for him to come immediately.[17]

On one occasion (Quintus) Sertorius[18] was engaged in a battle in which he was informed that his constable had been killed, but in order

16. Frontinus II, v, 18: "Memnon, the Rhodian, being superior in cavalry, and wishing to draw down to the plains an enemy who clung to the hills, sent certain of his soldiers under the guise of deserters to the camp of the enemy, to say that the army of Memnon was inspired with such a serious spirit of mutiny that some portion of it was constantly deserting. To lend credit to this assertion, Memnon ordered small redoubts to be fortified here and there in view of the enemy, as though the disaffected were about to retire to these. Inveigled by these representations, those who had been keeping themselves on the hills came down to level ground, and, as they attacked the redoubts, were surrounded by the cavalry" (Bennett trans., p. 143).

17. Frontinus II, vii, 4: "When the envoys of King Syphax told Scipio in the name of their king not to cross over to Africa from Sicily in expectation of an alliance, Scipio, fearing that the spirits of his men would receive a shock, if the hope of a foreign alliance were cut off, summarily dismissed the envoys, and spread abroad the report that he was expressly sent for by Syphax" (Bennett trans., pp. 171–73).

18. Quintus Sertorius (c. 122–72 B.C.), of Sabine extraction, served as a governor in Spain. When master of most of Spain, he created a senate of three hundred Romans to rival Sulla's. His general, Hirtuleius, overran Hispania Citerior, but was defeated by Metellus near Segovia. Sertorius was one of several Roman generals who tried to master Rome from the provinces, but in spite of his military skill and chivalrous behavior, he was unsuccessful.

that his men should not know it and thereby be frightened, he killed the messenger with the lance he was holding.[19]

Likewise, at that time when Hannibal descended upon Italy to advance to Rome, three thousand Carpetani that he was leading fled from his army in one night. Learning of this, and in order that his men should not be amazed, he had word circulated that they had been discharged by his order, and to make this more convincing, he sent away some others who could be of little use and were poorly armed.[20]

Once when Lentulus (Lucius Lucullus)[21] had assembled a great army to combat his enemies, he had included a cohort of Macedonians to help him. A cohort consists of 665 men. But when he expected to make use of them, they decided suddenly to leave his army and to join the other side. When Lentulus, who was well versed in strategy, saw this, he was not dismayed, but rather knew how to catch them in their own toils. Also, to keep his army from being upset at being diminished by so many men, he circulated the word that he had sent them ahead willingly to organize the head of the army. To make this more believable, he immediately set out to follow them, so that what he had in mind took place; for the enemy, seeing the Macedonians approach, truly believed that they were coming against them for the first battle. Those so threatened turned against them and began to attack vigorously and strike them down, so they were obliged to defend themselves whether they wanted to or not. Lentulus, with his troops, was in the meantime attacking his enemies elsewhere, so that in this way the Macedonians helped him, willingly or not, to the point that he was victorious.[22]

19. Frontinus II, vii, 5: "Once when Quintus Sertorius was engaged in battle, he plunged a dagger into the barbarian who had reported to him that Hirtuleius had fallen, for fear the messenger might bring this news to the knowledge of others and in this way the spirit of his own troops should be broken" (Bennett trans., p. 173).

20. Frontinus II, vii, 7: "When Hannibal entered Italy, three thousand Carpetani deserted him. Fearing that the rest of his troops might be affected by their example, he proclaimed that they had been discharged by him, and as further proof of that, he sent home a few others whose services were of very little use to him" (Bennett trans., p. 173).

21. Lucius Lucullus (c. 177–156 B.C.) served Sulla, campaigning successfully in the Aegean. He was later given an important command post in the war against Mithradates. He was known as a good strategist and administrator.

22. Frontinus II, vii, 8: "When Lucius Lucullus noticed that the Macedonian cavalry, whom he had as auxiliaries, were suddenly deserting to the enemy in a body, he ordered the trumpets to sound and sent out squadrons to pursue the deserters. The enemy, thinking that an engagement was beginning, received the deserters with javelins, whereupon the Macedonians, seeing that they were not welcomed by the enemy and were attacked by those whom they were deserting were forced to resort to a genuine battle and assaulted the enemy" (Bennett trans., p. 173).

VI.

CONCERNING SCORYLO, CHIEFTAIN OF DACIA, FULVIUS
NOBILIOR, EPAMINONDAS, GENERAL OF THEBES, FABIUS
MAXIMUS, THE SECOND SCIPIO THE AFRICAN, SERTORIUS, AND
ONCE MORE EPAMINONDAS, THE THEBAN GENERAL.

During a time when the Romans were in dissension among themselves
and fighting a civil war, a period of good fortune for others, several nations developed a disdain for them and were tempted to display it. It
seemed to the Dacians in particular that the time had come to get the
better of them, and they had on several occasions called this to the attention of their chieftain, Scorylo, who was not in agreement with them. Finally, however, because they were pressing him so hard, and in order to
teach them by this example, he had brought to the square before the
palace several dogs, who were set against each other until they began to
fight furiously. At the height of their battle, when they seemed so vicious
that nothing could separate them, he had brought into their midst a wolf
he had provided for the purpose. As soon as the dogs saw it, they stopped
fighting among themselves and all together attacked the wolf. By this example the chieftain pointed out to his people that whatever war a nation
might have within itself, it would not allow itself to be attacked by an out-
sider, but would rather join together to vanquish it.[23]

Likewise, Fulvius Nobilior, duke and leader of the Roman army, once
found himself so near to the Samnites that he could only expect a battle.[24] Therefore, because he knew that his men would be frightened, as
their enemies were in larger numbers than they, he decided on a scheme
to deal with that fear. He said to his men, and had it proclaimed throughout his forces, that he had bribed one legion of the Samnites with money,
so that they would come over to him once the battle had begun. To make
this more believable, he borrowed as much gold and silver from his men
as they could provide, as if to pay this bribe. One legion numbers 6,666

23. Frontinus I, x, 4: "Scorylo, a chieftain of the Dacians, though he knew that the Romans were
torn with the dissensions of the civil wars, yet did not think he ought to venture on any enterprise
against them, inasmuch as a foreign war might be the means of uniting the citizens in harmony. Accordingly he pitted two dogs in combat before the populace, and when they became engaged in a
desperate encounter, exhibited a wolf to them. The dogs straightway abandoned their fury against
each other and attacked the wolf. By this illustration, Scorylo kept the barbarians from a movement
which could only have benefited the Romans" (Bennett trans., pp. 69–71).

24. Samnites: inhabitants of Samnium in the southern Apennines of Italy. Primitive, but warlike, they lived mostly in agricultural villages.

men. It turned out that because of their confidence, the Romans had such great courage that they fiercely attacked the enemy, whom they found quite unsuspecting. They had little regard for them, because they represented a smaller number, and so were vanquished.[25]

Likewise, Epaminondas, the valiant Theban leader, who was once obliged to engage in battle with the Lacedaemonians,[26] devised this plan. To increase the strength and courage of his troops, he had them all come before him and said loudly to this audience that he wanted to tell them that what had been brought to his attention was true. This was that the Lacedaemonians had decided that if they were victorious, they would kill all Theban men and women, they would destroy the city and put all small children into perpetual bondage. Because of this threat, the infuriated Thebans fought like madmen and overcame the Lacedaemonians, even though these were more numerous.[27]

Likewise, Fabius Maximus, when he had to fight against his enemies, had his troops well protected by stockades and fortified lodgings. As a result, he feared that they would fight with less vigor because of the assurance afforded them by their fortifications. Therefore he had these burned before the battle.[28]

Likewise, when Scipio, the second African, led his army to Africa, it happened that as he was leaving the ship, he fell to the ground. As soon as he looked at his soldiers, he saw that they considered this a bad omen and were disturbed by it. Then the wise warrior thought of a clever way to reassure them. He began to laugh and said boldly: "Heaven be praised, this is a good omen. I am seized by the African land. It is ours without a

---

25. Frontinus I, xi, 2: "Fulvius Nobilior, deeming it necessary to fight with a small force against a large army of the Samnites who were flushed with success, pretended that one legion of the enemy had been bribed by him to turn traitor; and to strengthen belief in this story, he commanded the tribunes, the 'first ranks,' and the centurions to contribute all the ready money they had, or any gold and silver, in order that the price might be paid the traitors at once. He promised that, when victory was achieved, he would give generous presents to those who contributed for this purpose. This assurance brought such ardour and confidence to the Romans that they straightway opened battle and won a glorious victory" (Bennett trans., p. 71).

26. Lacedaemonians: inhabitants of Lacedaemon, ancient Sparta.

27. Frontinus I, xi, 6: "Epaminondas, general of the Thebans, on one occasion, when about to engage in battle with the Spartans, acted as follows. In order that his soldiers might not only exercise their strength, but also be stirred by their feelings, he announced in an assembly of his men that the Spartans had resolved, in the case of victory, to massacre all males, to lead the wives and children of those executed into bondage, and to raze Thebes to the ground. By this announcement the Thebans were so roused that they overwhelmed the Spartans at the first onset" (Bennett trans., pp. 73–75).

28. Frontinus I, xi, 21: "Fabius Maximus, fearing that his troops would fight less resolutely in consequence of their reliance on their ships, to which it was possible to retreat, ordered the ships to be set on fire before the battle began" (Bennett trans., p. 81).

doubt." So by these words he reversed the misgivings of his men, and it turned out as he had predicted.[29]

Likewise, once when Sertorius was obliged to fight, a marvelous sign appeared in his army, for the shields of the horsemen and the chests of their horses suddenly appeared to be covered with blood, which alarmed everyone greatly. But their valiant leader reassured them by saying, with a joyful expression, that it was a very good omen, and by it they should understand that the victory would be theirs, as these were the parts that were usually splattered by the blood of the enemy.[30]

Likewise, on another occasion Epaminondas, the valiant Theban leader, was about to engage in battle with the Lacedaemonians. As there was a certain delay, his chair was brought to him so he could sit down while waiting. By chance the chair gave way beneath him, which astonished his men, who considered it a bad omen. When the wise leader observed this, he rose quickly, saying with a brave face: "Up, up, my knights; the gods forbid us to sit, for by this sign they have admonished us to engage in battle immediately. The victory will be ours."[31]

VII.

THE SECOND PART OF FRONTINUS SPEAKS
OF THE LACEDAEMONIANS,
OF JULIUS CAESAR, OF PAPIRIUS CURSOR, OF POMPEY.

At a time when the Lacedaemonians were involved in a war with the inhabitants of the city of Messina, they learned through their spies as a certainty that the inhabitants of Messina were so angry at them that they would bring their wives and their children to battle to inspire them to

29. Frontinus I, xii, 1: "Scipio, having transported his army from Italy to Africa, stumbled as he was disembarking. When he saw the soldiers struck aghast at this, by his steadiness and loftiness of spirit he converted their cause of concern into one of encouragement, by saying: 'Congratulate me, my men! I have hit Africa hard' " (Bennett trans., p. 81).

30. Frontinus I, xii, 4: "Sertorius, when by a sudden prodigy the outsides of the shields of his cavalrymen and the breasts of their horses showed marks of blood, interpreted this as a mark of victory, since those were the parts which were wont to be spattered with the blood of the enemy" (Bennett trans., p. 83).

31. Frontinus I, xii, 7: "When the same Epaminondas was about to open battle against the Spartans, the chair on which he had sat down gave way beneath him, whereat all the soldiers, greatly troubled, interpreted this as an unlucky omen. But Epaminondas exclaimed: 'Not at all; we are simply forbidden to sit' " (Bennett trans., p. 83).

greater courage, or for all of them to die together. For this reason the Lacedaemonians withdrew and put off the battle.[32]

Likewise, Caesar had once driven his enemies, by cutting off their water supply, to the point where, dying of thirst, they were in despair of their lives and, enraged, came out to do battle with him. But he did not wish it at that hour and restrained his men, for it did not seem to him wise to fight when his enemies were driven by wrath and despair.[33]

Likewise, when Papirius Cursor[34] had to fight the Samnites, he learned through his spies that his enemies outnumbered him, whereby his troops feared to assemble. He immediately chose some of his men in whom he had the greatest confidence and commanded them to take a great quantity of wooden branches and drag these after them in order to stir up dust, and to go down the slope of a mountain so that the two armies could see them, and to make as much noise as they could. When this had been accomplished, Papirius, as soon as he saw them, shouted so loudly that both his own men and the enemy should hear him. He also had several others shout that it was his colleagues whom he had left in ambush, who had gotten the better of some of the enemies, and that they should make sure that his companions did not enjoy the glory of victory without him. So it turned out as he had intended, for his own troops were emboldened and shed their fear, and the Samnites, because of the great amount of dust, thought that all this must be true, so turned their backs and fled.[35]

Likewise, Pompey suspected that a certain city was more sympathetic

32. Frontinus II, 1, 10: "When the Spartans learned from scouts that the Messenians had broken out into such fury that they had come down to battle attended by their wives and children, they postponed the engagement" (Bennett trans., p. 95).

33. Frontinus II, 1, 11: "In the Civil War, when Gaius Caesar held the army of Afranius and Petreius besieged and suffering from thirst, and when their troops, infuriated because of this, had slain all their beasts of burden and come out for battle, Caesar held back his own soldiers, deeming the occasion ill-suited for an engagement, since his opponents were so inflamed with wrath and desperation" (Bennett trans., pp. 95–97).

34. Papirius Cursor: Roman hero of the second Samnite War. His victory in 309 B.C. marked him as a great general, a fit match for Alexander.

35. Frontinus II, iv, 1: "When Papirius Cursor, the son, in his consulship failed to win any advantage in his battle against the stubbornly resisting Samnites, he gave no intimation of his purpose to his men, but commanded Spurius Nautius to arrange to have a few auxiliary horsemen and grooms, mounted on mules and trailing branches over the ground, race down in great commotion from a hill running at an angle with the field. As soon as these came in sight, he proclaimed that his colleague was at hand, crowned with victory, and urged his men to secure for themselves the glory of the present battle before he should arrive. At this the Romans rushed forward, kindling with confidence, while the enemy, disheartened at the sight of dust, turned and fled" (Bennett trans., p. 125).

to his enemies than to him, and was giving them help. For this reason, before a showdown, he asked the inhabitants of that city if they would be willing to receive, until his return, a few injured men who could not follow his army, and to look after them and cure them; and he said he would bring them gold and silver and other assets to repay the favors the injured would receive. When this matter was arranged, Pompey had some of his best and bravest men wrapped up, bandaged, and put on litters as if they were seriously wounded, and he had their equipment brought along in chests and bundles as if it were clothing and great possessions. Thus, when they saw their opportunity, they rose up and managed to gain control of the city and to keep it.[36]

## VIII.

### THIS CONCERNS ALEXANDER THE GREAT, CAESAR AUGUSTUS, CRATES, DUKE OF ATHENS.

When the great Alexander had conquered a third of Asia, fearing that after he departed there might be rebellion, he led away with him, as if to honor them, all the kings and princes of the land, and those he thought to be the most upset at being conquered and subjected. For those who remained, he provided certain captains and chieftains from their own people. In this way he gained the love of the people because he left the government to them. Thus, even if they wanted to rebel, they could not do so, because they had no leaders. People who have learned about government from a leader can do nothing without him.[37]

Likewise, when Caesar Augustus had subjugated Germania, and the Germans had given themselves up to him, he had several castles built near their cities in order to dominate them better, but to pacify them

36. Frontinus II, xi, 2: "Gnaeus Pompey, suspecting the Chaucensians and fearing that they would not admit a garrison, asked that they would meanwhile permit his invalid soldiers to recover among them. Then, sending his strongest men in the guise of invalids, he seized the city and held it" (Bennett trans., p. 189).

37. Frontinus II, xi, 3: "When Alexander had conquered and subdued Thrace and was setting out for Asia, fearing that after his departure the Thracians would take up arms, he took with him, as though by way of conferring honour, their kings and officials—all in fact who seemed to take to heart the loss of freedom. In charge of those left behind he placed common and ordinary persons, thus preventing the officials from wishing to make any change, as being bound to him by favours, and the common people from even being able to do so, since they had been deprived of their leaders" (Bennett trans., p. 191).

for this move, he bought from them the lands on which he built these castles, whereby they were pleased with him and did not oppose his domination.[38]

Likewise, Chares, Athenian commander, was established in the field with few men, but he was expecting reinforcements. He feared that his enemies, of whom there were a great number, might attack him because they knew of his weakness. In order to avoid such a consequence, he sent out a large part of his troops by night with the order that the next morning they should return, coming down the slope of a mountain making a great deal of noise so that the enemy could see them and thus believe it was a reinforcement. So it came about that through this deception they remained safe until help arrived.[39]

IX.

IN BOOK THREE THERE IS THE CASE OF LYSIMACHUS,
KING OF MACEDONIA, AND OF FABIUS MAXIMUS.

Lysimachus, king of Macedonia, was besieging the city of Ephesus. He had the help of an arch-pirate, which is to say a great sea-thief, who did a great deal of harm to the king and his ships, often taking from him a great number of prisoners. However, the king took advantage of him through a curious scheme, for he managed to bribe him with money to the point where he filled his ships with the king's men, well supplied with equipment, and he took them into the city as if to prison. After nightfall, when those of the city were not paying attention, the king's men attacked the guards and killed them. In this way the city was captured and turned over to Lysimachus.[40]

38. Frontinus II, xi, 7: "When the Emperor Caesar Augustus Germanicus, in the war in which he earned his title by conquering the Germans, was building forts in the territory of the Cubii, he ordered compensation to be made for the crops which he had included within his fortifications. Thus the renown of his justice won the allegiance of all" (Bennett trans., p. 193).

39. Frontinus II, xii, 3: "Chares, the Athenian commander, on one occasion was expecting reinforcements, but feared that meanwhile the enemy, despising his small force, would attack his camp. He therefore ordered that a number of the soldiers under his command should pass out at night by the rear of the camp, and should return by a route where they would be clearly observed by the enemy, thus creating the impression that fresh forces were arriving. In this way, he defended himself by pretended reinforcements, until he was equipped with those he was expecting" (Bennett trans., p. 195).

40. Frontinus III, iii, 7: "When Lysimachus, king of the Macedonians, was besieging the Ephesians, these were assisted by the pirate chief Mandro, who was in the habit of bringing into Ephesus

Likewise, Fabius Maximus, when he wanted to lay siege to Capua, first laid waste to the planted fields all around it, so that it did not seem to be his intention to besiege the city. Then he went away and waited to return until the fields had again been planted and the inhabitants had used up all their seed, of which they had very little. Then Fabius returned and so conquered the strong city through famine.[41]

Likewise, Denis the Tyrant, after he had captured several fortresses in Sicily, came to Rhodes, which he knew to be well supplied with food and therefore very strong. Thus Denis pretended to make peace with the inhabitants, as if he intended to go elsewhere. Part of the agreement was that they would, for pay, supply him with food for a certain time. When he saw that their supplies were about to be exhausted—for they had paid no attention to this, thinking they were at peace—and their fields were almost ready for harvesting, Denis laid siege and conquered the inhabitants through hunger.[42]

When Alexander wanted to capture the city of Leucadia, which he knew to be well supplied with provisions, he first captured several outlying towns and castles and allowed the inhabitants to escape freely to Leucadia without harm, so that Leucadia's provisions would all be consumed. He took precautions that supplies should not reach them from elsewhere, and in this way he captured the city.[43]

Likewise, Iphicrates, who was holding Tarentum, found a sentry asleep, so he struck and killed him. When he was blamed for this, he

---

galleys laden with booty. Accordingly Lysimachus bribed Mandro to turn traitor, and attached to him a number of dauntless Macedonians to be taken into the city as captives, with hands pinioned behind their backs. These men subsequently snatched weapons from the citadel and delivered the town into the hands of Lysimachus" (Bennett trans., p. 217).

41. Frontinus III, iv, 1: "Fabius Maximus, having laid waste the lands of the Campanians, in order that they might have nothing left to warrant the confidence that a siege could be sustained, withdrew at the time of the sowing, that the inhabitants might plant what seed they had remaining. Then, returning, he destroyed the new crop and thus made himself master of the Campanians, whom he had reduced to famine" (Bennett trans., p. 219).

42. Frontinus III, iv, 3: "Dionysius, having captured many cities and wishing to attack the Rhegians, who were well provided with supplies, pretended to desire peace, and begged of them to furnish provisions for his army. When he had secured his request, and had consumed the grain of the inhabitants, he attacked their town, now stripped of food, and conquered it" (Bennett trans., p. 219). Christine was apparently not quoting directly from the Latin source here.

43. Frontinus III, iii, 5: "When Alexander was about to besiege Leucadia, a town well-supplied with provisions, he first captured the fortresses on the border and allowed all the people from these to flee for refuge to Leucadia, in order that the food-supplies might be consumed with greater rapidity when shared by many" (Bennett trans., p. 219). Leucadia (Leukas): a town and island in the Ionian Sea.

replied that he had left him as he had found him, which was to say that he considered a sleeping man dead.[44]

## X.
### CONCERNING HAMILCAR, LEADER OF CARTHAGE, HANNO, EMPEROR OF AFRICA, HANNIBAL, VALESIUS.

Hamulcar, or Hamilcar, Carthaginian general, knew well that the Romans were accustomed to receiving their enemies kindly when these turned toward them, and also were accustomed to receiving them kindly when these crossed over to their side, holding them in honor, especially soldiers from Gaul. Because of this, in order to catch them in their own toils, he commanded a great number of his men whom he knew to be the most loyal to him to present themselves to the Roman army, as if they had rebelled against him and gone over to the Romans. So it turned out that they, when they saw their opportunity, killed the Romans. Thus the general profited doubly from this deceit, which is to say that his enemies were killed because of it, and that they no longer dared to receive those who wanted to desert him.[45]

Likewise, Hanno, emperor of Carthage, had a large army in Sicily, opposing the Romans. He learned for a certainty that among his troops were four thousand Gauls who had decided to desert together to the Roman side because they had received no pay. As Hanno did not dare to punish them, he provided himself with a scheme for dealing with the problem. He called together the leaders of these people and spoke to them frankly, promising them that on a day he would set, he would give them satisfaction, but he, neither wanting nor being able to keep his word, knew that on the day before the promised date they would leave.

44. Frontinus III, xii, 2: "When Iphicrates, the Athenian general, was holding Corinth with a garrison and on one occasion personally made the rounds of the sentries as the enemy were approaching, he found one of the guards asleep at his post and stabbed him with his spear. When certain ones rebuked this procedure as cruel, he answered: 'I left him as I found him' " (Bennett trans., pp. 245–47).

45. Frontinus III, xvi, 2: "When the Gallic auxiliaries of Hamilcar, the Carthaginian general, were in the habit of crossing over to the Romans and were regularly received by them as allies, Hamilcar engaged his most loyal men to pretend desertion, while actually they slew the Romans who came out to welcome them. This device was not merely of present aid to Hamilcar, but caused real deserters to be regarded in future as objects of suspicion in the eyes of the Romans" (Bennett trans., p. 255).

So he sent to the leader of the Roman army one of his faithful knights, as if he were escaping from his army and in rebellion, who reported to the Roman that he should take note that the next night four thousand Gauls would strike his army. Because of this possible danger, the Roman leader put on watch for that night the major part of his army, which attacked the Gauls when they saw them coming. This was advantageous to Hanno, for the Romans lost many men, and he had avenged himself on the Gauls who had abandoned him, for they were all overcome and slaughtered.[46]

Likewise, Hannibal avenged himself on certain soldiers whom he knew had left his army by night to go over to the Romans. He had the word spread throughout his army that nobody should think badly of the valiant knights who had left his army. This had been done with his permission and orders so that they might know the plan of the enemy and carry out certain things he had ordered them to do. Hannibal did this because he well knew that he had Roman spies in his army, who would straightaway report all this. As they did so, the Romans immediately arrested the deserters, cut off their hands, and sent them back.[47]

Likewise, Valesius (Livius) commander of the Romans, who were in possession of the citadel of the Tarentines, sent a message to Hasdrubal, who was besieging it, that he would give up the citadel if allowed to withdraw safely. While this negotiation was taking place, during which time Hasdrubal felt quite confident and paid little attention, Valesius, seeing his advantage, went out with his army so cleverly that he overcame his enemies and killed Hasdrubal.[48]

46. Frontinus III, xvi, 3: "Hanno, commander of the Carthaginians in Sicily, learned on one occasion that about four thousand Gallic mercenaries had conspired to desert to the Romans, because for several months they had received no pay. Not daring to punish them, for fear of mutiny, he promised to make good the deferred payment by increasing their wages. When the Gauls rendered thanks for this, Hanno, promising that they should be permitted to go out foraging at a suitable time, sent to the consul Otacilius an extremely trustworthy steward, who pretended to have deserted on account of embezzlement, and who reported that on the coming night four thousand Gauls, sent out on a foraging expedition, could be captured. Otacilius, not immediately crediting the deserter, nor yet thinking the matter ought to be treated with disdain, placed the pick of his men in ambush. These met the Gauls, who fulfilled Hanno's purpose in a twofold manner, since they not only slew a number of the Romans, but were themselves slaughtered to the last man" (Bennett trans., pp. 155–57).

47. Frontinus III, xvi, 4: "By a similar plan Hannibal took vengeance on certain deserters; for, being aware that some of his soldiers had deserted on the previous night, and knowing that spies of the enemy were in his camp, he publicly proclaimed that the name of "deserter" ought not to be applied to his cleverest soldiers, who at his order had gone out to learn the designs of the enemy. The spies, as soon as they heard this pronouncement, reported it to their own side. Thereupon the deserters were arrested by the Romans and sent back with their hands cut off" (Bennett trans., p. 257).

48. Frontinus III, xvii, 3: "Livius, commander of the Romans, when holding the citadel of the Tarentines, sent envoys to Hasdrubal, requesting the privilege of withdrawing undisturbed. When by

What more can I tell you of the stratagems of Frontinus? There are many excellent ones in his book that would take a long time to describe, but let this suffice except for a few notable ones included in his fourth book.

XI.

FRONTINUS, IN HIS FOURTH BOOK, SPEAKS OF CAESAR, DOMINICUS, AEMILIUS, SCIPIO THE AFRICAN, GAYUS, SCIPIO.

Caesar used to say that one should use against one's enemy the advice doctors give for illness, which is to say, to use diet and hunger before steel.[49]

Likewise, Dominicus (Domitius) Corbulo said that one should wound the enemy in many ways with subtle devices rather than expose one's own body.[50]

Likewise, (Lucius) Aemilius Paulus (Macedonicus) said that it was important for all good military leaders to be old men in character.[51]

Likewise, Scipio the African replied to someone who reproached him for not being aggressive with his hands in battle: "My mother," he said, "bore me an emperor and not a warrior."[52] This meant that it ought to be sufficient for a prince or general to command his followers without exposing his body to danger.

Likewise, Gayus Maximus (Gaius Marius) replied to a German who called on him to do bodily combat, that if the German did not want to live, he, Gayus, would prefer to choose the way he should be killed.[53]

---

this feint he had thrown the enemy off their guard, he made a sortie and cut them to pieces" (Bennett trans., p. 259).

49. Frontinus IV, vii, 1: "Gaius Caesar used to say that he followed the same policy towards the enemy as did many doctors when dealing with physical ailments, namely, that of conquering the foe by hunger rather than by steel" (Bennett trans., p. 309).

50. Frontinus IV, vii, 2: "Domitius Corbulo used to say that the pick was the weapon with which to beat the enemy" (Bennett trans., p. 309).

51. Frontinus IV, vii, 3: "Lucius Paulus used to say that a general ought to be an old man in character, meaning thereby that moderate counsels should be followed" (Bennett trans., p. 309).

52. Frontinus IV, vii, 4: "When people said of Scipio Africanus that he lacked aggressiveness, he is reported to have answered: 'My mother bore me a general, not a warrior' " (Bennett trans., p. 309).

53. Frontinus IV, vii, 5: "When a Teuton challenged Gaius Marius and called upon him to come forth, Marius answered that, if the man was desirous of death, he could end his life with a halter. Then, when the fellow persisted, Marius confronted him with a gladiator of despicable size, whose life was almost spent, and told the Teuton that, if he would first defeat this gladiator, he himself would then fight with him" (Bennett trans., p. 309).

Likewise, Scipio said that one should not only offer one's enemy a way to escape, but also help him to find it.[54]

With respect to these matters, it seems to me useful to recall what the wise king of France, Charles V, said when told it was a great shame to recover with money his strongholds taken by the English, when he had sufficient strength to retake them by force. He replied: "It seems to me that what one can take with money should not be bought or retaken by human blood."[55]

XII.

THE BOOK OF VALERIUS SPEAKS OF HANNIBAL, OF A KING OF
GREECE, OF ANOTHER IN A SIMILAR SITUATION,
OF ROMANS WHO HAD TO DEAL WITH MERCENARIES.[56]

Valerius speaks of this matter in his sixth book, saying that Hannibal, who has been mentioned before, greatly disliked the very valiant general Fabius Maximus because the general had made problems for him in battle, and had done him much harm. Hannibal did not know how to get even with him. For this reason he tried to help himself through deceit, so he laid waste to all the fields around Rome and the dwellings of princes other than the brave knight Fabius, whom he did not touch or harm, in order to make the Romans suspect that there was between them some sort of link or agreement. As he saw that this trick accomplished little, he wanted to do more, so he wrote letters that he secretly sent to Rome, addressing the same Fabius, writing and discussing as if there were some sort of agreement between them and as if he were expected to commit treason against the Romans. Hannibal arranged the matter so that it

54. Frontinus IV, vii, 16: "Scipio Africanus used to say that a road not only ought to be afforded the enemy for flight, but that it ought even to be paved" (Bennett trans., p. 315).

55. Christine had already made this point in her biography of Charles V (Solente ed., I, p. 228).

56. The French translation of Valerius Maximus, *Facta et dicta memorabilis* (Deeds and memorable words) had been undertaken around 1375 by Simon de Hesdin at the request of Charles V and was completed in 1401 by Nicholas de Gonesse under the patronage of the duke of Berry. It was a principal source for Christine's *Livre du corps de policie*. Here she limits her use to book VII, devoted to military stratagems, several of which she had already included in her earlier work. In the *Corps de policie* she had included a chapter entitled "The Reason Why Valerius Is So Much Quoted in This Book," where she expresses her belief that deeds such as those recounted by Valerius inspire men more than mere words.

would come to the attention of the Roman senators, but they were convinced of the loyalty of Fabius to the point that nothing came of all this.[57]

Likewise, a king of Greece was very envious of the Romans;[58] for that reason and none other he hated them, and if it had not been for his fear of their great power, he would willingly have done them harm. The only way he could think of to accomplish that end was by trickery and pretense. So he pretended that he liked them very much, and several times wrote them letters expressing great friendship. Finally he made known to them that he would like very much to see Rome and its noble organization. When he came to Rome as a seeming friend, he was very warmly received, but the more he saw of the city's pleasures and magnificence, the greater grew his displeasure and the pricks of envy that he kept concealed within himself. The result was that before he left the city, he managed to stir up by his malice a great deal of division and discord among its leaders. He believed that in this way he could do much harm to the city.

Likewise, in the similar case of another who hated Rome, when he had fomented sedition and contention among the Roman leaders to the point where they were engaging in battle with each other, he sent his own men to help the group that was stronger, not at all to give aid to anyone, but to contribute to their greater destruction.

Likewise, the Romans in need of help took on foreign soldiers, but when it came time to assemble for battle, it seemed to these mercenaries that Rome would have the worst of it, so they deserted the army. But on the slope of a mountain where they went to join the stronger army, they encountered difficulties. This had been cleverly prepared by the Roman general, who, having seen that his men were panicking, had gone through all the ranks explaining that this departure had taken place with his consent in order to attack the enemy from the rear when it should be assembled. In this way he reassured his troops and was victorious.

Likewise, on another occasion foreign mercenaries abandoned the

---

57. Valerius Maximus VII, iii, 8: "With the same skill Hannibal, seeing Fabius Maximus enjoy the unconquered strength of his arms by healthful delays, desired to tarnish his reputation with the suspicion of seeking to prolong the war. While Hannibal was laying waste to all of Italy with iron and fire, he left intact only the property of Fabius. This false appearance of marked favor might have had some success if the Romans hadn't been quite aware of Fabius's love of his country and Hannibal's deceitful character."

58. This account of the king of Greece, already cited in the *Corps de policie*, does not appear in the original text of Valerius Maximus. It is an addition of the translator, as are the other examples in this chapter. This translation includes commentaries of other classical authors.

Roman army to join the other side. A wise general dealt with this skill-fully, for he followed them with his entire army in good formation, so that the enemy, when they saw the first group coming, thought it was to initiate the attack. They slaughtered them, so that they were the first ca-sualties. As so many of them were killed, they were of help to the Romans in spite of themselves.

XIII.

DEVICES OF THE BESIEGED ROMANS, OF THE ROMAN ARMY, OF
QUINTUS METELLUS, OF THE KING OF SICILY, AND OF HANNIBAL.

At the time that Rome was captured, the Gauls had besieged the Capi-tolium, a fortress truly unconquerable except by starvation. For this rea-son the Gauls intended to starve them, but the Romans, always clever in matters of war, in order to remove that hope from their enemy, took the small amount of food that they had and made a great many scraps of bones, crumbs, and other things and threw them out to the gleaners. When the Gauls saw this, they were astonished and, thinking the Ro-mans well provided for, began to sue for peace.[59]

Likewise, when Hannibal and Hasdrubal, Carthaginian leaders, were in Italy with a large army, the Romans sent against them two leaders, in charge of two large armies, who arranged matters so cleverly that they prevented the two Carthaginian armies from being able to make contact. If that had been possible, it would have ruined most of the Romans. But they arranged for their own two to join together one night, without mak-ing any noise, before the day that they were to give battle to one of those Carthaginian armies; thus it was defeated.[60]

59. Valerius Maximus VII, iv, 4: "Here again is an occasion where our ancestors were able to find a clever expedient with a happy ending. The Gauls, after capturing Rome, laid siege to the capi-tol but realized that they could not hope to take possession except by overcoming the besieged through starvation, but the Romans, by a clever strategy, took away from the conquerors the only hope that could move them to pursue their objective. They began in fact to throw down bread from different points on the ramparts. Seeing this astonished the Gauls greatly, and believing that our peo-ple had a great amount of wheat, they decided to negotiate the raising of the siege."

60. Valerius Maximus VII, iv, 4: "While Hannibal was laying waste to one end of Italy, Has-drubal invaded the other. It was hoped that the two brothers, joining forces, could not overwhelm our exhausted forces: this is what Claudius Nero dealt with by an energetic resolve and Livius Sali-nator by great skill. Nero contained Hannibal in Lucania. He had the skill that the plan for his un-dertaking required, that he was always present and, traversing a great distance with astonishing speed, he went to the aid of his colleague Salinator, who was to engage in battle the next day near the Metaure, a river in Umbria. Salinator received Nero at night in great secret. Without any tumult he introduced a second army into a space scarcely large enough for one. So Hasdrubal discovered that

Likewise, Quintus Metellus, being with an army in Spain, could not reach by force the city he wanted, so he left the siege and began to march his army here and there to places that were quite widely separated, so that even his own troops were astonished. His enemies laughed at him and thought him a fool. So he went along until he finally saw the opportunity he wanted, when all his enemies were tired of being on their guard. Then he took them unawares.[61]

Likewise, the king of Sicily was attacked by the Carthaginians, but when he saw that the whole country had been occupied, and that there was no help for it, he departed for Africa with as many men as he could assemble. There he began to set fire to everything. In that way the Carthaginians were quite happy to make peace with him and give back to him what they had taken.[62]

Likewise, when Hannibal had to fight against the Romans in the Battle of Cannae,[63] which was so devastating to them, he made use of three schemes: first, he positioned himself in a place where he was certain that he would have the sun and the wind at his back, for they were both in evidence that day, as well as dust; second, he ordered that when the battle had begun, a part of his troops should act as if they were fleeing along a byway where a trap had been placed to catch the Romans who would follow the escapees; third, he ordered that four hundred men-at-arms should likewise seem to be fleeing toward the Romans as if frightened by

---

he was dealing with two leaders through being overcome by their joint efforts. Thus the clever Carthaginian, so unhappily celebrated in the whole universe, was that time the dupe of Roman skill, which allowed Hannibal to fall into Nero's trap and Hasdrubal into Salinator's."

61. Valerius Maximus VII, iv, 5: "Quintus Metellus also merits being cited for his resourcefulness. As proconsul he was in Spain making war against the Celtiberians. Seeing that he could not take by force the city of Centubie, capital of that nation, he sought a means in long and serious reflections and found a way of achieving his ends. He moved about in forced marches, going in different directions, sometimes withdrawing from heights to go immediately to others, leaving his own men as well as the enemy ignorant of his unexpected and subtle objective. After he had made it impossible for his troops to know anything and had misled the Celtiberians, one day, when he was off in another direction, he turned around, surprised and overwhelmed them."

62. Valerius Maximus VII, iv, 1: "Agathocle, king of Syracuse, joined audacity to deceit. Seeing the Carthaginians already in possession of a large part of his city, he moved his army to Africa, in order to repulse terror by terror, force by force, and this diversion had its result. His sudden arrival upset the Carthaginians so greatly that they hastened to secure their own safety at the price of the enemy's safety and to make a retreat for the purpose of rescuing Africa from the Sicilian army and at the same time Sicily from the Carthaginian army. If Agathocle had persisted in defending the walls of Syracuse, Sicily would have been overwhelmed by all the calamities of war, while Carthage would have been left to enjoy in tranquillity the advantages of peace. But in taking to the others the ills he was suffering, in attacking the territories of the enemy instead of protecting his own, he found his kingdom more secure than when he had left it with such decision."

63. Christine had already made use of this episode in the *Corps de policie* (II, 19).

the battle, and should give up. When these commands had been put into operation and the battle begun, the Romans were troubled by the sun and the dust that distorted their vision; also by the trap that caught them and where many were killed; and by those who had surrendered to them and who, according to the custom of the day, were disarmed and placed behind the combatants. But those who had surrendered had secreted beneath their underclothes sharp instruments, with which they crippled the Romans who were fighting. Valerius comments that the Roman army was overcome more by malice than by battle.

Likewise, on another occasion, in order to destroy a battalion, pieces of wood wrapped in cork and dipped in oil were placed under the tails of oxen. This wood was then set on fire, and the oxen were chased toward the enemy, who were effectively scattered and destroyed.[64]

XIV.

HERE BEGINS A DISCUSSION OF THE WAY TO FIGHT IN CASTLES
AND TOWNS AND, FIRST, HOW TO CONSTRUCT THEM.

Having examined the best ways to carry out battles in the field and also chivalric deeds, according to military manuals and more recent information, we will now discuss what Vegetius and other authors have to say concerning suitable techniques for besieging cities, castles, and fortresses, and also for defending them. We shall also speak of battles at sea or on rivers. The aforementioned author speaks first of ways to improve security, as the ancients built enclosures of walls and dykes for their fortresses.[65] He offered this advice: whoever wishes to build an enduring fortification should pay particular attention to five aspects of the site. First, the situation should preferably be elevated, which is to say, well placed on some height in a good country, but if a certain terrain does not permit this, one would be well advised to try to build it with one of its sides by the sea, or on the bank of a navigable river. If it is possible to have the sea on one side and fresh water on the other, this is advantageous, especially if the river is navigable.

64. This example, cited by Frontinus (II, iv, 17), had already been used by Christine in Chapter IV of this part. See note 10 above.

65. Vegetius IV, i: "Cities and forts are either fortified by nature or by human hand, or by both, which is considered stronger. By 'nature' is meant places which are elevated, precipitous, surrounded by sea, morasses or rivers; by 'hand,' fosses and a wall. In places enjoying the safest natural advantages, judgement is required of the selector; in a flat place, effort of the founder. We see cities of great antiquity so built in the midst of spreading plains that in the absence of help from the terrain they were rendered invincible by art and labour" (Milner trans., p. 121).

In the second place, it should be in good, healthful air, far removed from swamps and marshes.

The third consideration is that it should be situated in a fertile and productive spot with all things necessary for human life.

The fourth, that a hill should not be so close that the fortification could be harmed by any dart from above, and the fifth, that the land should be free and unencumbered.

The author says that the ancients who were well advised did not make the walls of their cities in a straight line, as is done now, for they considered that in such a way they would be more vulnerable to blows from war machines, and also to being scaled.[66] So they made them curving, with steps well elevated and stone well joined with good sand and strong lime, and they included angles so that they could be defended in more places, with numerous strong and defendable towers all around them.

Along with this, the author teaches how walls can be doubly fortified against all machines, which is to say that two strongly masoned partitions should be built, one inside the other, at a distance of some nine feet, and that the earth dug from the foundations, which would be the same depth as the moats on the outside, should be put between these two walls and beaten and pressed down as much as possible with good mallets.[67] The first of these walls would be elevated and so thick that passageways could be made on them with openings and slits for firing cannons and hurling stones and other sorts of missiles, and on each side there should be suitable well-built emplacements for projectile throwers, if these should be needed to defend the place, and curtains and wooden barbicans could be attached outside the crenellations to protect against arrows. The ancients had tall and wide screens made in time of war, which were held together by good chains that dangled outside the walls. These broke the shots from machines so that they could not damage the walls. Or they made thick, rough barriers of briars and branches, which they coated with earth

66. Vegetius IV, ii: "The ancients refused to build the circuit of their walls in straight lines, fearing that it might be exposed to the blows of rams. Instead they enclosed cities within foundations laid out in sinuous windings, and put more frequent towers precisely at the angles so that if anyone tried to move up ladders or machines to a wall constructed on this system, he would be shut in before, on the flanks and virtually behind as though in an embrace and destroyed" (Milner trans., p. 121).

67. Vegetius IV, iii: "The wall is completed so that it can never be knocked down, on the following plan. Two internal walls are built at intervals of twenty feet each. Then earth which has been dug out of the fosses is dumped between them and rammed solid with piles, the first internal wall from the outer wall being built proportionately lower, the second far smaller, so that one can ascend from the ground-level of the city as if by stairs on a gentle slope up to the battlements. For no rams can breach a wall that is strengthened by earth, and if for some reason the masonry should be demolished the mass that has been compacted between the internal walls resists intruders in the wall's stead" (Milner trans., p. 122).

and dung, and these could protect the walls from being damaged by large stones from catapults. The gates, made of large planks, were covered with sheets of iron or raw leather on the outside so that they could not be set afire. Above these was a barbican, as there is today, where an opening was made in the wall and where a portcullis hung on iron chains and rings, so that if the enemy attacked, they might be surprised and entrapped by that portcullis dropped down on them. There were also other openings through which could be thrown large stones, boiling water, and other means of defense similar to the ones used today.[68]

Likewise, ditches should be dug very wide and deep, in case no river flows underground, or the fortress should be built on a strong rock so that the place cannot be mined from below. The ancients protected their fortresses well against this problem, for they sealed masonry thoroughly with good concrete and cement, especially the foundations, so that they could not be pierced. Also, moats should be made so wide and deep that they cannot easily be filled in by enemy forces. Sometimes formerly they were protected by a wall on the other side so that nobody could descend into them. There was also an abundance of iron hooks and sharpened metal bars called grappling irons placed down the sides, which were a great hindrance to anyone trying to climb down the side. Such matters are well enough known, I think. Likewise, there were many other enclosures and means of defense, which it does not seem necessary to describe further, as present-day experts in such matters are well aware of them.

XV.

HERE WE SPEAK OF THE PROVISIONS NEEDED FOR
A CASTLE OR TOWN IN TIME OF WAR.[69]

The wall of a castle, however well it is provided with all means of defense, is of little value if supplies are lacking when the castle is besieged.

---

68. Vegetius IV, iv: "Take care also that gates may not be burned by fires placed against them. To counter this they should be covered with hides and iron. But it is more useful, as antiquity discovered, to add a barbican before the gate, and place in its entrance a portcullis, which hangs on iron chains and ropes. Thus if the enemy enter, it is let down, and they are shut in and exterminated. The wall above the gate should be so designed as to admit openings through which water may be poured from the upper storey to quench a fire below" (Milner trans., p. 122).

69. It is evident that Christine's details of necessities to withstand siege mark a significant departure from her usual sources. She evidently had here the advice of the contemporary experts she later mentions.

This was evident in the stronghold of Perimeum, which had seven pairs of walls, based on rocks, surrounded by stout towers, well supplied with good men-at-arms, and which after a long siege was taken through hunger. For this reason enemy forces try to prevent supplies from reaching a castle. The defenders should therefore ensure in the construction of the place, if no river flows abundantly enough, that water cannot be taken from them. Good conduits should be dug so deep that they cannot run dry and carry enough water; for otherwise the structure will not be worth anything. Where water enters by conduits, the entrance can be easily destroyed, and the place could soon be conquered, as it is impossible to get along without water.

Likewise, along with this, those within, as soon as they feel the threat of war, and those who live on a frontier constantly, should provide themselves with wheat, flour, sea biscuits, wine, vinegar, sour grapes, salt, oil, salted butter, peas, dried beans, barley, oats, poultry (which keeps when salted), wood, coal, beef, mutton, salted fish with onions, pepper, handmills and windmills, spices, rose water, almonds, rice, and food suitable for those who are ill. Earthenware pots for the kitchen and for keeping wine, earthenware cups, tallow, candles, lanterns, wicks to put into them, linen, beds and covers, stretchers, water buckets, cauldrons, vats for water, casks, a great many planks, enclosures, thick and thin ropes, and all such things. It is true that where salt is lacking and wine abundant, all meat cooked in wine, even without salt, is preserved without spoiling. If there are small gardens within the walls, they should be diligently and carefully enclosed. In this regard particular care should be taken, for as has already been said, it is important that provisions are distributed with due care and proportions, for there is no way of knowing how long a siege will last, or what increase of population there may be, or what will need to be done. For this reason particular care must be taken to keep up the stocks, for this can be the greatest protection. Those in the fortress should want the enemies to be aware of their situation, and in particular to think them well supplied, even if this is not the case; for thus they would be more inclined to depart. Nor should it be forgotten that nothing the enemy might make use of should be left outside, but everything taken into the fortress before their arrival. It would be better, Vegetius says, to set fire to anything that cannot be disposed of than to leave it, for everything that helps the enemy is harmful to you. If it should come about, he says, that provisions are scarce and that they might give out before the end of the siege, old and feeble men, women and children, who are of no use for the defense, should be sent to other towns or cities so as to make the provisions last longer.[70]

Likewise, provisions for the defense: cannons, much gunpowder, and a quantity of stones, rams, crossbows, turning arrows, machines for firing them, leather belts, ropes called *damiers*, bows, arrows, arrow cords, raw and tanned leathers, and a well-equipped forge, iron, steel, coal, and sulfur.

Likewise, for countermining, picks, crowbars, hammers, axes, shovels, logs, iron hooks, ladders. It is a good thing to prepare a defense against machines, to be able to burn them; also concrete, cement, pitch and oil, and a quantity of tow.

Likewise, iron and steel to repair the equipment of the men-at-arms, wood to make longbows, large projectiles for them, and turning arrows, if shooting strength should be needed. In any case, the store of crossbows, handbows, and adequate arrows should not be small. A great number of stones should have been gathered from streams, for these are harder and heavier than other stones and more suitable for throwing by hand. There should not be small supplies of these on the walls, but great containers well fitted to throw down all at once, if need be, by specially made weights and instruments for firing stones from the towers.[71]

Likewise, in short, all sorts of machines for throwing, such as bom-

70. Vegetius IV, vii: "Fodder for horses above all should be stockpiled, and what cannot be carried in should be burned; stocks of wine, wine-vinegar, and other crops and fruits should be collected, and nothing which may be of use left for the enemy. Considerations of both utility and morale urge that gardening (for food) be conducted in the pleasure-grounds of townhouses and (public) open spaces. But there is little point in having collected large stocks without sensible issue from the outset by competent officials: men who began to keep a frugal diet while there was still plenty have never been in danger of starving. Also those unfit for fighting by reason of age or sex were often shut out of the gates because of the need to conserve food, lest hunger oppressed the soldiers guarding the walls" (Milner trans., p. 124). Christine is obviously more humanitarian than Vegetius with regard to the treatment of noncombatants.

71. Vegetius IV, viii: "It is advised to procure bitumen, sulphur, liquid pitch and the oil which they call 'burning-oil,' for burning the machines of the enemy. For making arms, iron of both tempers and coal are kept in magazines. Wood, needed for spear-shafts and arrows, is also laid in. Round stones are very carefully collected from rivers, because they are heavier in proportion to their density and more suitable for throwing. The walls and towers are filled with them, the smallest for casting by slings and 'sling-staves,' and by hand, the larger are shot by mangonels, and the biggest in weight and of a rollable shape are laid out on the battlements, so that, sent headlong below, they not only overwhelm hostile forces but smash their machines too. Huge wheels are also made out of green wood, and cylindrical sections, which they call *taleae*, are cut from very stout trees and smoothed to make them roll. These falling down with sudden impetus usually deter soldiers and horses. It is also necessary to have in readiness beams and planks, and iron nails of different sizes. Besiegers' machines are usually resisted by means of other machines, in particular when height needs to be added to walls and battlements by emergency works, so that the mobile towers of the enemy may not overtop and take the city" (Milner trans., pp. 124–25).

bards, and large stones should be prepared. With these a very good supply of gunpowder to make them function is necessary, and containers
and suitable vessels full of quicklime should also be provided so that
these can be thrown down if the enemy comes close to the walls. When
these break, the quicklime will enter the eyes and the mouth and thus do
some of the attackers in.

Likewise, such a stronghold needs a quantity of panels of screening,
fine and closely formed, in order to make supporting screens, if needed,
against machines that might be placed against the walls.

Likewise, lime, sand, stones, plaster, to make enclosures and second
walls, if necessary, and workmen to do this.

Likewise, there should be large supplies of strings for hand- and crossbows, and sinews to make them, and if it should happen that sinews are
lacking when needed for making ropes, horsehair is good and even the
hair of women will do. For, as Vegetius says, the Romans made good use
of this in their great need, when Hannibal pressed them so hard that in
defending themselves ropes and sinews gave out. Then, the brave women
of the city, may they ever be praised for it, who had long and beautiful
hair, preferred to be disfigured and shorn of their blond locks, even
though it was considered their greatest ornament, to save the city. Rather
than allow themselves to be captured with their blond hair and placed in
servitude to the enemy, they offered their hair to the marksmen, and so
Rome was saved.[72]

Likewise, there should be a supply of animal horns to repair the crossbows, and of rawhide to cover the machines and other devices so that
they cannot be set on fire. Above all, what contributes the most to success
is good men-at-arms and marksmen skilled in everything pertaining to assault and defense, in such numbers as are needed in relation to the situation and engagement. For, as the proverb says: The wall does not make
the castle strong without the defense of good men that make it impreg-

---

72. Vegetius IV, ix: "It is advisable to collect supplies of sinews with the utmost vigour, because
mangonels, catapults and other torsion-engines are of no use unless strung with ropes made of sinew,
although horsehair taken from the tail and mane is said to be useful for catapults. Indubitably, however, women's hair has no less virtue in such kinds of torsion-engines, as was demonstrated in Rome's
hour of need. For at the siege of the Capitol, the torsion-engines broke down from continuous and
long fatigue after supplies of sinews had run out. But the matrons cut off their hair and presented it
to their husbands as they fought, the machines were repaired and they repelled the hostile attack.
For women of the highest character preferred to disfigure their heads for the moment in order to live
in freedom with their husbands, than become slaves to the enemy with their beauty intact. It is also
advantageous to collect horns and raw hides for weaving cataphracts and other machines and armour" (Milner trans., pp. 125–26).

nable. Furthermore, it should not be forgotten that on the side that is the weakest should be placed the greatest defense, for that is the place where the attack is usually the strongest.

XVI.

PARTICULAR NEEDS FOR STOCKING A FORTRESS WITH
FOOD SUPPLIES AS WELL AS WEAPONS.[73]

As we have sufficiently discussed in general what is needed for living as well as for defense against enemies, it is useful to complete our work by mentioning in detail the proper estimate, more or less, of what would be sufficient to provide for a certain number of men-at-arms, which could be augmented or diminished according to the number involved. Let us consider then two hundred men-at-arms with their servants, which is to say, two for each man, to be fed for six months. One would need 110 measures of wheat according to the Parisian measure (1872 liters), a third of which would be in prepared bread and ten in flour. Likewise, four measures of dried beans, two measures of peas, one hundred twenty jugs of wine (c. 500 liters each), two measures of vinegar, one measure of sour grape juice, one measure of oil, one measure of salt, fifty pounds of spices (ginger, cumin, and other small spices), two pounds of saffron, two measures of mustard seed, and a mill to grind them to make mustard.

Likewise, salted and fresh meat: one hundred large oxen, both salted and alive, insofar as possible and when there is sufficient space and fodder; one hundred or one hundred twenty flitches of bacon, eight score of sheep, wherever there is a place to keep them; a supply of poultry, as many as can be kept and are wanted.

Likewise, salted fish if it is in Lent and for the days one does not eat meat, a thousand eels, twenty-five barrels of herring, cod, many hake, a cask of salted butter, eleven pounds of almonds, ten or twelve of rice, the same quantity of oatmeal, rose water and other things thought good for the ill, both to eat and as ointments, and other medicines. Ten dozen earthen pots, twelve dozen goblets for drinking, ten leather buckets to hold water, two hundred toises (six-foot lengths) of rope.

73. Here Christine takes complete leave of her usual sources to give a contemporary assessment of supplies needed for a specific number of defenders in a siege. Such specific detail is rather unusual in military writings of the Middle Ages. It must be supposed that she was here taking advantage of the military advisors she mentions elsewhere.

Likewise, for the kitchen, if it is in winter, two hundred cartloads of large logs, sixty loads of coal, or thousands of small bundles of wood that are called *esterels*; twenty dozen large earthen pots for making soup and cooking meat, six large cauldrons, two dozen pans—large, medium, and small—four dozen wooden spoons, two thousand wooden bowls, as many trenchers, goblets, and cups, empty caskets, twenty or thirty bellows, and other small necessities that one may think of and that have already been mentioned.

Now it is time to speak of provisions for the defense of the place. First of all, at least twelve cannons throwing stones, two of which will be larger than the others to break up machines, mantelets, and other coverings, if necessary; two bricoles and two other rock-throwing machines, each one provided with slings and ropes and a great stock of stones, and two or three large crossbows on wheels, provided with the necessary arrows.

Likewise, if it is thought that it will not be necessary to fire the cannons too frequently, a thousand pounds of powder should suffice, or fifteen hundred, a third in powder and two-thirds in ingredients, three thousand pounds of lead to make shot for the cannons, six dozen iron-tipped lances, twenty-four good crossbows well equipped, six others on wooden bases, six dozen strings for arrows, with a hundred sheaves of arrows, twelve score crossbows with hooks, twelve machines for bending crossbows plus two other machines for bending them, eighteen leather belts with four dozen strings for them, sixty or eighty large shields, twenty-four thousand spinning arrows, twelve thousand of them for longer distances, two hundred round stones for the cannons and a great many others, enough wood to make four hundred tampons (plugs) and a carpenter to make them and give help where it might be needed; three masons to make stone cannon balls and other things as needed.

Likewise, two horse-operated mills, two ovens, a well-provided forge, four thousand pounds of iron, a half thousand of steel, four hogsheads of coal, twenty-four horseloads of charcoal, four kettles with feet, eight bellows for countermining, two dozen equipped baskets, six dozen wooden shovels, eight dozen stretchers, vats and adequate tubs, as is said.


XVII.

HOW A FORTRESS SHOULD BE PROVIDED WITH WATER.


Vegetius says that although it is a great advantage for a city when live sources of water, such as fountains or wells, are available, nevertheless, if the nature of the place is such that none exist, the best remedy possible must be provided. If the fountains and wells are outside the walls, but nearby, the people within must skillfully protect their water in case an enemy should try to destroy it or keep them from making use of it. If a spring is so far away that the water comes to them through a conduit, a small fortified cover must be built over it, which can be protected by soldiers and marksmen. Along with this, in all such cities and fortresses cisterns should be provided, which should be situated in places where the rainwater that falls and comes from the eaves of houses and from gutters can flow into them, and these should be kept as full and well provided as possible. The same with other water from rivers, for it keeps very well in the sand and is safe to use.[74] Furthermore, Aristotle says that salt water from the sea, or from briny sources, becomes sweet if it is passed through wax conduits. Along with this, it is useful to have a good supply of vinegar, especially in summertime, for it greatly refreshes the body when drunk with water; this is well known in Italy. If the fortress is located on the seashore and it happens that salt is in short supply, sea water may be taken and put in vessels that are broad and shallow, and set in the heat of the sun, or boiled over fire until the water evaporates. In this way salt will be found on the bottom of the pan.[75]

XVIII.

HOW LOYAL PEOPLE ARE NECESSARY FOR THE GARRISON
OF A CITY, WITH SOME EXAMPLES.

In setting forth all things, or even the greatest number, that are necessary for the defense of a city or fortress, it should be known that the most es-

74. Vegetius IV, x: "It is a great advantage for a city when its wall includes perennial springs within it. But if nature does not provide, wells have to be dug to whatever depth and draughts of water extracted by rope. Sometimes places are too dry if built upon mountains and rocks. Fortifications erected on such places may discover sources of water outside the wall, lower down, and protect them with missiles shot from battlements and towers so as to allow free access to waterbearers. But if a source is beyond the range of missiles but on the hill below the city, it is advised to build a small fortification which they call a *burgus* between the city and the spring, and station there catapults and archers to defend the water from the enemy. Also, under all public and many private buildings cisterns should be constructed very assiduously to provide reservoirs for rainwater that flows off roofs. It has proved difficult to overcome with thirst those besieged who used water only for drinking, however little there was" (Milner trans., p. 126).

75. Vegetius IV, xi: "If a city is on the coast and salt runs out, water is taken from the sea and poured into troughs and other flat vessels; in the heat of the sun it hardens to salt. But if the enemy denies access to the sea, as does happen, people sometimes collect up sand which the sea stirred up by the wind has flowed over. They then wash it in fresh water, and this evaporated in the sun equally well turns to salt" (Milner trans., p. 127).

sential element is the presence of good, loyal men who are well united, and worthy leaders, without greed, who are attached to the place; for where other needs are provided for and this alone is lacking, nothing is of avail. To witness that this is true and the opposite a great misfortune, we will speak of several examples, as they usually penetrate the ears better than arguments or reason. First of all, repeating what authorities say, the greatest good a community can enjoy is peace and undivided affection. They also say that it is a great wonder that such qualities as these can be destroyed by any force. This is demonstrated by the reply of the wise magician Troisiaux to Scipio the African when asked how it was that the city of Numantia[76] could hold out so long against the great power of the Romans. He replied that it was because of the great solidarity that existed among the inhabitants there.

Along with this, it is great good fortune in a country, city, or castle to have princes or sovereigns who have a great love for the place. This was well demonstrated by Camillus among the Roman leaders when Duke Brennus of Siena had destroyed Rome in a war, and had gone off with much booty and riches. But when the noble Camillus learned of this situation, he was distressed, even though the Romans had wrongfully exiled him and made him live outside the city, and immediately assembled as many people as he could. He enjoyed great authority, and he attacked Brennus, who did not expect it, defeated him, and took back the spoils, which he restored to Rome, and he also brought back the refugees. Because of this he was called the second Romulus.[77]

Just as great good, joy, and happiness are to be found in a country or city where there are union and peace within it, all is utter desolation and peril when there are discord and dissension, which are its very destruction, as the Holy Scripture says. Such contentiousness usually arises in a community or city through some very unfortunate movement that can arise, which is to say, from the pride and arrogance of some against others because of envy and greed. This happened in Rome because of the pride of their leaders, which is to say, Sulla and Marius, whose competition was

76. Numantia was a strategic site on the Duero River in Spain. It played a significant role in resistance to Roman conquest, but after an eight-month siege it finally capitulated, in 133 B.C., to the overwhelming forces of Scipio, marking the end to the organized resistance to Roman Spain. Christine describes this situation in the *Mutacion de fortune* (Solente ed., III, pp. 255–59), where her source is the *Histoire ancienne*.

77. According to a somewhat legendary account Brennus, a Gallic king, overcame the Romans and entered Rome. The consul Camillus, then in exile, raised an army that overcame the invaders and restored the gold that had been removed from Rome. This was recounted in the *Mutacion de fortune* (Solente ed., III, pp. 195–16), based on the *Histoire ancienne*.

supported by Pompey, Certorius, and many others of great valor and authority and brought about a civil war that was so harmful to the Romans that they were nearly destroyed.[78] In this, in several battles before it was over, twenty-three of their generals, six of their rulers, forty great noblemen, and one hundred thousand Romans were killed, not to mention foreigners who came to their aid. Thus such accursed contention and disagreement should be avoided.


## XIX.
### ON THE SAME SUBJECT.

Continuing on the matter of placing loyal people in castles and cities: this should be given careful attention, and they should not be unduly greedy, for in that way many cities and towns have been betrayed, sold, and robbed. This is illustrated by the example of Sinope,[79] which was large, strong, rich, and well inhabited, and which King Mithradates put under the protection of two knights whom he considered faithful to him. They, however, protected it badly, for they and their men pillaged and robbed it, and when they had set fires all over the place, they went off, whereupon a remarkable incident took place. Just then, as the leader of the Roman army arrived there to lay siege, he was astonished that such a thing could have happened, and when the situation had been explained to him, he had the citizens called to the gates and reassured them, and when the gates were opened, he ordered his men to put out the fires. So it was attacked by those who should have protected it, and rescued by those who intended to destroy it.

That greedy people can exercise a great power in a city or castle is made evident by the words of King Jugurtha,[80] who, under cover of pretended affection, felt great envy and ill-disguised hatred for the Romans. But the better to deceive them, he gave great gifts to some of their leaders, and in doing this spread discord and sedition among the citizens; so their enemy, who claimed to be their friend, waged war on them without their noticing it. On his departure from Rome, where he had gone pre-

78. Christine speaks of this civil war, based on the *Histoire ancienne*, in the *Mutacion de fortune* (Solente ed., IV, pp. 4–13).

79. The example of Sinope, based on the *Histoire ancienne*, is cited in the *Mutacion de fortune* (Solente ed., III, pp. 267–71).

80. The case of King Jugurtha, likewise inspired by the *Histoire ancienne*, appears in the *Mutacion de fortune* (Solente ed., III, pp. 267–71).

tending great affection, he could not resist saying, in passing: "This strong city could be easily captured by anyone who gave enough gifts."

With these matters, it should be known that on a number of occasions great misfortune has overtaken a city or country, or even an army, through having a great number of foreigners present. This happened to Rome in the time of their conquests, when they were in the habit of putting into their service the prisoners they captured, making them serve and perform labor for them. From this circumstance, it once came about that there were so many that more than twenty thousand of them rebelled, and did a great deal of harm before it was possible to destroy them.

XX.

HERE WE BEGIN TO SPEAK OF LAYING SIEGE AND ATTACKING
A FORTRESS, ACCORDING TO VEGETIUS.[81]

When the time has come for the army to lay siege to a city or fortress, this is best done in the harvest season or shortly thereafter. If the commander in charge is wise, he will know that this is a profitable time for two reasons: one, that he will find more food in the fields; the other, that he will harm the enemy doubly, by the siege and by taking or preventing them from making a harvest of the grain and of other commodities. Thus the army in question will establish itself as near to the objective as possible. Before this they will have observed the layout and situation of the place, or will have been advised by others who are well informed, so that the siege will be undertaken to their advantage and they will know how to attack and place their machines. (In the margin of the Brussels MS: If it is possible that the place can be besieged on all sides, it is all the more advantageous, but if there is a mountain or something that protects it, they will nevertheless establish themselves on all possible sides and will make

---

81. Vegetius IV, xii: "When however a violent assault is prepared against forts and cities, deadly battles are fought with mutual danger to both sides but greater bloodshed for the assailants. For the side wishing to enter the walls doubles the sense of panic in hopes of forcing a surrender by parading its forces equipped with terrible apparatus in a confused uproar of trumpets and men. Then because fear is more devastating to the inexperienced, while the townspeople are stupefied by the first assault if unfamiliar with the experience of danger, ladders are put up and the city invaded. But if the first attack is repelled by men of courage or by soldiers, the boldness of the besieged grows at once and the war is fought no longer by terror but by energy and skill" (Milner trans., p. 127). Despite Vegetius, however, the development of this chapter is primarily based on contemporary practice. For an illuminating discussion of Christine's contribution to the history of siegecraft, see B. S. Hall, "So Notable Ordynaunce: Christine de Pizan, Firearms, and Siegecraft in a Time of Transition," in *Culturhistorische Caleidescoop aangebodenaan Prof. Dr. Willy L. Braekman* (Gent, 1992), 219–40.

trenches or palisades from one spot to another, so that those within cannot come out without risk.)

Thus the besiegers will have made good trenches and fortified the position with strong stockades, like a true fortress, in order to oppose those who might come to raise the siege, or even those from within the walls, if they should come out to engage them. If they decide on scaling ladders, they will arrange as many as they think they will need in double ranks, and these will soon be raised against the walls, rolled there on good wheels attached to the ladders to make them slide better against the walls, and they will be strongly weighted below, if need be, so that they cannot be knocked down from above. Then straightaway they will begin the assault, strong and sharp on all sides. Likewise, they will provide sure defense on all sides and a good watch at all hours. Then they will decide by what means the place is most likely to be taken. If mining seems a good idea, they will immediately put in place the workmen they have brought along for the purpose to start digging in the earth. They will do this before the shelters are put in place, and this will be done so far away that those within the walls will in no way be able to see the men who are carrying out the dirt. This mine will be dug so deep that it will surpass the depth of the trenches and will be supported by strong wooden boards until the foundations of the walls or a lower depth have been reached. By this means they will find some way of entering, unless there is some impediment. While the mine is being dug, the wise commander will not be idle, but so that those within the walls can neither feel nor hear the miners, he will keep them busy with all sorts of assault so that the sounds, the activity, and the noise will keep their bodies as well as their ears occupied, for arrows thicker than flies from crossbows, bombards, cannon shots, the terrible din of stones being thrown by engines against the walls, the shouts of the attackers, the sound of trumpets, and the fear of those who may be scaling the walls will keep them sufficiently occupied.

Therefore, if it turns out that the miners can pierce the walls without being detected and get to the outer buildings of the castle, the men-at-arms will enter by that means and set fires everywhere; so the place will be taken. They will even have put dry wood against the walls, which they will set on fire so that all will collapse at one time. Then there will be a general entrance.

But if this plan cannot succeed, and if the place is very strong and well supplied, the wise commander who is determined must find a way to overcome the situation.

## XXI.

### HERE BEGINS A PRESCRIPTION FOR LAYING SIEGE: WHAT IS NECESSARY FOR ATTACKING AN IMPORTANT STRONGHOLD ACCORDING TO PRESENT-DAY CUSTOM.

Vegetius, on whose book on chivalry we have based the greater part of this present work, spoke in general terms of usages in the times of the heroic conquerors of the past, yet sufficiently for those who understand warfare well, as much about what concerns or may concern battle in the field, with its variations, as what is involved in attacking castles and cities, by land or by sea, as will be explained later. Nevertheless, to give more particular instruction, not to those who are already informed, but to those who in the future may read this or hear it read through desire to learn (as what is written in books is one of the most enduring things in the world), it seems to me a good idea to show in the work in greater detail things that may be good and useful for attacking strongholds, castles, and towns according to present-day usages, in order to provide more comprehensible examples. Thus, as we have been helped in what has been said by the book of Vegetius, we will be assisted in this by the advice of wise knights, experts in these military techniques. Although they deserve great praise for this, as they also merit honor and respect for other kindnesses, and for the chivalric values and noble virtues they represent, it does not please their humility to be mentioned here by name. So if it should happen that anyone has already read the passage that follows, either having seen it in writing or heard it, may he not in any case hold it in disdain, but rather be pleased with it, thinking it would be a pity if the fragility of a small piece of paper that disappears in so short a time should have destroyed the memory of such a noble ordering, quite worthy of being preserved so that it could perhaps be useful in the future, perchance even in this realm.[82]

Let us suppose, then, a very great stronghold, situated in part on the

---

82. In the summer of 1406 the French government agreed that John of Burgundy was to lay siege to Calais, while Louis of Orleans besieged Bordeaux. Money provided to support these enterprises was to be divided equally between them. Burgundy's intention was to be before Calais by the end of November. The troops assembled were reviewed at St. Omer at the end of October, but the duke was never able to obtain the promised money for the undertaking, so by the middle of November the project had to be given up. A Burgundian financial officer, Jean Chousat, wrote to a colleague in Dijon, describing the magnificent equipment prepared for the undertaking, which was subsequently stored away for future use. See Richard Vaughan, *John the Fearless* (London: Longman Green, 1966), 39–40, and Dijon ACO B1554, fol. 213. Engerrand de Monstrelet speaks, in his *Chroniques*, of Burgundy's displeasure at not being able to carry out his plans, and of his blaming the

sea or on a mighty river, large, strong, and very difficult to capture, but to which one wants to lay siege with a great deal of equipment, which is needed however long the siege might last.[83] One must first consider and decide on the pieces of machinery and cannons, which is to say, two large machines and two of medium size, armed and entirely ready to throw projectiles. Item, four entirely new catapults (trebuchets), completely equipped, each one with two cables and four slings to change when needed. Item, four large cannons: one called Garite, another Rose, another Seneca, and the other Maye, the first firing four to five hundred pounds in weight, the second firing around three hundred pounds, and the other two firing two hundred pounds or more. Item, one more cannon called Montfort, firing three hundred pounds in weight, and according to the experts, this is the best one of all. Item, one cannon called Artique, firing one hundred pounds in weight. Item, twenty other ordinary cannons firing stones. Item, other small cannons firing lead and ordinary stones of one hundred to a hundred and twenty pounds. Item, two other large cannons firing three to four hundred pounds and four smaller ones, three other cannons, one large and two small. Item, twenty-four other large cannons firing stones of two hundred to three or four hundred pounds and sixty other smaller ones. All should be stuffed with plugs of wood (for gunpowder chambers) and all that is needed, the total number of these cannons being two hundred forty-eight, which are named separately because they should be placed in various positions according to the situation of the fortress.

XXII.

OF THE SAME, SPEAKING OF THE POWDER NEEDED FOR THE
CANNONS MENTIONED, CHARCOAL, AND OTHER MATERIALS.

First, about thirty thousand pounds, more or less, of cannon powder, half of which should be put into the prepared product.[84]

Item, three thousand sacks of charcoal from willow wood, two thou-

---

duke of Orleans, in particular, for his failure to get the money he expected. Monstralet, *Chroniques,* ed. Douet d'Arcq (Paris: SHF, 1857), I:135–36.

83. A useful table of this artillery is to be found in Hall, "So Notable Ordynaunce," 234.

84. Hall points out that this is a rather small amount of ammunition for the number of guns specified, suggesting that these weapons had weaker walls than later versions ("So Notable Ordynaunce," 235).

sand sacks of charcoal from oak trees, twenty large braziers with three feet and a handle to light the fire for the guns, twenty bellows.

Item, for each of the large cannons mentioned above, to transport them from one spot to another, a reinforced cart; to carry the powder and these other necessities, twenty-five carts, each drawn by three horses and furnished with all the necessities.

Item, three to five hundred wooden tampons for the cannons.

## XXIII.
### NEXT COME THE MANTELETS (OR SHIELDS).

First, six large mantelets for the large cannons already mentioned, fashioned on an axle with supports, each of them ten or twelve feet wide, thirty feet long and a handsbreadth thick.

Item, two large flat shields, each thirty feet long and sixteen feet high, all made of white wood a half foot square and five inches in breadth, and each with five wheels of elm wood with spokes on each side.

Item, another large pointed mantelet similar to the other two, and one of the three can be made when one wishes.

Item, ten other small mantelets, each of them twelve feet long and eight to ten feet high. These will be similar to the other large mantelets, and each will have a window for firing the cannons when necessary. The boards will in general be four inches thick, and each will be on two wheels like carts, made of light boards more or less an inch thick.[85] These will protect against shots while the others are being set up. Two other pointed mantelets, each one on four wheels.

Item, in addition eight other large mantelets for the already mentioned large cannons and stone-throwers. These will be made of wooden squares a half foot in width, each of these being thirty-six feet long and eighteen feet high.

Item, three large engines with arms to lift and set up these pieces of equipment.

---

85. Some contemporary German works, such as Conrad Keyser's *Bellefortis*, give illustrations of machines with a porthole or retractable shutter through which guns could be fired. Christine is unique in supplying dimensions that other descriptions lack. See B. S. Hall, *The Technological Illustrations of the So-Called Anonymous of the Hussite Wars* (Wiesbaden: Reichert, 1979).

## XXIV.
### WHAT IS NEEDED TO TRANSPORT AND ARM THE EQUIPMENT REQUIRED FOR ASSAULT.

Now we suppose that the fortress about to be besieged, for which these preparations are being made, would be in part on the ocean or on a large river, and then we can suppose that this wooden equipment would be made in some nearby forest and that it could reach the designated location or a nearby spot in boats or other water-borne vessels. Let us consider other machines suitable for transporting the boards, pieces of wood, stones, and other things beyond the boats: the carts that would be suitable and other necessities. First would be a machine to carry the stones from the boats, load them onto the cart, and then unload them where they would be needed.

Item, three small ironclad mechanical devices to take the wood for the machines and mantelets from the boats to the place where they will be set up.

Item, two large reinforced ironclad sledges to take the rods of the machines from the boats to their places.

## XXV.
### OTHER USEFUL EQUIPMENT.

In the nearby forest, as has been mentioned, the order will be given to fashion five hundred sixty boards for palisades, in panels thirty-four feet long and twelve feet wide. Five hundred and sixty panels come to about twenty-four hundred feet. On each panel there will be two trestles, one of which will be attached with mortar onto the panel, with the other end two feet away; these will be lined with screens to make passages.

Item, five hundred six panels of small boards, ten feet high and twelve wide. Five hundred six panels make eleven fathoms (sixty-six feet) to be placed before the panels mentioned above and the others. Those who know best where to place them will so advise, making the fortification according to the wishes of masters and workmen. There should be four gates and a closing device for one, with sentry boxes all around to defend the enclosures from shots and from cannons.

Item, with these there should be five hundred trestles, each ten feet long and eight feet high, which will serve to make covered alleys for the already mentioned mantelets, for the cat, and for the siege towers that will be made if need be.

Item, there should be eleven thousand hurdles (bundles of interlaced twigs) to cover the trestles and mantelets and form bulwarks if needed.

Item, eight full tons of wooden pins to put everything together.

Item, with all this a shelter will be built in this forest, one hundred forty-four by forty-eight feet, to house the mills and other necessities for those in the army who will be ordered for combat duty in the battle.

## XXVI.
### EQUIPMENT FOR FIRING.

To begin with, two hundred crossbows, thirty other crossbows with spanning devices, and one hundred others with hooks.

Item, two hundred thousand quarrels, or bolts, and one thousand large bolts. Twelve quite new spanning frames for shooting the crossbows, thirteen strong lever spanning machines for bending crossbows, fifty leather belts.

Item, four hundred pounds of Antwerp cord for making bow strings. Fifty other spanning frames to bend crossbows.

Item, three hundred handbows, each provided with three strings.

Item, a provision of eight hundred strings for the bows.

Item, twelve hundred thousand arrows.

Item, ten thousand iron hooks to be placed on the ground (for defense).

## XXVII.
### OTHER EQUIPMENT.

First of all, thirteen hundred shields, two hundred lanterns, and thirty other lanterns, sixteen feet tall, bound with great bands of iron to place in the ground.

Item, twenty-seven thousand ropes covered with pitch to burn in these lamps.

Item, four hundred battle-axes, some with falcons' beaks and others.

Item, for mining, four hundred pointed spades for the foot soldiers, if they break theirs, one thousand wooden shovels, four hundred scoops to empty water, twelve large iron hooks, each with two loops.

Item, fifteen hundred baskets, all with provisions, two lanterns.

Item, a thousand large iron bars a foot and a half long and twelve smaller ones.

Item, four barrels of nails; those in one of which will be a half foot long, another four fingers, another three, and the other two.

Item, three equipped forges, two ropemakers, two leatherworkers, wheelwrights, two wood turners to make plugs for the cannons. Two carts filled with elm wood to make these plugs, three thousand bundles of iron, sixty bundles of steel, sixty measures of charcoal from dirt, of which three measures make two-sixths, two hundred sacks of wood charcoal for the workmen, two thousand pounds of spun rope to make cords for the machines.

Item, for the leatherworkers, forty tanned cowhides to make bases for the machines, twenty-five rawhides to make slings for these machines, twenty-five rawhides to make girdles for those slings.

Item, for the wheelwrights wood will be taken when needed from what has been brought on the carts mentioned above.

Item, to attach the ropes of the machines, leather strings bound with iron and other small things necessary for the machines will be prepared.

Twenty-two barrels that can be locked.

Item, eighty wheelbarrows shaped like stretchers to put the stones in the cannon barrels.

## XXVIII.

### HERE FOLLOW STONES FOR THE CANNONS.

First, one hundred fifty stones ready dressed and rounded for the cannon Montfort.

Item, one hundred and twenty stones ready dressed for the other large cannons.

Item, three hundred other stones prepared for the small guns.

Item, six hundred other stones that will not be rounded, for three cannons.

Item, for the stone-throwers (trebuchets) four hundred stones, all ready to be thrown, and five to six hundred that will only be broken up and placed in piles, altogether around twenty-two hundred stones.

Item, six thousand pounds of lead to make pellets.

## XXIX.
### SMALL EQUIPMENT FOR THE ATTACK.

First, one hundred picks, fifty goats-feet grappling hooks, sixteen bridge joinings, twenty-four large and strong double ladders with four levels to support four men-at-arms together, from thirty-four to forty feet high, and on each ladder three pulleys at the upper end.

Item, seven to eight score of other ladders from twenty-four to twenty-six feet high and still other smaller ones.

## XXX.
### THE SQUARE WOOD NEEDED TO MAKE
### THE FOLLOWING EQUIPMENT.

To make a bearded cat (mobile shelter) and a belfry (siege tower) forty-eight to fifty feet high and two feet wide, there should be ordered twenty-four hundred feet of boards, twenty-four wheels, and a great quantity of smaller pieces. The nails needed for this have already been mentioned.

Item, six masts sixty to eighty feet high to serve the belfry and the cat in a manner to be prescribed.

Item, four horse-drawn mills fashioned so that there will be only two wheels, each wheel to make two mills turn, and these will be placed in the shelter described above.

Item, four casks of tallow to grease the engines, carts, mantelets, mills, and whatever else necessary.

Item, three dozen wooden pulleys and twelve other copper pulleys.

## XXXI.
### THE WORKMEN NECESSARY FOR THIS EQUIPMENT.

First of all for the machines, each one requires two people, one and the other as equals, then the masons, in this case also two.

Item, six carpenters whose duty it will be to raise the walls, construct the mantelets, projectile throwers, cats, and siege towers as well as other pieces of equipment, these to be organized in groups of ten. Groups of fifty and thirty will have supervisors over them to keep them in better order through organized commands. These will be designated by knights and squires to raise the aforementioned stockades, each in its designated place, as will be explained later.

Item, six hundred other men to assist these carpenters, grouped in assigned numbers.

Item, two thousand workmen to dig ditches for the stockades and other necessities, all organized in orderly fashion, as has already been said.

Item, a hundred knights and squires will be chosen and ordered to set up five panels of stakes and dig around them, and each will have for this purpose a group of ten carpenters and ten assistants, and three groups of ten workmen with six carts and their drivers to unload the stakes from the boats and put them in their assigned places. Each of the squires and knights will have a written list of their companions. Each group of ten will have a lantern for nighttime, equipped with fifty wicks (ropes dipped in pitch), and they will have the names of those designated to deliver to them shovels and spades of various sorts.

Item, fifty carpenters and twenty common soldiers will be designated to erect mantelets for the cannoneers, dig ditches, and emplace the cannons, whose names they will have. There will be others to supervise them, and these will have their assigned carts to transport their cannons and other equipment from the boats to the location where they will be placed.

Item, those in charge of the stone-throwers will have twenty common soldiers assigned to them to dig ditches, to establish the machines, and also to put the mantelets in place. They will likewise have their own people and carts and will be organized in the same way by the person in charge of the large machines, who will be assigned sixteen carts.

Item, those who will be in charge of the gunpowder, artillery, and other equipment will be given eight carts to transport these provisions. Another group of carts will serve to transport food and other such necessities from the boats to where they will be distributed.

Item, the one in charge of the mantelets will have twenty-five carts to bring them and the lumber from the boats to where they will be needed, and fifty workers in the manner already described.

## XXXII.

### HEREIN IS EXPLAINED HOW FOOD AND EQUIPMENT WILL BE TAKEN CARE OF AND THEIR DELIVERY PROTECTED.

For these matters, certain knights and squires, outstanding people, will be designated to protect the routes and passages, as well as to transport these supplies. One of the officers will be the commander, with one hundred men-at-arms, one hundred archers, and two hundred pikemen to guard the path from the river. He will be given one hundred large shields, ten cannons, and the powder needed to fire them.

Item, another knight or squire will be charged to guide around six score boats loaded with artillery and food, cannons, shields, and other equipment, and he will have two hundred men-at-arms, one hundred bowmen, and two hundred carpenters, as many of them as possible archers.

Item, another wise and experienced knight or squire will guide the large boats that will carry the machines, stone-throwers, large cannons, and all other sorts of equipment. He will be assigned one hundred men-at-arms and one hundred archers.

Item, to look after the food supplies that will come by land, and other necessities, there will be another competent knight or squire, who will take care that the merchants are not robbed or plundered. He will have at his disposal two hundred men-at-arms, a hundred archers, and a hundred crossbowmen. From another place on land there will be another who will oversee the same sort of necessities in a similar manner. He will have with him such men-at-arms and archers as are deemed necessary.

## XXXIII.

### HERE ARE DISCUSSED OTHER NECESSITIES.

Six or eight other wise knights and squires, experienced in arms, will be appointed to choose and inspect that place where the siege will be undertaken and fortification established with machines, cannons, and other equipment.

Item, marshals will be designated to assign lodgings as best they can, and to provide for the merchants to be amply and well lodged, and also the craftsmen, so that the army can be better served.

Item, it will be announced throughout the neighboring towns that food should be bought for all parts of the army, and that the good people will be paid and protected, and so it should be carried out.

Item, it should be announced that on pain of death the merchants should not be mistreated, or spoken against, nor anything taken without being paid for, nor should anyone be so bold as to enrich himself by charging more than a proper price, nor should anything be sold to be taken to any place except the army.

## XXXIV.
### HERE IS DISCUSSED BLOCKING THE HARBOR.

As we have already said, the fortress in question is large, strong, and mighty and is to be attacked in the hope of taking it. If it should have on one side the sea or a large river, the following equipment would be useful. It is also useful to consider how aid or any rescue that might come to it could be prevented. Thus it should be considered helpful to have ten or twelve big, old oceangoing vessels, to which could be attached strong, pointed masts, well sharpened, ironclad, and cutting across each other in a considerable quantity, two thirds of which would be inside the boat and the other third outside. These would be loaded with as many stones as they could carry without sinking. They would then be towed into the harbor of this fortress, where they would be sunk, so that they took up the available space for a considerable distance and so that no other boat could approach by taking advantage of bundles of brush from the tide or an increase in the water level. To arrange this so that it could in no way be disturbed, there should be a good commander with three thousand men-at-arms and five hundred or more archers. These would be in another boat, which would break up the loaded boats. If there should be an embankment, bridge, or another large river that might fill the ditches, this company could break up the former and make a way for the water to go elsewhere. On the two sides of the harbor, on the submerged ships, two fortifications could be built in the form of bulwarks, which is to say, buildings made of great poles of whatever height one might wish. These could be made quickly if there were enough help. Around these would be attached enclosures, covered with well-packed earth and put on wheels if desired. Such structures need not fear fire or cannon shots, because stones thrown sink into dirt, which is soft, and fire cannot affect them. Next the barrier of stakes, that has already been described, should be begun around the earthen fortress and should go from there to the other earthen fortresses. Thus by turning aside the river and following these directions, if the place is properly prepared, the ditches remain dry, and an embankment can be formed around the city, like a bulwark, as is said, so that cannons and other guns cannot injure the army. In this way, the city or fortress can be mined, as the water will be kept away. When the cat and the belfry have been raised and put in place, and the cannons have worked on the walls, an attack can surely be made.

XXXV.

MACHINES USEFUL FOR ASSAULT, AS DESCRIBED BY VEGETIUS.

One should know that, as Vegetius says, in attacking all fortifications there are five principal machines by which they can be taken: in one of these, through the force of powder composed of carbon, saltpeter, and other useful things, large stones can be launched with such great force that they break up and throw down towers and walls, houses, roofs, and everything they strike.[86] From these comes marvelous force, from some more than others.

Item, they made other machines that, according to ancient custom, Vegetius says they called *musculi* (mantelets). These are covered like large, flat houses, and there is dung on top so that the stones cannot break them or fire affect them. They are taken on wheels wherever one wishes. Inside this machine are men who guide and drag it, and they have before them branches of trees and other things useful for filling trenches, so that in this way it can be used where one wishes. Thus it makes a path for other machines to be dragged up to the walls.[87]

Item, the third machine is called a ram; it is made of planks like a covered house, and to this cover and all around it are attached rawhides, so that it will not catch fire. At the front of this structure is a large beam, the end of which is covered with heavy and massive iron. This beam is controlled by iron chains, and it is made to be set so that those inside can

---

86. Vegetius IV, xv: "The siege-mound is built from earth and timbers against the wall, and from it missiles are shot" (Milner trans., p. 129).

87. Vegetius IV, xvi:

MANTELETS.

They call *musculi* the smaller machines which shelter soldiers who remove a city's blockade; they also fill the fossework with stones, timber and earth that they bring up, even making it solid so that mobile towers can be joined to the walls without obstruction. *Musculi* are named after the sea-creatures; for as they, though quite small, provide continuous support and assistance to the whales, so these diminutive machines are assigned to the big towers and prepare the way for their advance, building roads ahead" (Milner trans., pp. 129–30).

produce great blows against a wall, knocking everything down. It delivers these blows like a ram, which backs off when it is about to strike; for this reason it is called a ram.[88]

Item, the fourth is called a vine. One does not use this one except with great effort. It is made of great planks and is eight feet wide and sixteen feet long, and is covered with a wicker screen and dung to protect it against stones, with rawhide on top and all around it so that it cannot be set on fire. Beneath this machine are men-at-arms who, on drawbridges they have with them, pierce the walls and place ladders against them.[89]

Item, the fifth machine is still more powerful and the last used, as it is suitable only in an assault on large and important cities, or much-coveted fortresses where there has been a lengthy siege. This is called a tower. It is a structure made of large planks with platforms on several levels. Because it is such a large structure, Vegetius says, it must be well protected. It is necessary, in order that fire cannot be set by the enemy's guard, that it be covered by fresh rawhides. Light and brightness must be provided for these machines, for they are tall, some thirty feet and others forty or even fifty. Sometimes they are so tall that they not only overreach the walls, but even the highest towers. So this machine is placed on wheels and pushed as close to the walls as possible by men and horses, and there are

88. Vegetius IV, xiv:

THE RAM, SIEGE-HOOK AND "TORTOISE."

The "tortoise" is made from timbers and planks with a covering of hides, goat's hair mats and fire-blankets to save it from destruction by fire. It holds within it a beam which is either tipped with an iron hook and called a *falx* because it is curved for tearing stones out of the wall, or else the head of the beam itself is covered in iron and called a "ram." This is either because it has an extremely hard brow for undermining walls, or because it backs off like a ram in order to strike harder at speed. The "tortoise" takes its name from its resemblance to the real tortoise. Just as it now withdraws, now thrusts out its head, so the machine at one moment withdraws its beam, at another sends it out to strike more strongly. (Milner trans. pp. 127–28)

89. Vegetius IV, xv:

The ancients called "vines" what are now called in military and barbarian parlance *cau[s]iae*. The machine is made of light wood, 8 ft. wide, 7 ft. tall and 16 ft. long. The roof is constructed with a double protective covering of boards and hurdles. The sides also are fenced with wicker against penetration by impact of stones and missiles. To avoid combustion from fire-darts the outside is covered with raw and freshly flayed hides and fire-blankets. When a number have been made, they are joined together in a line, and under their shelter besiegers make openings to undermine the foundations of walls in safety.

"Screens" refers to apse-shaped structures made from wicker, covered with goat's hair mats and hides, and fitted with three wheels, one in the middle and two at the ends, so that they can be moved up in whatever direction you wish, like a wagon. Besiegers bring them up to walls and sheltering under their cover dislodge all defenders from fortifications by means of arrows, slings and missiles, so as to provide easier opportunity to mount by ladders. (Milner trans., pp. 128–29)

movable bridges that can be attached to the walls. If it comes about that this tower can actually be brought up against the walls, it is very probable that the city can be taken shortly, for within the tower there are a great many men on all the levels.[90] Those at the top can fight vigorously with those on the walls and easily get the better of them; those on the other levels pierce the wall, and the city or fortress is invaded on all sides so that those within do not know what to do; they are dumbfounded and easily captured. This is what Vegetius teaches when he says that the fortress should be assaulted all at once in many places, with many machines. In this way the more frightened the defenders are, the sooner they give up. The ladders serve this purpose and so are very useful, as are all engines made to reach high.

To reach and establish such heights, one must know the height of the walls. Vegetius teaches that this may be done in two ways, explaining that with an arrow to which a sufficiently long string has been attached one can learn this, which is to say that it should be shot up to the height of the wall. In this way the measure of the string can be taken according to how far it has been extended. The other method he teaches is that when the sun moves, and throws the shadow of the towers and the walls on the ground, one can measure the length of this shadow with two stakes marking the two ends, and with the opinion of a good and wise observer one can estimate the height required for the ladders or other machines.[91]

90. Vegetius IV, xvii:

MOBILE TOWERS.
"Towers" refers to machines constructed from beams and planks looking like buildings. They are very thoroughly armoured with raw hides and fire-blankets, lest all this work be burnt by enemy fire. Their width increases in proportion to the height, for sometimes their dimensions are 30 ft. square, sometimes 40 ft. or 50 ft. Their height is sufficient to overtop not only walls but even towers built of stone. Many wheels are placed under them by mechanical skill, so that by their rolling motion such a great bulk may be moved. The danger to a city is immediate once a mobile tower is moved up to the wall. (Milner trans., p. 130)

91. Vegetius IV, xxx:

HOW THE MEASUREMENT IS OBTAINED FOR MAKING LADDERS AND MACHINES.
Ladders and machines are most useful for capturing walls if they are made to such a size that they surpass the height of the city. The measurement is worked out by two methods. Either a thin, light thread is tied at one end to an arrow, and when it reaches its mark having been aimed at the top of the wall, the height of the walls is found from the length of the thread. Or else when the slanting sun casts a shadow of the towers and walls on the ground, the length of the shadow is measured without the knowledge of the enemy. At the same time a ten-foot rod is fixed upright in the ground and its shadow measured in the same way. With this information, the height of the city is undoubtedly revealed by the shadow of the ten-foot rod, as it is known what height casts what length of shadow. (Milner trans., p. 139)

## XXXVI.
### DEFENDING CASTLES AND CITIES, ACCORDING TO VEGETIUS.

It is a certainty that one could easily take and conquer any stronghold if there were nobody to resist or oppose the attack. So, as Vegetius put in his book of military doctrine, with the ways of assaulting cities, castles, and fortresses, there are also ways of defending them.[92] So he said that if there are defenders aware of their chivalric skills, there are also many remedies against the aforementioned machines and perils along with many others that can be used in an assault, for there is no ill for which there is no cure. Skill in arms is very valuable, often more so than strength, even in the taking of castles and cities, as the Romans demonstrated when they captured by skillful art and ingenuity the rich city of Capsa, from King Tigran of Armenia.[93] He was at war with them, and one night, as the ambassadors from that city came and went, thinking they were discussing peace, the crafty Romans lay in wait in the gardens along the walls, and just as the messengers expected to enter the gates, the Romans swarmed onto the bridge so suddenly that they captured the gate and held it long enough for the army to pass through it. Thus that city, so strong and well protected, was taken by a trick when this could not have been done by assault.

Vegetius says further that the advantage is usually with the defenders rather than the assailants for several reasons, even in the event of combat, for regarding what is thrown from above—whether stones or arrows shot from ballistae, or stones from mangonels or other catapults—the greater the height from which they are thrown, the more they injure. Nothing can protect the attackers against such objects, if they are skillfully thrown, any more than against lightning.

In the first place, those within the city can be rescued by their lord. If he is not there, he can come with armed men to raise the siege and rescue them, or else they can be rescued by the help of friends from whom they may have requested aid. This happened when Lucullus, commander of the Roman army, was opposing King Mithradates.[94] He commanded his men, who were in the city of Mycenae, which was very strong because the sea beat against it and two enclosures of walls sur-

---

92. Vegetius IV, xxiii: "There are also a number of remedies against rams and siege-hooks" (Milner trans., p. 135).

93. This episode of King Tigran of Armenia, son-in-law of Mithradates, is recounted by Christine in the *Mutacion de fortune* (Solente ed., IV, pp. 15–17), based on the *Histoire ancienne*.

94. This episode concerning Lucullus is also told by Christine in the *Mutacion de fortune* (Solente ed., IV, pp. 13–17), following the *Histoire ancienne*.

rounded it, that they should not be dismayed by the great strength of King Mithradates, for they would soon be rescued. It was a great challenge for the messenger to make his way through so many people, but he accomplished it by swimming at night. He put two large bottles in his armpits and swam seven thousand strokes, thus entering the city. Soon after this Mithradates was countersieged, and in great misfortune his army was deprived of food, which could not reach them from any side, a device that is possible against those who are carrying on a siege.

Likewise, they, or a part of them at least, if they feel strong enough, can go out in good order at some hour when the enemy is not expecting them, so does not see them, and attack them as they are being attacked, for in this way a besieging army has many times been conquered and undone.[95]

Likewise, it is necessary for all who engage in battle for the defense of their country or city to have great faith in God that they will be victorious because their cause is right, for otherwise they will not be able to fight bravely. Such hope is essential, as it has been shown many times, by the apparent result, that God is favorable to such combatants, as even seemed to be the case with Rome, one of the many times that Hannibal, with a large army, arrived before the city to destroy it. But as the Romans went out very bravely to meet him, although they had one-third the number of men, our Lord, who did not wish for the city where He intended in the future to establish His church to be destroyed, sent a heavy rain just at the hour they intended to assemble, so that their equipment was so filled with water they could not use it, and they were obliged to withdraw.[96] When this happened three more times, as if miraculously, Hannibal said that he did not want to make war against the gods, for he saw that they were favorable to Rome.

Likewise, because of pacts and arrangements that are sometimes less useful to the honor and profit of those within than those without, it finally comes to the point, as it is said, where those within have no choice but to defend themselves with bodily force. They should take courage, following the example of the Carthaginians, who, before giving up to the Romans, preferred to destroy their city.[97] When they discussed it, they

---

95. This chapter was suggested by Vegetius IV, xxviii: "WHAT THE BESIEGERS DO TO AVOID SUFFERING SURPRISE ATTACKS FROM THE BESIEGED" (Milner trans., p. 138).

96. Based on the *Mutacion de fortune* (Solente ed., III, pp. 220–22), after the *Histoire ancienne*.

97. Likewise in the *Mutacion de fortune* (Solente ed., III, pp. 249–53), following the *Histoire ancienne*.

chose to die, to the point where they forged armor from gold and silver, bronze and other metals, because they had run out of iron and steel, and thus they defended themselves and their city to the death.

The besieged must help and protect themselves with machines, fire, iron, and stones, which is to say with well-aimed crossbows and large stones hurled with force from catapults. If they are provided with pitch, oil, sulfur, and wads of material for large hurlers, they can fire often and rapidly at the weapons of their enemies so that they set them on fire. Rods to be thrown at these weapons can be made of dry wood, hollow inside, filled with fire, cement, oil, and wads. The weapons can also be destroyed using a machine with a sling of iron rings. Beside that machine can be a forge in which there is a large piece of very red and burning iron. This piece of iron can be thrown by the machine just as it is. Against this iron there is no defense, or any rawhide that this fire does not ignite.

## XXXVII.
### CONCERNING THE SAME THING.

Likewise, at night one can let down certain men in baskets that have inflammable material all prepared for lighting, so that they can set fire to machines in various places.[98]

Likewise, it has been seen many times that those within the walls have come out suddenly to destroy by fire and sword the weapons of their enemies.

Along with these matters, Vegetius says once more that those within should take note of that part of the wall where the aforementioned large machine called the tower is to be placed. If there is such a machine, the wall should be raised so that it is higher than the tower. On the top of the wall should be placed planks and boarding the better to raise it, for it is certain, as he says, that if the wall is higher, the machine is ineffective. But besiegers have usually devised such a stratagem as this, that first they construct the tower in question so that it seems lower than the walls, but then they construct secretly within it another tower of planks that, when

98. Vegetius IV, xviii: "Men are also let down on ropes while the enemy are asleep; carrying lights in lanterns they set fire to the machines and are hoisted up onto the walls again" (Milner trans., p. 131).

the machine is attached to the wall, is suddenly pulled up with ropes and pulleys and placed on top of the other. In this way the men-at-arms attack the wall so suddenly that great defense is required to keep them from climbing over it.[99]

To impede this those within should be provided with very long iron-clad beams, by which with great force they can drive the tower away.

Likewise, he says that once when the city of Rhodes was besieged by such a movable tower of amazing height, much higher than the walls, those within, on seeing the great tower coming toward them, devised a great stratagem. On the night previous to the tower's expected arrival, they had dug underground at the foundations of their walls and hollowed out the earth at the spot where they thought the tower would be moved. They made a great ditch and wide cave, so that when the day came and the machine on its large and heavy wheels approached the walls, the earth gave way and the machine collapsed in such a manner that it could not be raised up again. Thus the city was saved.[100]

It should be stated that the movable parts of these machines formerly had proper names, as will be explained later. With them, when these towers were attached to the walls, the archers, the slingers, and the spearsmen, and all the men-at-arms, each in his own way, tried to take

99. Vegetius IV, xix:

HOW HEIGHT IS ADDED TO THE WALLS.
. . . [T]he part of the wall which the machine attempts to reach is made higher by building it up with cement and stones, or mud or bricks, and finally with hoarding, so that the machine cannot destroy the defenders of the walls by attacking the city from above. Naturally the machine is rendered ineffective if it is found to be lower. But besiegers are in the habit of using the following kind of stratagem. First they build a tower in such a way that it looks smaller than the battlements of the city. Then they secretly make another turret inside out of planks and, when the machine is joined to the walls, suddenly the turret is pulled up from the middle on ropes and pulleys. From it emerge soldiers who, because it is found to be higher, at once capture the city. (Milner trans., pp. 131–32)

100. Vegetius IV, xx:

HOW THE GROUND MAY BE UNDERMINED SO THAT THE MACHINE CAN BE RENDERED HARMLESS.
Sometimes very long iron-clad beams are opposed to an approaching machine and push it away from the vicinity of the wall. But when the city of Rhodes was under attack by enemies and a mobile tower higher than all the walls and towers was in preparation, the following remedy was invented by the genius of an engineer. During the night he dug a sap under the foundations of the wall and, removing the earth without any of the enemy realizing, hollowed out inside the place to which the tower was to be advanced on the following day. When the mass was moved on its wheels and reached the place that had been undermined, the soil gave way under such great weight and it subsided and could not be joined to the walls or moved farther. So the city was liberated and the machine abandoned. (Milner trans., p. 132)

the walls from those within, who challenged them as best they could. The walls were everywhere invested with ladders, and those on the outside who climbed them took serious risks. The use of ladders for such a purpose was initiated at the city of Capua, and those within hurled vessels full of stones at the climbers, so that they and the ladders fell down and the stones thrown killed many of them. So there were machines called *sambuca, exostra, tolleno*. The *sambuca* is a machine fashioned like a harp capable of piercing the walls, and it is attached to a mobile tower by ropes. The *exostra* is the name of the *bridge* that is thrust suddenly from the tower onto the wall, by which men-of-arms were able to go inside the walls. The *tolleno* is a machine with a pole planted into the earth. At the top is fixed a longer beam similar to a balance, at the ends of which can be attached ropes and chains as desired. When one end is lowered the other is raised up like scales. On the end toward the fortress is fashioned a little enclosure of nails and boards well joined together. On the lower end are loaded men-at-arms, and when the other end is pulled down, they are raised above the walls.[101]

The defense against these machines was good: mangonels, catapults, large stones hurled by torsion machines, mounted crossbows strung with cords made of good sinews, which, it is said, if there were good bowmen who knew how to use them, could pierce whatever they might strike.[102]

---

101. Vegetius IV, xxi:

LADDERS, DRAWBRIDGE, "THRUST-BRIDGE" AND SWING-BEAM.

When mobile towers have been moved up, men are cleared from the walls by the action of slingers with stones, archers with darts, hand-catapultiers and crossbowmen with arrows, and darters with lead-weighted darts and javelins. This done, they put up the ladders and occupy the city. But those climbing up ladders are often put in peril. For example, Capaneus-reputedly the first to discover storming by escalade-was slain with such violence by the Thebans that it was said he had been blasted by a thunderbolt.

For this reason besiegers get across onto the wall of the enemy by means of the drawbridge, "thrust-bridge" and swing-beam. The *sambuca* is named after its likeness to the zither. For corresponding to the strings on the zither, there are ropes on the beam which is placed on the side of the mobile tower, and these let the drawbridge down from the upper storey on pulleys, to descend onto the wall. Warriors immediately exit from the tower and cross over by it to invade the walls of the city. The *exostra* denotes the bridge we described earlier, because it is suddenly thrust out onto the wall from the tower. The *tolleno* is the term for a very tall pole placed in the ground, which has attached to its top end a cross-beam of longer dimensions, balanced at the middle so that if you depress one end, the other is raised. On one end is constructed a machine made from hurdles and boards, and in it a few soldiers are placed. Then the other end is pulled and lowered by ropes, they are lifted up and deposited on the wall. (Milner trans., pp. 132-33)

102. Vegetius IV, xxii: "CATAPULTS, MANGONELS, "SCORPIONS," CROSSBOWS, "SLING-STAVES" AND SLINGS, TORSION—ENGINES BY WHICH THE WALL IS DEFENDED" (Milner trans., p. 133).

## XXXVIII.
### REMEDIES AGAINST THE ASSAULT WEAPONS DESCRIBED.[103]

Against the machine called a ram, Vegetius teaches us that there are several sorts of protection, namely quilted blankets and mattresses, or sacks full of dung as large as quilts, that can be let down against the wall in the spot where the blow is expected to strike, and by the softness of these objects the blows will be weakened.

Likewise, there is another instrument called a wolf, which has a curved iron hook with sharp teeth. It is placed on the wall in such a way that it catches the arm of the ram and holds it firmly so that it cannot be moved either forward or backward, and sometimes it catches it, hanging it up with ropes, so that it cannot do any more damage.

Likewise, if it happens that in spite of everything the wall is pierced or taken by force, those in the city or fortress, if well provided with what is necessary, may make and build another wall in that spot, and if the besiegers attempt to rush in and the defenders can entrap them between the two walls, they can kill them.

## XXXIX.
### PROTECTION AGAINST MINES.

Against other methods of attacking fortresses, which is to say, the mine that is dug underground, these are the defenses: in the first place, the moats should be dug so deep that no mine can pass under them.

Likewise, those within should mount up to the summit of the towers and observe if there are men to be seen anywhere carrying earth, or any other indication that might arouse suspicion, and along with this, one

---

103. Vegetius IV, xxiii:

MATTRESSES, NOOSES, GRAPNELS AND HEAVY COLUMNS ARE USEFUL AGAINST RAMS.

There are also a number of remedies against rams and siege-hooks. Some people let down on ropes quilted blankets and mattresses, putting them in front of the places where the ram strikes, so that the impact of the machine, weakened by soft material, may not destroy the wall. Others catch the rams in nooses and, using gangs of men, drag them from the wall [up] at an angle, overturning them sheds and all. Many attach ropes to a toothed iron instrument like a pair of pincers, which they call a "wolf," and catching the ram they either overturn it or they hang it up so it loses the impetus to strike. Sometimes marble bases and columns launched with great impetus from the walls smash rams. But if such force is used that the wall is pierced by rams and, as often happens, it falls down, one hope of safety remains, and that is to demolish houses and build another wall inside. The enemy may then be wiped out between the two walls if they attempt to enter. (Milner trans., p. 135)

should frequently listen night and day at the walls below to find out if there is any sound of hammering. If any is noticed, the defenders should immediately begin a countermine, and continue it until it reaches the enemy's mine, and the invaders should be challenged there with lances, their progress fought with great vigor. If the besieged have put at the entrance to the countermine great tubs of water or urine, they first pretend to withdraw but rather go out, if possible, then suddenly throw that water inside the mine, and if with the help of the women it can be boiling, all the better. In this way, Vegetius says, many miners have been caught and killed.

Likewise, let us suppose that in spite of everything the enemy army has succeeded in reaching the walls, the towers, and the gates of the city. Should those within allow themselves to be killed like animals and captured through fear and astonishment, as the quail is taken by the hawk? By no means, but rather as vassals defending themselves until death, they should go up to the windows of their houses and onto the rooftops, and with good large stones and tiles, boiling water, ashes, and quicklime kill, if they can, or crush their enemies who stealthily go about plundering the city. If these enemies intend to light fires, they should throw down on them such large stones that they break the heads of them all, for in throwing, as is said, the high have greater advantage than the low. In this way they will sell themselves as dearly as possible, for with courage so emboldened, never doubt it, many cities and towns surprised by their enemies have been victoriously delivered from them. For it is too great an undertaking for soldiers to fight in another city if it is well provided and the inhabitants have good courage in defending what is their own.[104]

O! what marvelous fervor and courage against their enemies had those of the city of Numantia when they saw that they could no longer hold out against the Romans, who had besieged them for a long time.[105] Then, as those preferred to die, destroying themselves, their city, and all their possessions rather than allowing their enemies to be masters and enjoy their great treasures, for their city was very rich, they set fires everywhere; then they went out and sold their great wrath and their sorrowful death dearly to the Romans, who lost so many of their own before they overcame them that nothing was gained.

---

104. Vegetius IV, xxv: "WHAT THE BESIEGED SHOULD DO IF THE ENEMY BREAK INTO THE CITY" (Milner trans., p. 136).

105. The Romans' conquest of Numantia in Spain is recounted in the *Mutacion de fortune* (Solente ed., III, pp. 255–58), according to the *Histoire ancienne*.

One thing Vegetius teaches is that if the inhabitants are brought to this state of affairs, the besiegers should carefully avoid keeping the gates of the city closed, for, as he says, one should allow the enemy in such a situation to leave if he wishes. Keeping him enclosed could double his strength, as he could not hope to leave if he needed to.[106]

Likewise, it sometimes happens that those of the besieging army pretend as a trick that they are leaving, and even go away, as did once those of Greece before Troy after a pretended peace. Later, when they think that those within feel confident and are making little effort to maintain a watch or be on their guard, then, silently by night or secretly, they return, and scale the wall where the guard, tired of keeping watch, is merely passing the time; and now the defenders are found asleep, thinking they are safe, and the invader suddenly surprises them and kills them all.[107] By this deceit have many cities and towns been captured, as was the great Troy. Likewise, Rome would have been taken the time that Hannibal, prince of Carthage, was before the city, had not the cry of the geese, as it happened, awakened the guards. As such things happen often, a good guard should be maintained continually. Little shelters should be constructed on the walls to protect the watchmen from cold in the winter and the sun in the summer. In ancient times it was the custom to raise very fierce and brutal dogs in these buildings and in the towers, by whom the arrival of enemies could be sensed.

With such ways of defense as these, Vegetius teaches us that those who are enclosed and besieged should take care to search out and be made aware of their enemy's organization by some means and spies.[108] Nothing is more profitable or useful than this, for in this way it is possible to be better aware of their affairs, to know if they are of good courage and, if possible, the hour when these adversaries may not be on their guard, either seated at their meals or moving about in recreation, so that they do not suspect that those within might make a sortie.[109] If it is possible to de-

---

106. Vegetius IV, xxv: "Countless examples demonstrate that enemies have often been slain to a man after they had invaded a city . . . To avoid this fate, the besiegers frequently open the city gates in order to induce resistance to stop by conceding the chance to escape" (Milner trans., p. 136).

107. Vegetius IV, xxvi: "WHAT PRECAUTIONS SHOULD BE TAKEN TO PREVENT THE ENEMY OCCUPY-ING THE WALL BY STRATAGEM" (Milner trans., p. 136).

108. Vegetius IV, xxvii:

WHEN SURPRISE ATTACKS ARE MADE ON THE BESIEGED.

   Not just in sieges but in every kind of warfare it is deemed of the highest importance to spy out and get to know thoroughly the habits of the enemy. (Milner trans., p. 137)

109. Vegetius IV, xxviii: "When negligence intervenes, besiegers are equally subject to surprise attack. For whether they are preoccupied with food or sleep, or dispersed to rest or on some other necessity, then is the time when the citizens suddenly break out and kill them unawares, setting fire to

scend on them suddenly, and especially if it is possible to go out through some false gate in the rear of the enclosure, that is their best chance of escape. But they should take care that their intention is not revealed, whereby a trap can be laid for them so that they are killed as they go out, but if the besiegers can be surprised in the way described and the inhabitants are inspired by great courage, they can in this way destroy the enemy.

Good heavens! what marvelous courage was shown by the citizens of the city of Numantia in Spain at the time when, though they had defended themselves very well through several battles, the Romans had brought them to such a point that they no longer dared to leave the strong enclosure of their city walls. Nevertheless, they decided that they would prefer to sell themselves at a high price to their enemies. For this reason, from a certain amount of grain that they had on hand, though it was very little, they brewed a drink so potent that when they had drunk it, they were all intoxicated. Then they went out and fought so well that before they could all be killed, they had killed all their enemies, and as they were in equal numbers, the Romans were not successful.

But if it turns out, as Vegetius says, that Fortune does not favor them, so that they are heavily pushed back, they should be sure to have left word that the gate be opened for them quickly. If the adversaries are so bold as to follow them onto the drawbridge, or even within the gate, it should follow that they are immediately enclosed, and that there are enough stones and good marksmen upon the walls to fire them from all sorts of machines, so that all the adversaries, or at least most of them, do not return, and no advantage whatsoever is gained by them. Nevertheless, it is very dangerous to fight on a bridge, as in the case of the king of Gaul, Vituitus, who, with all his great army opposing the Romans, weighed down the wooden bridge they had constructed over the Rhône River, so that it broke down and his men perished.

Likewise, if it should come about that a pact or any sort of agreement or treaty should be discussed regarding the taking of the fortress, great care should be given that the disloyalty and deceit of some evil and malicious person is not able to take advantage of the ignorance of the simple-minded, for many times feigned peace and bad proposals in the guise of

---

the rams, machines and even the siege-mounds, and overthrowing all the works constructed for their own ruin. Against this the besiegers make a fosse beyond the range of missiles, and equip it with a rampart, stockade and turrets, so that they can resist sorties from the city; they call this work a "breast-work." Often in descriptions of sieges in historical works one finds that a city has been surrounded with a breastwork" (Milner trans., p. 138).

agreements have been more injurious than the superior strength of armies.

## XL.

### HERE VEGETIUS SPEAKS OF SEA BATTLES.

In accordance with matters spoken of at the end of his book, Vegetius touches briefly on some that pertain to battles fought at sea or on rivers. Speaking first of all of the construction of ships and galleys, he says that in March and April trees are full of sap and should not be cut down then to build ships, but they should rather be cut down in July and August, when sap has ceased to run. They may then be sawed and left to dry out until they are no longer green and can shrink no more.[110] Furthermore, he says that to nail together the boards, brass is better than iron, even though iron is stronger, for brass withstands moisture better without rusting.[111] He also states that those who wish to fight at sea, either in an army or by whatever other arrangement, must be provided with expert night sailors, masters in the art of nocturnal navigations, skilled in knowledge of the source and dangers of winds, in the perils of the sea, familiar with channels and dangerous places as well as harbor facilities, in reading maps and celestial signs and stars. Without such knowledge sailors set out to their woe. They should be able to recognize those signs that indicate the fortunes of the sea, what the future holds with regard to the sun, the moon, the winds, the birds, and even the fish; they should be masters of the sails and ropes, and know how to drop and weigh anchor. All of

---

110. Vegetius IV, xxxvi:

THE MONTHS IN WHICH TIMBER SHOULD BE CUT.

Timbers are best cut after the summer solstice, that is, through the months of July and August, and through the autumnal equinox until the 1st January. For in these months the moisture evaporates and the wood is drier and therefore stronger. Avoid sawing timbers immediately after felling, or putting them into the ship as soon as they have been sawn, because both trees that are still whole and those divided into "double" planks deserve a truce for further drying. Those fitted when still green exude their natural moisture and contract, forming wide cracks; nothing is more dangerous for sailors than for the planking to split. (Milner trans., p. 143)

111. Vegetius IV, xxxiv:

THE CARE WITH WHICH WARSHIPS ARE BUILT.

. . . So the warship is constructed principally from cypress, domestic or wild pine, larch, and fir. It is better to fasten it with bronze nails than iron; for although the cost seems somewhat heavier, it is proved to be worthwhile because it lasts longer, since iron nails are quickly corroded by rust in warm, moist conditions, whereas bronze preserve their own substance even below the water-line. (Milner trans., p. 142)

this is necessary, for many times armed men find themselves in sea battles under perilous conditions and faced with unforeseen adventures.

If all provisions are duly made to arm ships or such vessels, they must be manned by skilled men-at-arms. It is said that those who depart to fight at sea should be better and more strongly armed than those who fight on land, for the former are more interested in their movement, and they should send little corsair vessels ahead to reconnoiter and to find out as much as they can about the enemy by means of spies. When they close in, they must "greet" the enemy with a bombardment of stones hurled from various devices, such as strong crossbows; and when the ships have been joined together, the valiant men-at-arms who are confident of their strength jump the decks and pass over to the ships of their adversaries and there, using good swords, axes, and daggers, engage in violent hand-to-hand combat. Also, in the largest vessels, towers and barbicans are erected, so that objects can be hurled down from on high to injure and kill as many as possible. Inasmuch as a battle is indeed a cruel thing, in which men perish not only by force of arms, but also by fire and water, without any possibility of freeing themselves or even turning aside, whole and living creatures are often cast overboard to feed the fish. There are burning arrows and darts wrapped in pitch and oil; the railings of the vessels, made of seasoned wood, may be covered with pitch, which easily catches fire. So it is that some perish by iron, others are burned, still others are mercilessly forced to leap into the water; hence by these means many who fight at sea perish; it is a most piteous and bitter affair.[112]

---

112. Vegetius IV, xliv:

ON NAVAL WEAPONS AND TORSION—ENGINES.
    Land warfare requires many types of arms; but naval warfare demands more kinds of arms, including machines and torsion-engines as if the fighting were on walls and towers. What could be crueller than a naval battle, where men perish by water and by fire? Therefore protective armour should be a particular concern, so that soldiers may be protected with cataphracts, cuirasses, helmets and also greaves. No one can complain about the weight of armour, who fights standing on board ships. Stronger and larger shields are also taken up against the impact of stones. Besides drags and grapnels and other naval kinds of weapons, there are arrows, javelins, slings, "sling-staves," lead-weighted darts, mangonels, catapults, and hand-catapults, shooting darts and stones at each side. More dangerously still, those confident of their courage move up their warships alongside, throw out bridges and cross over to the enemies' ships to fight it out there with swords hand-to-hand, or *comminus* as it is called. On larger warships they even erect fortifications and towers, so that they may more easily wound or kill their enemies from higher decks as if from a wall. Arrows wrapped in "burning-oil," tow, sulphur and bitumen are planted blazing by catapults in the bellies of hostile ships, and soon set light to the planking payed with wax, pitch and resin-so much kindling for fires. Some are slain by steel and stones, others are forced to burn to death in the water. Among so many forms of death the bitterest fate is that the bodies are left unburied to be eaten by fish. (Milner trans., pp. 149–50)

## XLI.
### DEFENSE GARRISONS TO EQUIP MEN WHO FIGHT AT SEA.

Those who fight at sea must be equipped with vessels full of pitch, resin, sulfur, brimstone, all of which must be melded together and bottled. These vessels must then be set afire and sent in the direction of enemy ships and galleys, which should be attacked immediately, before there is time to extinguish the fire. It must be remembered that this is one way of making a certain fire, which some call Greek fire, invented by the Greeks during the siege of Troy. Some have been heard to say that this fire burns even in water; stones, iron, and all manner of things burn, nor can it be extinguished except by certain mixtures devised for this purpose, but not by water. In addition, certain poisons can be made that are so powerful and lethal that if they contaminate iron, a mortal wound will be the result. But such things should not be taught, because of the evil that results from them; they should rather be forbidden and cursed. It is not good to put them in books or record them otherwise in writing, because no Christian soldier should make use of such inhumane weapons, which are in fact contrary to the laws of war.[113] Furthermore, those who fight must always do everything in their power to drive the enemy toward land, while maintaining their own position in deep water.

Additionally, a topcastle should be attached to the ship's mast,[114] completely armored with iron, and maneuvered with a device that can raise or lower it, thereby striking great blows against the enemy ships, like the aforementioned battering ram, so that in this way they may be hacked to pieces. In addition, there must be an abundant supply of arrows with iron tips, to pierce a sail so badly that it cannot contain the wind and so can no longer advance. Also a crooked piece of iron fashioned like a sickle, with a sharp edge, with which the sailors can cut a ship's ropes. Also, if one has the upper hand, one should use iron hooks to lash enemy ships to one's own, so that they cannot escape. Also, it is well to have a great

113. The origin of Greek fire is uncertain. This incendiary mixture, based on crude oil, was first heated to increase its flammability and then pumped through tubes onto attackers and ignited. It continued to burn even in contact with water. It was first used by the Byzantine navy and continued to be a factor up to the fall of Constantinople. It was not, however, much used beyond this navy, possibly because other Europeans shared Christine's view of it. See J. B. Partington, *A History of Greek Fire and Gunpowder* (Cambridge: W. Heffer, 1960).

114. A topcastle was a small railed platform, a sort of "crow's nest," from which projectiles and rocks could be thrown onto the decks of an enemy ship in preparation for boarding it. It could be reached by climbing the rigging, and missiles were taken up by rope pulleys. I. Freel, "Winds of Change? Ships and the Hundred Years War," in *Arms, Armies, and Fortification in the Hundred Years War*, ed. A. Curry and M. Hughes (Woodbridge: Boydell Press, 1994), 184–85.

supply of pots full of soft soap, which can be hurled onto the enemy ship, with the result that the sailors cannot stand up, but rather slip and fall into the water if they are near the ship's edge. And then it is good to throw pots of quicklime, which upon breaking may fill their eyes and mouths, so that they can scarcely see. Additionally they should be equipped with certain men trained and outfitted to plunge into the water and remain beneath the surface.[115] As long as the battle lasts, these men swim under the water and with great augers pierce the enemy ship, so that water enters it in various places. Also many large stones and sharp irons should be hurled as well as anything else that might damage the ship.

Having stated the above things, I can use the very words of Vegetius at the end of his book: "I think that henceforth I can remain silent on the discipline of arms, for in these matters common practice often reveals more of the art of warfare than ancient doctrine demonstrates."[116]

115. Some idea of the costumes and devices of these divers can be gained from the illustrations of Conrad Keyser's *Belliforis* (codex Latinus Monacensis 197). Hall, *Technological Illustrations*, 77–81.

116. Vegetius IV, xlvi: "I feel I should keep quiet, because their [river patrol-boats'] use has discovered a more advanced science for them than ancient theory had to show" (Milner trans., pp. 151–52).

# PART III

HERE BEGINS THE THIRD PART OF THIS BOOK, WHICH DEALS
WITH THE RIGHTS OF ARMS ACCORDING TO WRITTEN LAW.
THE FIRST CHAPTER TELLS HOW CHRISTINE ADDED TO THIS
BOOK THE LAWS GOVERNING DEEDS OF ARMS.

While I was waiting to begin work on the third part of this book and my
brain was weary from the great weight of the first two parts, there appeared before me, as I lay drowsily in bed, someone resembling a solemn
man in clerical garb;[1] he spoke to me as a right authorized judge might,
saying: Dear friend Christine, whose love of deed and thought result in
the labor of studying, which is ceaseless, in consideration of the great
love you have for things represented by letters, especially in exhortation
of all noble works and virtuous conditions, I have come here to lend a

---

1. The personage introduced here is undoubtedly Honoré Bouvet (or Bonet), the author of the
*Arbre des batailles* (The tree of battles), the treatise on warfare written probably shortly before 1390
and dedicated to King Charles VI. It is not known if Bouvet lived beyond 1405, but it does not seem
probable that he was still alive when Christine introduced him into her book. Although she does not
name him, there can be little doubt regarding his identity. Christine's borrowing all comes from
book IV of this work, and her use of the dialogue to present the problems under discussion cleverly
simplifies them. The titles here are based on *The Tree of Battles of Honoré Bonet: An English Version
with Introduction by G. W. Coopland* (Liverpool: Liverpool University Press, 1949).

hand in the composition of this present book of knighthood and deeds of arms, with which you have occupied yourself very diligently and with goodwill. Therefore, in conformity with your great desire to give material to all knights and other noble men who can read or hear it, for employment and improvement in accomplishing those deeds required of them, which is to say, the aforesaid exercise of arms, by physical training of the body and according to the rights authorized by written law, it is good for you to gather from the Tree of Battles in my garden some fruit that will be of use to you, so that vigor and strength may grow within you to continue work on the weighty book. In order to build an edifice that reflects the writings of Vegetius and of other authors who have been helpful to you, you must cut some branches of this tree, taking only the best, and with this timber you shall set the foundation of this edifice. To do this, I as master will undertake to help you as disciple.

Having heard these things, it seemed to me that I said to him: O worthy Master, I know that you are one whose work I admire greatly and have admired as long as I can recall; your haunting and virtuous presence has already helped me, thanks be to God, to bring to a successful conclusion many fine undertakings. Certainly, I am very glad to have your company. But it ought not to displease the master if the disciple, desirous of learning, asks questions. I pray you tell me if my work can be reproached for your counseling me to make use of the aforesaid fruit.

Dear friend, in this matter I reply that the more a work is seen and approved by people, the more authentic it becomes. Therefore, if anyone should murmur, according to the ways of detractors, saying that you took material from others, I answer them by saying that it is common usage among my disciples to exchange and share the flowers they take from my garden individually. And even though they help themselves, they are not the first to do so. Did not Master Jean de Meun make use of the works of Lorris, and likewise of other writings in his *Romance of the Rose*? It is therefore not a rebuke, but a lawful and praiseworthy matter when material is suitably applied, wherein is the mastery of the material, for therein is the indication of having seen and read many books. But it is wrong to take material without acknowledgment; therein is the fault. So do boldly what you have to do and do not doubt that your work is good. I assure you that it shall be commended and praised by many a wise man.

## II.

### CHRISTINE ASKS WHETHER THE EMPEROR HAS THE RIGHT TO MAKE WAR ON THE POPE.[2]

Then it seemed to me that I spoke thus: Seeing that it pleases you, most solemn judge, that I should add to my book of arms and of knighthood the fruits gathered from your garden by your command and make use of them, I shall ask you some questions pertaining to the aforesaid matter of arms, which is to say, concerning the rights pertaining thereto according to customary law and to written law.

First of all, on entering into this matter, I ask you if it is true, as I said at the beginning of the book, and you will not deny it, that wars and battles by right must not be maintained or judged except by earthly princes who hold their lands from no one except God, as emperors, kings, dukes, and others who are called lords. The question is whether the emperor of Rome, who in his temporal capacity is the first in the world, may rightfully engage in and wage war against the pope and whether, if he should undertake to do this, his men and other subjects are bound for this reason to come at his beckoning. For it seems that they should do so, because that jurisdiction and lordship is due him more than any other lord of this world. Another, stronger reason is that his subjects must be obedient to him or else be declared forfeit and forswear what they have promised him, be he ever so good or wicked or even schismatic.

Dear friend, my answer to this question is that he may not wage such war according to law, and here are the reasons that the law assigns: first, that he is the procurator of the Church. It would be a great outrage for the procurator to move against the master, whom he ought to defend. Besides, the emperor is a subject of the pope; he cannot deny this, for it clearly appears that his election pertains to the pope, and in the case of election the pope has the authority to crown him or not. Therefore, seeing that he is a subject of the pope, it would be a grievous wrong for a subject to go against his sovereign. I say further to you that if the emperor does not govern himself and rule his empire properly, the pope may remove him from the imperial dignity and establish another in his place. Thus the subjects should not in these circumstances properly obey the

---

2. *Tree of Battles* IV, v: "WHETHER THE EMPEROR CAN DECLARE WAR AGAINST THE CHURCH."

summons to war if they do not wish to disobey God in persecuting His church.

### III.
#### WHETHER THE POPE MAY DECLARE WAR ON THE EMPEROR.[3]

Seeing that it is so, dear Master, that the emperor may not or ought not to make war on the pope, I ask whether the pope may move against him. It should seem not, seeing that he is vicar of Jesus Christ on earth; so he should follow in his footsteps, which were always peaceful and in no way warlike. Furthermore, He said to His apostles that they should never assume lordship as do princes.

Item, along with this, Saint Paul said that churchmen ought not to take vengeance but rather to overcome by sufferance.

Friend, I answer you that, aside from these reasons and all others, the pope may without fail move against the emperor under some circumstances, for instance, if he should be a heretic or a schismatic. Also, if he were to usurp the right of the Church by taking its patrimony and its inheritance and jurisdiction. Indeed I say unto you that in these instances he may not only make war against him but should even be helped by all the Christian princes of his empire, as happened to Pope Alexander III, who, being persecuted by the emperor, sought refuge with the king of France, who restored him to his place. And even though some say that God told Saint Peter that he should put his knife in its sheath, which is to say, that the Church should not strike with a sword, He did not say that Peter should throw it away but that he should sheath it again, signifying that it should be kept, although he did not want to use it at that moment.

---

3. *Tree of Battles* IV, vi: "WHETHER THE POPE CAN DECLARE WAR AGAINST THE EMPEROR."

IV.

## HERE IS EXAMINED THE POWER AND AUTHORITY OF THE PRINCE'S COMMANDER OF CAVALRY ACCORDING TO LAW, AND FOR WHAT OFFENSES MEN-AT-ARMS MAY INCUR CAPITAL PUNISHMENT.[4]

Master, I have heard enough about this case. But please inform me whether I have heretofore spoken sufficiently of the office of chief commander of the prince's army; although I have already been informed of many things pertaining to his office, I should like to hear more from you about this.

Fair friend, to this I respond that you have dealt fairly and completely with this matter. But you may add to it other authorities that the laws give him along with the certain duties allocated to him, that is, to give permission to his men-at-arms to go where needed, both for their own affairs at an appropriate time and also for military duties; for without this permission they should undertake nothing. So it is his duty to commit his men, now here, now there, to the profit of war, in accordance with good advice and counsel available to him. It is also his duty to take care that men-at-arms do not leave for another place without the lord's permission to do so. He should keep the keys of the castles and towns where he is lodged on military expeditions. It is further up to him to order those who are to do guard duty; he must diligently take account of grain and wine and make certain that the weight of these items is correct and punish those who use them improperly. He must hear and understand the debates and questions of his men, being careful to do what is right for every one of them, whether the man be a gentleman, a merchant, or anyone else who comes to him to lodge a complaint. These and sundry others that would take a long time to explain are the duties expected of the commander in chief.

But with all this, in order to explain to you better, I will speak to you of cases that by law may result in capital punishment. The law decrees that whoever strikes the captain with evil intent should be beheaded. Likewise, anyone who rebels and contradicts while in battle formation ought to be beheaded. Similarly, he who runs away from battle if the others remain. Also he who is dispatched as an envoy to the enemy or is sent to

---

4. *Tree of Battles* IV, ix: "THE DUTIES OF THE COMMANDER OF THE ARMY."

spy on him, if he in any way reveals secrets of his side. Also he that makes false excuses for not wanting to take part in battle with his lord. Likewise, he who does not defend his captain to the best of his ability if he sees him assaulted by another. He who deserts the army without leave in order to join another army. Such as these incur by law capital punishment, however good or virtuous their deeds may be elsewhere. He who will not allow peace to be made, he who causes dissension and mortal rioting in his army, he that steals army provisions—all these may incur capital punishment.

## V.

### WHETHER THE VASSAL IS BY RIGHT OBLIGED TO GO TO WAR FOR HIS OVERLORD AT HIS OWN EXPENSE.[5]

Because it is customary for a king, a prince, or an overlord to call up one of his vassals to be of assistance to him in time of war, I ask you, Master, whether the said vassal is obliged to obey, according to the laws of the land, the lord's calling and, being bound to do so, whether it would be at his own expense or that of the lord.

Dear friend, the better to answer your question, we should note what is contained in the oath of fealty that one takes upon entering into possession of some land or other thing under the jurisdiction of his lordship. There are six principal covenants according to civil law: The first is that by his oath he shall never seek on any day to damage his lord, nor will he be in any place inadvertently where such a thing is intended.

The second is that he shall never reveal a secret that would be prejudicial to his lord.

The third, that he shall in every way be for him just and reasonable against all men, exposing his body and his strength where needed in wartime whenever and as often as this is needed.

The fourth, that he shall never consent to damage to his lord's goods, possessions, or heritage or to his well-being.

The fifth, that if his lord requires him to do something that is within his capacity, he shall not make excuses, saying that the job is too hard and difficult for him.

5. *Tree of Battles* IV, xv: "WHETHER VASSALS SHOULD GO TO WAR FOR THEIR LORD AT THEIR OWN EXPENSE."

The sixth, that he should not seek in any way to excuse himself from going to his lord at his command.

Such are, or should be, according to law, the promises made by good faith and oath by the vassal to his lord. By these premises it clearly appears that vassals are bound to be with their lord and serve him in time of war well and truly, with all their strength, under threat of losing the fiefs that they hold from him and that are capable of being confiscated. And as God says in the gospel: He who is not with me is against me. This should be the case with their lord if they fail him, and for this they deserve to be despoiled of the lands they hold from him. Nevertheless, no law is binding on them to serve the lord at their own expense, but rather at suitable wages from the lord, if the land has not obligated them from the distant past to serve their prince at their own expense for a certain time, with a given number of men for his wars. But there is good reason not to do this. For why should the lord take from his men levies for his lands for various expenses except to maintain his estate and put in his treasury to support his wars, if need be? But nevertheless, if it should happen that the lord no longer has enough to maintain them and that his resources are not sufficient to protect and defend his lands, his subjects, and his rights, the vassals are obligated to tax themselves or put aside a certain sum to assist him, and they can rightfully be obliged if they do not do it willingly, especially if the enemy has invaded his lands to attack him. For according to law defensive warfare is more highly privileged than offensive war. But in truth, if a prince or lord has need to resort to such help, he ought to see to it that this should not be excessive or impoverishing for his men, nor should he put such a levy to other use lest it be charged against him. He should carefully avoid the counselor who would advise him to do otherwise, for it would be his downfall. Nor should a good king or prince listen to the words of such a counselor, but rather dismiss him as the enemy of his soul, his body, and his honor, for such a one would counsel his ruin and put him on the way to losing the love and goodwill of his subjects.

## VI.

### HEREIN IS EXAMINED WHETHER FEALTY MEN OR VASSALS ARE MORE OBLIGED TO HELP THEIR SOVEREIGN LORD THAN THEIR NATURAL LORD. AND IF A GENTLEMAN HOLDS TWO FIEFS FROM TWO LORDS WHO ARE AT WAR WITH EACH OTHER, WHICH OF THESE SHALL THE GENTLEMAN HELP.[6]

Kind Master, solve this question for me. I say this because a vassal is obliged to help his lord from whom he holds fiefs against all other men. Therefore it seems that if a king or prince were at war with one of his barons, the subjects of the baron would be obliged to support their lord against the king or prince, for they would not have made a promise of fealty to the king, but only to the lord from whom they held their fief, without any exception.

Dear friend, without fail I can answer this question briefly, although arguments could be raised saying that the vassal should as rightfully help the small man with affairs as the great one, so why wouldn't the men who have promised loyalty to the baron help him, for they haven't promised it to the king, and so forth and several other things that you could add to the question. Nevertheless, I say to you on the contrary that all these reasons are void with regard to our laws, for in good faith no subject is obliged to help the one from whom he holds a fief against his sovereign lord; quite the opposite, he makes a mistake under pain of death if he does, by *lèse-majesté*. For although the baron is the subject's natural lord, nevertheless the king or prince is sovereign over both, and if you ask me how this comes about, I reply to you that they do it not, because no oath can allow them to do evil, which they would be doing by wrongfully supporting their lord against his sovereign.

Dear Master, another more difficult question that is related to this I would ask you. I am supposing that two barons of the kingdom of France or elsewhere are at war with one another; for this war they call up their men. It soon happens that the king, for his wars and the defense of the country, has need of his people, so he makes his call for them, among them being included the subjects of the two barons. I ask you if these subjects are obliged to obey the command of the king or to go to their lord.

6. *Tree of Battles* IV, xvi: "WHETHER THE SUBJECTS OF A BARON ARE BOUND TO AID THEIR LORD AGAINST THE KING"; xvii: "WHETHER THE SUBJECTS OF TWO BARONS WHO ARE AT WAR SHOULD AID THEIR LORD OR THE KING."

To this question, in confirmation of the preceding one, I reply that according to right and law they are obliged to go to the king and leave their lord. There are three reasons for this: the first is that the war of a king or sovereign prince concerns the common welfare of the realm; the second is that they are obligated to the king in general jurisdiction, which is of greater authority and more powerful than the smaller jurisdiction of the baron; the third reason is that the less important official should not have the power or authority to be obeyed before the lord and that his power is diminished as soon as the authority of the sovereign prince comes before it, just as the glow of the candle is small as soon as the sun's rays appear.

I ask you one more question: I am supposing that a count or baron of the kingdom of France has land from the king of Aragon or some other king. It comes about that the king of France summons him by his command to come to his assistance in his wars. Likewise, at the same time the king of Aragon sends for him. Which one should he then obey? It is impossible to be in both places, and it would seem that he should be excused from going to either the one or the other.

I reply to you that he cannot be excused from either the one or the other, if he does not want to lose the right to the fief, so he should go to one, whichever pleases him, perhaps the one from whom he holds the most, and he should send his people to the other.

A more difficult question. I ask you, if it should turn out that the two kings are at war with each other, I do not understand which one he should help without losing one of his lands.

I tell you that the preceding answer can serve for this question according to some opinions, which is to say, to go to one and send men to the other. But this solution cannot really be properly carried out, for if it were done, then his own men would have to oppose him, as the two kings would be adversaries and one would have the people he sent and he would be with the other. Therefore there is no better remedy than to choose one and leave the other altogether or to have permission from both not to take up arms for the one or the other. But do you know what such a vassal must do, in God's name? He should make every effort to bring about peace.

## VII.

### WHETHER ALL SOLDIERS MAY LAWFULLY GO TO ANY KIND OF WAR, AND CONCERNING THE PERIL TO WHICH A MAN OF WAR EXPOSES HIMSELF IF HE GOES TO AN UNJUST WAR AND TAKES UP ARMS OTHERWISE THAN LAWS OF WAR REQUIRE.[7]

Master, if I understand you correctly, all subjects are bound to go to war with their lord if they are called upon to do so, not at their expense but accepting their lord's wages. If you please, I have another question. I ask you whether men-at-arms, from the same place or perhaps strangers, may properly and without burdening the soul accept wages from lords, towns, or countries to which they are neither native nor subject, even though such is the generally accepted custom. It would seem not, in view of the fact that war involves killing others and various other kinds of evil, things forbidden among Christians by God's law.

To this question, friend, I answer as follows: You yourself have touched on it enough at the beginning of this book, that every man may go to a just war and accept wages for serving there. For a just war may keep on to recover what is right, of which the limits may not be overstepped by any means, which is to say, by pillaging friendly lands and various other sorts of grievances that men-at-arms carry out frequently, thereby misbehaving seriously. This is unjust and is not sanctioned by law, yet it is allowed. For it is in the very execution of justice that God suffers and permits it, to the end that wrong may be made right, even though God suffers wars to be fought sometimes against all right and reason; this is like the scourge of God and the punishment for the sins of the people.

But to return to the first question: I say to you that every man who quite properly wishes to expose himself to war should, before he becomes involved, be well informed of the nature of the quarrel in order to know whether the challenge is just or not. If you ask me how he shall be able to know this, as all parties that wage war insist that their cause is just, let him inquire if this war has first been judged by competent jurists or lawyers, or whether it may be for the cause of defense, for all wars are just in case of defense, which is to say, defending one's country when it is attacked. In this matter the warrior should be well informed before he engages in it. You should know that if the quarrel is unjust, he that exposes himself in it

---

7. There is no chapter that is an exact source for this discussion of mercenaries in war, an important question when the book was being written.

condemns his soul; and if he dies in such a state, he will go the way of perdition without great repentance through divine grace at the last. But many make light of this, for there are plenty who care not a whit what the quarrel is, so long as they have good wages and may commit robbery. Alas, the sorrowful payment often arrives, for a single stroke suddenly struck can send them to hell forever. And along with this, all, or most of them, forget that those who pass in the exercise of arms the limits of proper warfare, whatever the quarrel, just or not, as limited by law, condemn themselves to perdition.

VIII.

HERE IS DISCUSSED SOLDIERS' PAY AND
WAGES FOR MEN-AT-ARMS.[8]

In order that noble men, who may hear this book read to them, whether at the present time or that to come, may know what things are allowed by law and those that are not, and as, dear friend, you have already reminded me of wages that soldiers ought to be paid in time of war, and likewise in what manner the lord is obliged to pay them and in what way not, consider that such matters are written into the law.

First, every nobleman, or city, town, or seignorial commune, that engages people by paying wages is bound to pay them for the whole time they are taken, whether or not they are put to work, even supposing they are at leisure and doing nothing, if the fault is not theirs and they are always ready to be employed. If payment is lacking after the agreement has been made, I say that by right and reason they may request it as a matter of pure justice.

Now, Master, as we are embarked on this matter, and you say the lord is bound to pay the soldiers their wages, suppose that they are always in one place and doing nothing; in this event I put to you some questions: first, I am supposing that a captain and all his company are retained at the king's wages and by his command to go to Guyenne against the English, if there is war there. It so happens that in going there they are lodged in a certain place where the townspeople have maliciously poi-

8. *Tree of Battles* IV, xlii: "AS TO WHETHER A SOLDIER WHO IS SICK IN WARTIME SHOULD BE PAID"; xxxviii: "WHETHER A SOLDIER WHO WITH HIS LORD'S LICENCE GOES OFF ON LEAVE FOR A CERTAIN TIME SHOULD HAVE WAGES FOR THAT TIME"; xxxix: "IF A KNIGHT OR SOLDIER HAS TAKEN OR RECEIVED WAGES OF THE KING FOR A YEAR AND WISHES TO DEPART AFTER THREE MONTHS, CAN OR SHOULD HE ASK FOR ANY WAGES FOR THESE THREE MONTHS?" xl: "IF A SOLDIER HAS ACCEPTED WAGES FOR A YEAR MAY HE PUT ANOTHER MAN IN HIS PLACE DURING THIS PERIOD?"

soned both the bread and the wine, whereby some of the men die and others remain ill during the time they were to serve, or even longer, wherefore it is not in their power to serve the king as they had promised; I ask you whether they should forfeit their wages for the time lost.

To this question I reply certainly not, seeing that their malady was service-connected, for illness rightfully excuses a man, and in this case he ought not to lose any part of his wages, as the malady occurred after he had been retained.

I have another question: If a soldier should be retained on the payroll for a whole year but in the meantime something arises to which he must attend in his house, he may therefore go to the captain and take leave of him in order to go to see his wife and his household for the space of one month. I ask you whether by right he is entitled to his wages for the time he is absent, for it would seem not, in view of the fact that during that time he would not be serving the lord, but rather going about his own business. Why should he then be paid for what he does not do?

I reply to you that the nature of the law of arms is such that great weight is attached to the leave and permission granted by the captain; indeed it is so privileged that seeing that the captain willingly grants the leave, the said man ought to be considered resident and present, for he still remains in the service of the lord in his wars, having been retained for a whole year. But it is indeed true that if he were bound by a certain interval of time, which is to say, if he were retained only by the month for a certain sum, I should respond differently.

I have another question: A knight is accepted to serve the king in his wars for a year. It happens that after he has served only three months, he wants to leave, asking for his wages for the time served. The captain denies the request, saying that he had been hired for a whole year; that if he had no intention of serving the full term, another man would have been taken; and that one who does not serve the period agreed upon loses his wages, and by going away forfeits his hire.

To this I answer that the captain is in the right, for if the man-at-arms fails to keep his promise, it is unreasonable for him to expect the agreement to be kept. I might add that if through his own fault he has lost his horses or his harness and is unable to recover them, for which reason he cannot serve, he should lose all the time he has served, for service is not to be paid for until the end unless other agreements have been made. Coveting and bargaining are well established in law. Thus you can see that evil mingled with good turns the good into evil.

Master, now answer me this: A valiant man-at-arms is taken to serve a whole year. Soon afterward it happens that his presence is needed at home. On taking his leave, he says to the captain that he will put another in his place to serve as he should himself. The captain denies the request, saying that he had taken him on because of his worthiness, honor, and wisdom; he would have difficulty finding an adequate replacement. The soldier replies that certain affairs have arisen whereby he would lose his land and his inheritance if he were not personally present. Furthermore, it is only reasonable that he is more obliged to help himself with his judgment and strength than anyone else; for that reason he cannot be compelled to stay. The captain replies that he is bound by his oath upon the Holy Gospels, so a man is not truly free who has bound himself to another. Now, Master, solve this question. In view of the reasons given by this man-at-arms and the fact that in his place he wants to put an able person, it should seem that he might go freely.

I answer you that to settle this question, a great consideration must be taken into account. There is no doubt that any man can replace a common man-at-arms. But this one was so able that another could scarcely take his place; thus replacing him with someone less able would not be reasonable. But if it happened that he did arrange for a replacement as good as he, then I would not refuse his leaving. For as I have told you before, a man-at-arms is not his own master when he is bound to another by oath. Therefore I say that such a man would not be truly free, whatever need he might have to be so, if through special favor the prince or captain in command did not release him from his oath. There is good reason for this, for if you had taken on the obligation to pay for ten ells of scarlet cloth and you paid instead for coarse burel, you should not be free of the obligation even if both are cloth.

IX.

WHETHER A CAPTAIN OF A CERTAIN NUMBER OF MEN
CAN CHANGE THEM AROUND AS HE SEES FIT
WHEN THEY ARE RETAINED AT WAGES.[9]

Master, I have another question that is related to an earlier one. Let us suppose that a captain, wherever he may come from, is committed with

9. *Tree of Battles* IV, xli: "AS TO WHETHER A CAPTAIN MAY MAKE CHANGES AMONG THE SOLDIERS WHOM HE HAS PRESENTED AT A MUSTER."

wages for a year for a hundred men-at-arms under his command, all of whom have been chosen and inscribed at a muster. It so happens that a month later he decides to transfer all or part of the men and put others in their places. I want to know if he can indeed do that. It would seem so, if he can have one hundred suitable men as he promised. If he may not do this without authorization, the result could be prejudicial, for if among his men some turned out to be evil or perverted, thieves or unruly and harmful to the others, or through whom shame could come to all, would it not therefore be wiser to transfer them out of his company than to leave them there?

To this I respond that what is right is both just and reasonable and that all would understand that no wrong would be done to anyone. For this reason I tell you, however, that a simple captain, who is subordinate to the chief commander, may not rightly do this without the permission of his superior. For if it were so, it would be in his power to indulge in extortions from his lesser companions, if he wanted to, that is, to take on another soldier through some favor or through greed to usurp a part of his wages or fraudulently to boot out some who might be his soldiers. So he would be well advised to take only soldiers he would never have any need to replace. And if he had to replace them later, through some perversity on their part, it would be dishonorable on his part to have taken them in the first place. But if to all intents and purposes he must make a change and replace one with another, he should certainly not do this without the consent of the overall commander and even so only after careful deliberation. If he did this on his own authority, there can be no doubt that the soldier who was dismissed could complain to the commander, especially if he was capable and had right on his side. But to return to covetous captains who practice all sort of cheating and play other tricks on their lesser companions, there are plenty of them who receive their companions' pay, keeping it for themselves and only giving their men a little of it. These would perhaps not dare to complain, because this was the agreement, such a bargain being made in order for them to be taken; this poses a great problem because in this way the soldiers are obliged to rob and pillage more than if they were properly paid. The overall commander should take notice of such things, for at the very least the poor soldiers, whether those on foot or on horseback, archers or others, should have the poor pay and salary that they earn at the peril of their lives and with such great effort of their bodies. It would be a great pity if their pay were withheld or diminished. The ancients would never have permitted this, for they were anxious that what was gained should be to the profit of the soldiers rather than their own, for those wise ones wanted to give the soldiers the profits while keeping the honor for themselves.

## X.

IF A LORD SENDS A MAN-AT-ARMS AS PART OF THE GARRISON OF
ONE OF HIS FORTRESSES WITHOUT PROMISE OF ANY WAGES,
AND IT HAPPENS THAT ON THE WAY HE IS ROBBED,
FROM WHICH OF THE TWO CAN HE DEMAND COMPENSATION,
FROM THE LORD WHO SENT HIM OR THE PERSON
WHO DESPOILED HIM? ITEM, IF A MAN-AT-ARMS TURNS UP TO
SERVE A WARRING LORD WITHOUT ANY AGREEMENT
REGARDING WAGES, IS THE LORD OBLIGED TO PAY HIM?
ITEM, IF A KING SENT HELP OF MANPOWER TO
ANOTHER KING WHO HAD NOT REQUESTED IT, WOULD
THE LATTER BE OBLIGED TO PAY THE MEN WAGES?
LIKEWISE, A WIDOWED LADY TO WHOM SOMEONE CAME
THROUGH COURTESY TO HELP IN HER WAR?[10]

I have another question: Let us suppose that a lord is at war with someone else. If he sends a knight to one of his fortresses to guard it, without having made any arrangement about pay, and it should happen that en route the knight is robbed of his belongings, his harness and horses, to which of the two should he demand recompense for his loss, the one who robbed him or the one who sent him?

I respond that he may ask both of them; that is to say, to the one who sent him he can respond by way of a demand, to the other by way of violence and action. But if the lord who sent him makes restitution, he is bound not to pursue his demand to the attacker, whom his lord could then sue freely to make him give back the stolen property.

Now tell me further: A baron is waging a certain war, and there comes to his aid a knight who does so out of courtesy, without having been asked to do so. I should like to know whether the knight is entitled to ask for wages or recompense, if it pleases him to do so, for it would seem not,

---

10. *Tree of Battles* IV, xxviii: "WHO IS REQUIRED TO RECOMPENSE A KNIGHT WHO LOSES HIS GOODS WHILE CARRYING OUT THE ORDERS OF HIS LORD?" xxix: "WHETHER A KNIGHT WHO AIDS ANOTHER IN HIS WAR WITHOUT BEING CALLED UPON TO DO SO SHOULD RECEIVE WAGES"; xxx: "IF THE KING OF SPAIN SENDS HELP TO THE KING OF FRANCE WHO HAS FORMERLY SUCCOURED HIM, CAN THE SPANIARDS DEMAND PAY?" xxxii: "CAN A MAN WHO GOES TO WAR FOR VAIN GLORY DEMAND PAY?"

inasmuch as he was not called upon and it would seem that his intent was to serve out of courtesy.

I reply that if he is not of the lineage of the one he helps or greatly beholden to him, but came out of charity, he can without fail courteously request recompense for his expenses, if he wishes, for in law it is written that no one is required to take up arms at his own expense for anyone else. The lord should be satisfied that the knight came to his aid. As he came of his own accord, he is all the more entitled to recompense in wages or other benefits.

Master, let us suppose that the king of Aragon should tomorrow send a large contingent of his army to the aid of the king of France in his war, for a certain time, out of pure courtesy, doing this without having been in any way asked to do so, but simply to return an act of courtesy that had been done for him formerly. I ask you whether the soldiers, following their services, could ask for wages, for it would seem not, as they were sent as a sort of obligation. How could they ask for payment since they came as recompense for an earlier act of courtesy?

My answer, friend, is that if the king of France had at some time in the past served the king of Aragon or some other king with a certain number of men-at-arms paid for a certain time, as it is commonly the custom among princes who are good friends to help each other, so the latter is bound by gentlemanly civility to help the king of France if he needs it. Not that the king of France, without other agreements, can rightfully ask him, for he who gives freely cannot insist on being remunerated, but in some other manner the king of France is bound by the law of nobility for such gifts. Let us suppose that the soldiers come already paid: in no way by written law would they have the right to ask the king for payment, since he had not asked them to come.

Again I ask you: I am supposing that by the sinful act of some lord or knight in the course of war a widowed lady who holds certain land is wrongfully oppressed, to whose rescue there comes a gentle knight moved by pity to protect the rights of ladies and to increase his own fame for valiance and chivalry. The outcome is that he does so well that by his skill he restores peace for the lady and forces her opponent to make full restitution. Could he, after this generosity, ask recompense for his good deeds, as one who well deserved it?

I answer no, because he was not commanded or offered wages, so he cannot expect them. And if you want to say to me that he handsomely protected the lady, I reply to you that he did more for himself as far as honor and renown are concerned, so he is rewarded according to the reason he came. He has received the pay he wanted. But it is indeed true that if the lady is powerful and has the means to pay him, she should do so, thereby setting an example to others similarly helped.

## XI.

WE EXAMINE WHETHER THE LORDS THROUGH WHOSE COUNTRY
A KING MUST PASS WHEN HE IS AT WAR WITH
ANOTHER AND INTENDING TO ATTACK HIM WITH A LARGE FORCE
CAN RIGHTFULLY CHALLENGE HIS PASSAGE,
ASSUMING THAT HE DOES NO HARM
NOR TAKES SUPPLIES EXCEPT FOR MONEY.[11]

In matters concerning arms, I wish to pose further questions. Let us suppose that the king of France, moved by a certain challenge or quarrel, wishes to make war on the king of Hungary. To that end he assembles his army to make an attack. He writes to the duke of Austria that he wishes to pass through his country, but he assures him that no evil or grief will befall either him or his people, but rather good and profit insofar as he will pay with his money for supplies wherever he passes. The duke of Austria, who has doubts about these promises, replies to the king that he wants to be assured of this by taking hostages, so that restoration will be made for any harm or damages. I ask you what is the right thing to do? For the duke says that he is ruler in his own country, so nobody will pass through it in arms if he does not wish it. On the other hand, let us suppose that he gives his consent, would it be possible that such an army could pass without causing considerable damage? For this he wishes to have good assurance of restitution.

Friend, I answer you that it is written in law that he who within his rights and with just quarrel sets out armed may and ought to have passage on public roads through all lands and kingdoms without harm being done to him or his men. Thus, as it is his right, there is no need, nor is it suitable, for him to give hostages for what is proper for him to do. In testimony to this there is a decretal that recounts a history in which the Is-

11. *Tree of Battles* IV, lxi: "WHETHER ONE PRINCE CAN REFUSE TO ANOTHER PASSAGE THROUGH HIS COUNTRY"; li: A MAN DETAINS MY GOODS WRONGFULLY AND REFUSES SATISFACTION. I MAKE HIM PAY BY FORCE OF ARMS. CAN I THEN FURTHER PURSUE HIM BY WAY OF LAW?

raelites, when setting out against their enemies, had to pass through the country of the Amorites, who wished to prevent their passage. But when it came about that neither through love nor ability to pay could they gain passage, they accomplished it by force, as God ordered them to do. Therefore I say to you that it would be both right and reasonable to do likewise in any similar case.

Also I ask you, Master: I take the case of a baron of France who is moved because of wrong done him and outrage to make war on a knight, in the course of which he does him much grief and damage, yet at the time cannot find the right way to have justice from him. Nevertheless, the knight gathers together his friends and allies with a great number of men-at-arms to attack the said baron. The latter, for his part, defends himself so well that they cannot enter his lands or damage them. So what else does the knight do? He damages and fouls the lands neighboring those of the baron, lands belonging to those favorable to and supporting his enemy. So he takes booty on all sides to such an extent that he enriches himself as much or more than the amount of the damages he has suffered. There comes a time afterward when the two men find themselves in Paris, where the knight has the baron summoned to the court of Parliament. There he asks restitution for the damages that have wrongfully and without cause been done him in the aforesaid war. To this demand the other answers that what he has gained because of it should suffice him, for although before he was a poor knight, through the booty he has seized he has become rich. The knight replies that this is no concern of his, for what he gained pursuing his rights was nothing of his. And if his neighbors had been punished for the sin of wrongfully standing up for him, there was no reason that what had been taken from them should count for payment of his debt. I ask you, what is to be done in this matter?

To this I reply that if the knight had done so much that he had recompense from the baron or his friends, certainly that should suffice. But though the knight carries away what he has won and seized from his neighbors, as he says, which is a right of war, the baron is in no way exculpated, but is still responsible for such damages as he may have caused wrongly. The knight is within his rights in his argument. For if the other wished to say that it is unnecessary to pay a debt twice, and that having been paid once, the knight should be satisfied, all this is worth nothing, for what the knight has gained pertains not to the baron, but is rather for punishment of those who gave aid and comfort to the baron against him.

## XII.

### A CASE IN WHICH A MAN IS INJURED BY ANOTHER, WHO AFTER DEALING THE BLOW FLEES, BUT THE INJURED MAN FOLLOWS HIM AND HURTS HIM IN TURN. THE QUESTION IS WHETHER THE FIRST MAN SHOULD BE PUNISHED. LIKEWISE, IF A MAN-AT-ARMS BORROWS HARNESS AND HORSES TO GO TO WAR AND LOSES THEM, SHOULD HE REPAY THE LOSS.[12]

Master, I recall that you once said that a man may injure another in self-defense. As all blows and injuries are sometimes called acts of war, I wish to put this question to you: A man has injured another, and soon after striking the blow, he flees as far as he can. But the injured party goes after him, overtakes him, and injures him. I ask you whether the pursuer should be punished. From what you have said, it would seem not, in view of the fact that he did not exceed the limits of justice. As he was the first one to be assaulted, he has the right of self-defense and should be excused, even if he has killed his adversary. Also he did not wait, for if he had waited until another day, I would not say this, for that would be vengeance.

I answer that the case you bring up is quite different from just defense, which is privileged. This is to say that according to law, as the first assailant fled after delivering the blow, the law does not permit the injured one to pursue him and injure him in turn; for this he deserves to be punished. But it is true that the first one did the other a great disservice, and whether the second deserves a greater or lesser punishment is a matter of disagreement among the masters. Yet there can be no doubt that the first movement caused by being assaulted and by the heat of the moment excuses a great deal, for which the second should be only moderately pun-

---

12. *Tree of Battles* IV, lxxi: "IF ONE MAN WOUNDED BY ANOTHER PURSUES HIM AND INFLICTS INJURIES ON HIM DOES HE INCUR PENALTIES?" xxvi: "WHETHER BORROWED HARNESS AND HORSES, LOST IN BATTLE, MUST BE RESTORED"; xxvii: "IF HIRED HARNESS BE LOST IN BATTLE MUST ITS VALUE BE RESTORED?"

ished. But if he had killed the other when the other struck the first blow, and it can be proved that said other struck first, justice has no part in the affair, because he was struck by a sword. To protect one's life the law permits one to kill another. If you tell me that perhaps the assailant had no intention of killing, I reply that the one struck did not know this, and blows are not struck according to a pattern. One strikes only to kill, so that the first to strike may be the first killed. But notwithstanding these matters, from conscience a man must make every effort not to kill another. Nothing is so displeasing to God as that a man should kill his fellow. He is the judge of all things, who punishes everything according to its due, nor can anything be hidden or concealed from Him.

I have another question: A German knight, or one from somewhere else, comes to Paris, where he finds the king ready to go into combat. The aforesaid knight, who is not aware of this, does not at the moment have any equipment suitable for his needs. But being desirous of serving the king and enhancing his own honor, he hunts up a gentleman he knows, who lends him a fine mount and very good equipment of a suitable sort. It turns out that in the battle the German loses horse, equipment, and everything else and barely escapes, quite naked. After this, the gentleman who had lent him all this asks to have what he had lent returned. Now the question is whether by the law of arms the knight is required to restore them.

I say to you that this matter is clearly set forth in the applicable laws; and in this way, to show that restoration is not required by any other reason, I say to you truly that as the knight went straight into the battle for which he had borrowed the harness and horses mentioned and in no way deceived the other, which is to say that he did not make him think one thing while planning to do another, certainly he is not bound to restore them. But if he had gone somewhere else and had borrowed these things with the intent to deceive and had pretended to have lost them, I would say otherwise.

Master, if he had hired these things from merchants, that is to say, the equipment from an armorer and the horses from one or two merchants, and had lost them, as has been said, would he not be bound to make restitution and pay for the loan?

I tell you what I said before: no. In the event that no other special agreement has been made to return them no whatever happens to him, he would not have to do it.

## XIII.

### HERE INQUIRY IS MADE REGARDING THE GOODNESS AND JUSTICE OF TRICKS AND SUBTLETY USED WITH ARMS IN COMBAT.[13]

I would put to you another question, different from the last one: is it reasonable and right for a king or prince to resort to trickery to subdue and overcome his enemy, whether in battle or elsewhere? The answer would appear to be no, considering what is right and reasonable. It is in no way right for someone to deceive another. Furthermore, any person who has a just quarrel ought to have good hope in God, whose good fortune should be with him if he pursues his objective with effort and diligence. Therefore, he who has a just quarrel should follow, it would seem, a straight path in war without resorting to wiles.

Daughter and dear friend, you speak very well, but nevertheless I must point out that in accordance with the laws of arms, what is indeed more important, according to God and Holy Scripture, is that one should conquer one's enemy by ruse, wiles, or tricks without doing wrong in arms, seeing that war is judged and involves both sides, and so it is true that this is possible. Even our Lord gave an example of this, when he ordered and showed Joshua how by wile he could surprise his enemies. Such tactics are commonly used to help in arms. But I must confess that there are certain kinds of tricks that are unacceptable and forbidden in deeds of arms as well as in all other cases. For instance, were I to assure somebody that if he came to see me in an allotted place, I would be there to speak with him, and he came according to my assurance, and I surprised him there by some trick to harm him or kill or capture him, such an act would be right evil treason. Or if by feigned truce or peace I should take my advantage to injure another when his guard is down and he thinks he is safe, in all such cases I would do evil and bring dishonor and reproof on myself. In these cases I would do wrong, to my great dishonor, reproach, and sin. Therefore the law says that as faith is given to one's enemy, it should be respected. But it is another matter if a valiant man-at-arms or some wise commander knows how to set up ambushes the enemy must pass through, not being on his guard, or other sorts of tricks, provided these

---

13. *Tree of Battles* IV, xlix: "WHETHER IT IS FITTING FOR A KING OR PRINCE BY DECEIT OR SUBTLETY TO OVERCOME ANOTHER PRINCE HIS ENEMY AND IN WHAT WAY HE MAY OFFEND IN THIS MATTER."

are not contrary to promises or assurances that have been given. And nothing is to be said about the reason you give, that one should wait on God, although basically I agree with you. But however much right is on the side of the king of France against the English king, or in another such case, he must help to sustain his own cause, and so it is that whenever with intelligence and diligence men do their duty, they should put their hope in God that He will allow the matter to be brought to a good and suitable conclusion.

XIV.

HERE IS DISCUSSED WHETHER A MAN-AT-ARMS WHO IS ROBBED
ON SOME HIGHWAY MAY RIGHTFULLY ASK
RECOMPENSE OF THE LORD BY WHOM HE HAS BEEN SENT.
ALSO, IF A LORD SENDS MEN-AT-ARMS TO HELP
ANOTHER LORD IN HIS WAR WITHOUT BEING REQUIRED TO SEND
SUCH AID, WHETHER THE ONE TO WHOM
IT IS SENT IS REQUIRED TO PAY FOR IT. ALSO WHETHER
WELL-PAID SOLDIERS MAY LAWFULLY
TAKE RATIONS FROM THE COUNTRYSIDE.[14]

Master, from our earlier conversation, it seems to me that you have already concluded that if a knight or some other man-at-arms is sent from some lord to help garrison a fortress without any arrangement concerning wages, and it happens on the way that he is robbed, he may ask restitution from the lord who has sent him, if it pleases him. I will put another question to you: Let us suppose that a captain from Lombardy, or from some other place, was brought to France, and with him one or two hundred good brigands, and he and his men were accorded pay of five francs each a month and sent to a certain place but on the way were attacked by enemies, so that he lost his banner, his plates, his harness, his fife and drum, and his companions lost their cuirasses, their *boucliers*, and all their rings. I ask you whether they can ask the king for recompense.

I respond at once no, without there being any other sort of agreement,

---

14. *Tree of Battles* IV, xxxiii: "CAN A CAPTAIN WHO, WHILE CARRYING OUT THE KING'S COMMISSION, LOSES HIS GOODS, LAWFULLY DEMAND THEM FROM THE KING?" xxvi: "ANOTHER INTERESTING CASE WHICH MAY EASILY ARISE" (a duke of Brittany engages soldiers in Germany); xxxiv: "CAN A MAN-AT-ARMS WHO GOES TO WAR FOR THE SAKE OF PILLAGE LEGALLY ASK FOR WAGES?"

except for their wages. If nothing further was agreed upon, they may not ask for anything more. And if you ask me why the captain in so great an affair did not ask for such an agreement from the lord who sent him, as has been said before, I tell you that in law a greater favor is done for the one who is not bound by an agreement. For example, you may see this in the case of a man who has lived with a merchant or someone else for a year and a day, without being bound by any agreement. He may make a much greater demand for services from the lodging if there is no other previous agreement that the master, excused by any other sort of bargain, has made. Therefore I say that a man is not well advised to take on a servant in his house without making an agreement with him, for the law presupposes that a man dwelling with another is his equal insofar as gains and losses are concerned.

I have another question: Let us suppose that a lord had sent for and hired men from a foreign country for a year, to come to help him in his war, which he thought would be of long duration. It so happened that before the help could arrive with their commander, even though they made as great haste as possible, the lord lost his land, so that no amount of help would do him any good. I ask you if these soldiers so retained are entitled to wages for a whole year or only for the time the commitment was in force; it would seem the year because the law says that if a king's or some lord's counsel taken on wages has begun to exercise his office, the wages for the whole year are due him. If he were to die, his heirs could ask for them, so why might not these men profit from the same right? For it can also be that they have forfeited wages they should have had for the whole year elsewhere. Many other reasons could be mentioned that I will not discuss now.

And I answer you briefly that these reasons and all others you might mention are of little value, for I assure you that the men should be content to be paid only for the time in which they served. And here is the reason: they were retained as soldiers to protect the country before it was lost, but as it is lost, they cannot serve there. For that reason, they do not deserve wages for a service they cannot perform, which is to protect the country that is now destroyed. No law obliges a man to do something impossible. If they insisted on being paid, it could be said to them: And that would oblige you to protect what is lost; how would this be possible? Let that be the end of it.

Now, Master, hear me out if you are so disposed: if men-at-arms are given wages and there is no irregularity in their payment, can they, in addition to their wages, take supplies from the countryside, and take anything else, as they commonly do nowadays in France?

I assure you absolutely not, for such things have nothing to do with war but are wicked and violent extortions visited on the common people. As you yourself have said before, a prince who is bent on waging a just war should take into account beforehand where and how it will be financed. Above all he must give the order that his men are to be well paid, so that they may pay properly for their necessities and whatever they take. It would also be just to punish those who take anything without paying for it. But by way of argument you might say to me: True, but what of the unexpected case in which the enemy came into the land suddenly, requiring a sudden defense before the prince had set aside a sufficient amount of money to pay the men month by month, so that in his treasury there were not sufficient funds?

I assure you that in every case of need they must do the best they can, even if in this case the prince might be excused for allowing them to take only absolute necessities on their way to sustain life, causing the least possible grief to the poor laborers. They should not be like wolves, who are not satisfied with one sheep when they enter the fold, but must kill the whole flock. Many of our men do likewise: when a chicken or a sheep might suffice, they kill ten or twelve and create such a waste, as if they were true ravishing wolves without consciences, as if there were no God or they should never die. Alas! those who do this are utterly blind, for they are in greater peril of death than others, and take less heed than others in such matters.

XV.

THE QUESTION OF WHAT SHOULD BE DONE WITH WAR BOOTY.[15]

I should like to propose a different sort of question. I ask you what should be done with the goods taken in battle from the enemy.

Fair friend, the answer to that question depends largely on the cases involved. First of all, according to civil law, it must be ascertained what is the status of the person who has conquered by arms, and there is a way of understanding in what case and in what sort of wars these laws apply. For if a war is conducted by command of a king or prince who has the power to declare and carry out a just war, some rights are reserved for such a lord that others do not enjoy. This is to say that whatever has been seized

---

15. *Tree of Battles* IV, xliii: HOW THE SPOIL OF BATTLE IS TO BE SHARED.

in war should be disposed of according to the will of the prince or his lieutenant in charge. As the armed men are rightfully paid by the king or prince, whatever they capture should belong to the lord, whether it be a prisoner or other booty. So it was formerly, although by grace at the present time, through long custom in France and elsewhere, what they conquer may be left to the warriors if what they capture is not of such great value that it surpasses the sum of ten thousand francs. In this case, whether it is a prisoner or some object, it is turned over to the king, who is obliged to give to the soldier in question, whoever he may be, the amount of ten thousand francs. This is a good custom in any land. But the law in question affirms plainly that all the booty should belong to the will of the prince, and he should divide it justly among those who have won it, or helped to win it, to each according to his merit. Nobody could maintain that anything else is true, for the custom is supported by written law, which even assigns it a reason. This is that if the prisoners or booty should go to the men-at-arms, for the same reason so should the castles or towns that they might capture, which would not be just or reasonable, that they, being in the pay of the king or prince, should gain land, for what they do is carried out as his men put to that task for him and in his name. For this reason booty should not be theirs, along with their wages, except what the prince wishes to give them as a gift. To tell the truth, it does indeed belong to them in large measure, as those put on the line such precious belongings as blood, limbs, and life. To reward well those who have deserved it is an ancient noble custom. The valiant noble men of old did not keep for themselves any of their winnings in war, but rather it was sufficient for them to have the honor, and their men could have what was captured. In this way they acquired such great devotion of their men-at-arms that they achieved the great and marvelous undertakings for which they are known.

## XVI.

### HERE BEGINS A DISCUSSION OF PRISONERS OF WAR AND WHEN A POWERFUL MAN CAPTURED IN BATTLE SHOULD BE TURNED OVER TO A PRINCE, AND WHEN NOT.[16]

As I have told you before with regard to the aforesaid law, which is to say, that regarding the status of the person who has been conquered in arms,

---

16. *Tree of Battles* IV, xiv: "IF A SOLDIER HAS TAKEN A PRISONER WHOSE PRISONER SHOULD HE BE, THE SOLDIER'S OR HIS LORD'S?"

and I have explained to you a part of this, now let us suppose, in another case, that one baron wages war against another, whether or not the war is just, or whether or not he seeks to defend his land against the other, for defending himself and protecting his land, whatever the case may be, is commonly considered a just war, and is permitted by any law and right. If the baron who is defending himself captures and imprisons the one who is invading him, would you say that the one caught is the captor's own prisoner?

I assure you that he would not be, nor would the captor have any other right according to law, except that he could hold his prisoner safely until presenting him to the overlord from whom the captor holds his barony, who should make the judgment. But there is another aspect to consider. If he who captures the other should be one who exercises sovereign justice or has the power to do justice to evildoers and is accustomed to doing this as the true lord, as there are many lordships that have such authority, I say to you that as he finds the other overrunning the country robbing and killing men, he can punish him according to justice. Let us suppose further that he is greater in degree than the other. Despite the fact that one can insist in this case that no man may be the judge in his own cause, I say that he can do so for two reasons: first, by virtue of his own justification he may punish or otherwise bring to justice evildoers; and second, he may punish the crime of the one who commits it on his own property, where he has the authority of the law for such punishment, for if one man assails another, intending to harm him, the one attacked can do to the other whatever the other intended to do to him. I say that this is in accord with reasonable defense. But I confess to you that if the one who is assaulted should, though lacking jurisdiction to do so, punish on his own his adversary or hold him in prison, he would do wrong to his sovereign lord and would risk losing whatever he holds from him. So he should turn him over to his sovereign lord. This would even be praiseworthy for a churchman in order to recover what belonged to him.

## XVII.

### WHETHER A CHIEF COMMANDER OF AN ARMY SEIZED IN THE COURSE OF A BATTLE OUGHT TO BE KILLED, OR WHETHER HE OUGHT TO BE HANDED OVER TO THE PRINCE; ALSO WHETHER IT IS LAWFUL TO FORCE SUCH A MAN TO PAY RANSOM FOR HIS DELIVERANCE.[17]

Master, as we have turned to the subject of prisoners of war, I ask you whether a captured commander, or some important man, who has been very damaging to his captor or could be so if he escaped, can rightfully be put to death, for according to the law of nature it would appear so, as everything tends to destroy its opposite.

Certainly, friend, I answer that even though civil law says that one who is captured in battle is serf or slave of the one who takes him, he should not be killed. The decree affirms this by saying that as soon as a man is in prison, mercy is due him. Then it follows that if mercy is due him, how may he be put to death without wrong being done him?

But there is more to be said. Another decree states that if one man overcomes another, he is obliged to pardon him, especially his life. So I say to you that it is against right and gentility to slay the one who gives himself up. And the man's relatives might pursue the killer for doing wrong. But if a prince should take charge of him and remove him from the hands of the one who had captured him, and if for a good reason the prince, being advised that great harm might come to him and his own land if he let the prisoner go, should have him put to death, he had well deserved it, but otherwise it would be inhuman and excessively cruel. But if you tell me that the ancients had a law permitting them to kill their prisoners if they liked, or to sell them as slaves or put them to work in their service, I reply to you that among Christians, where the law is based on mercy and pity, it is not proper to use such tyranny, for it is denounced and reproved.

Now I ask to whom a prisoner should belong, to the lord or to the one who has captured him, for it seems to me that you have said before that one law bears witness to the fact that the prisoner is at the disposal of the

---

17. *Tree of Battles* IV, xiii: "IF THE DUKE OF THE BATTLE IS TAKEN PRISONER, OUGHT ONE TO HAVE MERCY ON HIM AND PARDON HIM?" xliv: "WHETHER I MAY LAWFULLY RETAIN WHAT I HAVE TAKEN FROM A THIEF WHO HAS TRIED TO ROB ME OF MY BELONGINGS" xiv: "IF A SOLDIER HAS TAKEN A PRISONER WHOSE PRISONER SHOULD HE BE, THE SOLDIER'S OR HIS LORD'S?" See xlvii: "WHETHER RANSOM OF SILVER OR GOLD MAY JUSTLY BE DEMANDED OF A PRISONER."

one who has captured him; and as he is at his disposal, it would seem that he belongs to him.

Fair friend, you seem to have forgotten what I told you before, so I say it again, that although in truth there are several opinions from various masters for and against this case, nevertheless the upshot is that everything captured and all booty ought to be at the disposal of the prince to whom belongs the responsibility of distributing it according to his discretion.

I understand you very well, Master, but now tell me, as we Christians have now abandoned the laws of the ancients that permitted placing in servitude or slaying their prisoners, I ask you whether a demand may be made of a prisoner for gold or silver or some other thing of value of the sort that is customary in matters of war. For if I rightly remember, you have said before that mercy is properly due a prisoner. It seems to me that as this is a right, it would be a wrong to make him pay a ransom, as in this way he is not being shown mercy.

I say to you in further response that truly mercy is due him in two regards: this is to say that his life should be spared, and more important, the master is obliged to defend his prisoner against anyone else who would harm him. Likewise, mercy is due a man-at-arms who should have on him at the time of his capture all his valuables, which failing such exercise of mercy would all be for the captor. But according to written law the captor should act so that in exacting ransom, which is permitted according to military custom, especially when one nation is fighting against another, as French against English, and others likewise, care should be taken that the ransom is not so excessive that the man is ruined by it, his wife and children destroyed and reduced to poverty. That would be tyranny against conscience and all military custom, for it is not proper that a gentleman should be reduced to beggary after paying his ransom, but rather he should be allowed to keep enough to live on and maintain his position. It is a good thing to note the custom in Italy, where a man-at-arms taken prisoner in its wars generally loses only his horses and equipment, so he is not obliged to sell his land or be despoiled of his worldly possessions to pay his ransom. So you can see how a suitable ransom is just according to military custom, where it is permitted. But to put a man in a terrible prison and force him by torture to pay more than he can is an inhuman horror and makes for a wicked Christian tyrant worse than a Jew. Be certain that whatever is gotten in that way is very wrongfully obtained, and it should be given up, or it will be his damnation. Let every man beware.

## XVIII.
### HERE INQUIRY IS MADE REGARDING THE RIGHT TO SEIZE IN ENEMY TERRITORY SIMPLE PEASANTS WHO ARE NOT ENGAGED IN WARFARE.[18]

I ask you whether a king or prince, when warring against another, even though the war may be just, has the right to overrun the enemy land and take prisoner all manner of people, including common people, that is, peasants, shepherds, and such like; it would appear not. Why should they bear the burden of the profession of arms, of which they know nothing? It is not for them to pass judgment about war; common people are not called on to bear arms; rather, it is distasteful to them, for they say they want to live in peace and ask no more. They should be free, it seems to me, just as all priests and churchmen are, because their estate is outside military activity. What honor can accrue to a prince in killing, overrunning, or seizing people who have never borne arms nor could make use of them, or poor innocent people who do nothing but till the land and watch over animals?

To this I would answer with a supposition like this: Let us suppose that the people of England wished not to aid their king in injuring the king of France, and the French fell upon them instantly, with right and reason on their side. In accordance with lawful practice they should not in any way cause bodily harm to, or injure the property of, such people or those who did not come to aid the king, offering either goods or counsel. But if the subjects of that king or of another in a similar situation, be they poor or rich, farmers or anything else, give aid and comfort to maintain the war, according to military right the French may overrun their country and seize what they find, that is to say, prisoners of whatever class, and all manner of things, without being obliged by any law to return the same. For I tell you that this is determined as a matter of law, the law of war. For if a war is judged by the counselors of both kings or princes, the men-at-arms are free to dominate each other. And occasionally the poor and simple folk, who do not bear arms, are injured—and it cannot be otherwise,

18. Continues *Tree of Battles* IV, xlvii.

for weeds cannot be separated from good plants, because they are so close together that the good ones suffer. But in truth it is right that the valiant and good gentlemen-at-arms must take every precaution not to destroy the poor and simple folk, or suffer them to be tyrannized or mistreated, for they are Christians and not Saracens. And if I have said that pity is due some, remember that not less is due the others; those who engage in warfare may be hurt, but the humble and peaceful should be shielded from their force.

XIX.

HERE IT IS ASKED WHETHER AN ENGLISH STUDENT
STUDYING IN PARIS OR IN SOME OTHER ENEMY TERRITORY
MAY BE SEIZED AND HELD FOR RANSOM.[19]

As we are engaged in a discussion of prisoners of war, I wish you to be the judge of a little debate, herewith proposed. It is well known, even notorious, how the kings of France and England frequently are at war with each other. Let us take as an example a student given leave by the city of London to come to Paris to study for a graduate degree in law or theology. It happens that a French man-at-arms realizes that the student is English and takes him prisoner, an act formally resisted by the victim. The matter is finally brought before justice. There the English student, basing his reasons on law, says that it is expressly stated by the law that on account of the great privileges accorded students, no harm may be done them, but rather honor and reverence. Here he states the underlying reasons: Who would not recommend scholars, who have abandoned riches and all bodily comforts, their close friends and their country, have taken on poverty, and given up all worldly goods and everything else for the love of knowledge? He would resist anyone who would do such a student evil. To this line of reasoning a man-at-arms would reply in these terms: Brother, I tell you that among us French we do not enforce the laws of the emperor, to whom we are neither subject nor obedient. The student responds: Laws are nothing more than the right reason ordered in accordance with wisdom, and if you do not care about this, it is not because the king and lords of France do not use reason concerning reasonable

---

19. *Tree of Battles* IV, lxxxvi: "WHETHER AN ENGLISH STUDENT DWELLING AT PARIS FOR PURPOSES OF STUDY COULD BE IMPRISONED"; lxxxviii: "WHETHER AN ENGLISHMAN COMING TO SEE HIS SON, A STUDENT AT PARIS, SHOULD BE IMPRISONED."

matters that they themselves have commanded. For when at the pope's request Charlemagne transferred the General Study of Rome to Paris, the lords gave great and notable privileges to this school. For this reason the king sent out into all parts in search of masters and students of all languages, and all were agreed on these privileges. Why, then, can they not come from all countries, when they are given royal permission to do so, as all kings swear on their assumption of power to maintain these privileges? In God's name, says the man-at-arms, assuming what you have said is true, you should know that since the general war has been waged between your king and ours, no Englishman has been allowed to come into France for such a reason as you gave, or any other person without a safe conduct; and the reason for that is a good one, for you could, under pretext of studying, write down or make known in your land the state of affairs here and commit all sorts of undercover deeds if you wished. Indeed it is not right that any kind of privilege should turn into prejudice against the king or his realm.

Hear these reasons and tell me, my dear friend, what you think.

Directly, my master, as it pleases you that my humble opinion may serve the cause, I say to you that the person of whom you speak is a true student. That is to say, he did not come under false colors to spy or to do harm. I consider his motive to be good and believe that he should not be taken prisoner unless the king has issued a special order that no Englishman of any sort should come to study in his kingdom, and unless such an order has been widely published and made known in all places.

You have shown excellent judgment and have made a wise distinction. For even if the bishopric of Paris or the archbishopric of Rouen, or Sens, or any other should become vacant and an English priest were to be elected, the king would have the right to quash the election for the reason that is not expedient for the king or for his realm to have enemies in their midst.

But still another question. Answer me this: Suppose the student may not be taken prisoner. What about his servants, if he brings along several from England? After all, the privilege given to students was never extended in good faith to servants.

Master, subject to your correction, the reason notwithstanding, it seems to me that part of the privilege of the master, if he be a true student, would be that his servants should be included, as is the case where the king grants privileges to his officers: their servants and their whole families are included.

But Master, I should like to ask something that may cast doubt upon this matter. Suppose the student were ill. Could his father by right come to visit him without danger?

To this I respond that according to written law, even if he came under false pretenses, he should be able to come safely. The reason is that the law of nature is greater than that of war. Love of father and mother for a child is privileged; no right of arms can take precedence over it. An even stronger argument may be advanced: if the father, to take his son books and money, were to go and see him, who was quite well and at work at his studies, even elsewhere than at Paris, he might not for that reason be arrested, seized, imprisoned in any country whatsoever, friendly or enemy. This judgment is set forth in written law, just as I have said. And for the same reason are included brother, other relative, or servant, who may take money or books to him, under the provisions of the aforesaid clauses; and all this is by virtue of privileges reserved for students generally.


## XX.

### WHETHER A GREAT LORD OF ENGLAND, OR SOME OTHER COUNTRY AT WAR, WHO HAS BEEN FOUND ALONE IN A FOREST, OUT OF HIS MIND, MAY RIGHTLY BE CAPTURED AND HELD FOR RANSOM WHILE HE IS OUT OF HIS MIND.[20]

Another question I put to you, kind Master. I am supposing that a duke or an earl departs from England and goes to France with his men to wage war against the king. It happens that he loses his mind and becomes mad, so that mad and raving he flees to the woods and hedges, where he is found by our men, who easily recognize him. I ask if he should be confined to prison, for that would seem fitting in view of the fact that he came with the intention of making war on the king and harming his realm.

To this I respond that we find in written law that a madman during his fury cannot be considered an enemy, for he is totally lacking in free will, where reason can operate; wherefore, if he should kill a hundred men, he would not be punished by justice or considered homicidal. Further, such a man cannot pay or promise to pay a ransom. How can he then be

20. *Tree of Battles* IV, xci: "WHETHER A SOLDIER WHO GOES OUT OF HIS MIND SHOULD BE IMPRISONED."

a prisoner? To imprison an ill man whom all noble men should try as best they can to help, how would this be courageous? So I say to you that he could not and should not be imprisoned or pay a ransom, but should rather be returned to his friends. I say even more strongly that if while in prison he should be cured, he should not be retained or obliged to pay. The reason for this is that nobody, when taken into custody, should be taken prisoner if he does not give himself up by a word or a sign. But how could he do that? According to what the law says, such a man cannot make a will, marry, or enter a monastery, all of which require free will. He also could not be baptized, if he were unbaptized, for this is not given to a man if he does not freely request it. For this reason there is no proper reason to retain him.

What wonderful things you are telling me, Master! If I had my mortal enemy in my power, however that might have come about, then perhaps, if he departed from me, he would kill me or injure me seriously if he could. At least I know that he would do what he could with plenty of will. Would it then be good sense for me to let him go freely?

Fair friend, I respond that this man of whom we are speaking, supposing that he was your enemy as described, you would not release except to have money through his ransom. And when the money had been paid, which you received for no good reason, how would you be more sure of him than before? Certainly in no way. Military custom does not require that one party or the other should be put in the wrong; rather, all noble men should protect the rights of others so that they can expect and require others to do the same. So I tell you once more that the most one could do to such a man is to make him promise and swear never to take up arms against the king of France—and, in the case leading up to this one, that the man-at-arms or the city or country that held him should not be afraid of being reproached for letting him go. If he is such a powerful man that he could still injure the kingdom, the best thing one could do to escape responsibility would be to turn him over to the prince, who would follow the advice of his good counsel. You should of course understand that what I say of the Frenchman with respect to the Englishman, I also mean in the case of the Englishman and the Frenchman and in every other similar case.

## XXI.

HEREIN IS ASKED WHETHER, AS MAY HAPPEN, AT SOME
FRONTIER AN ELDERLY ENGLISH CITIZEN,
WHO NEVER HAD ANYTHING TO DO WITH THE WAR, SHOULD BE
SEIZED; WHETHER SUCH A PERSON SHOULD
HAVE TO PAY RANSOM; LIKEWISE A CHILD OR A BLIND PERSON.[21]

I inquire about another case. Let us suppose that a French knight is posted at the frontier of Calais or Bordeaux, and it happens that a very old citizen of the city of Bordeaux should by chance come to hear mass or for some other matter on French territory; the French knight immediately seizes him and tells him that he is his prisoner. But the captive replies that this is not proper, for in the king of England's wars he has never taken up arms against the king of France, nor has he put on a sword or offered advice or aid, but has rather always been regretful and annoyed about the war, which he had advised against as best he could. And he further replies that he can prove this. "And with this fact I say that an old man like me, who is not able to bear arms, should not properly be imprisoned. You should take neither the possessions nor the persons of those who do not take part in the war, except those who of their own free will give aid and favor in maintaining the war against your king; for if this were by force, they should still rightfully be excused. But in all this I have done nothing through force or through affection and I can undertake to prove all this." I ask you, Master, if according to military custom such a man should be imprisoned.

I say to you, as before, that truly he should not be imprisoned if the truth of what he says can be suitably proved. But if it turned out that he had given or was giving in any way advice that was useful for the war, as certain old men do because their advice is more useful than what other younger men do with their arms, I would say otherwise.

Then tell me, if a Frenchman had taken the child of an Englishman, could he rightfully ask ransom for him? It would seem so, as someone who can do the largest thing can do the least, and he could indeed imprison the father if necessary. Why should he not then do the same with the son? Likewise and more important, as he could indeed take the possessions of the father, should the son be included among them?

I tell you with certainty that the child cannot and should not rightfully

21. *Tree of Battles* IV, xciii: "WHETHER AN OLD MAN CAN LAWFULLY BE IMPRISONED OR PUT TO RANSOM"; xciv: "WHETHER A CHILD SHOULD BE MADE PRISONER AND PUT TO RANSOM"; xcv: "WHETHER A BLIND MAN CAN BE TAKEN PRISONER AND PUT TO RANSOM."

be imprisoned, for reason does not agree that innocence should be trifled with; for it is evident that the child is innocent and not guilty in anything connected with war. Nor has he helped with either advice or possessions, for he does not have any. Therefore he should not suffer the pain of something he is not guilty of.

True, Master, but suppose that the child in question were rich in his own right, left without father or mother, should he then pay? For perhaps his guardians would pay a subsidy from his possessions to help to maintain the war.

I still say no, for whatever his guardians might pay, it would not be at the wishes of the child, who has not reached the age of discretion.

Nevertheless, Master, that law is not well observed today.

I confess to you, fair friend, that no longer are the noble early rights preserved that the valiant warriors observed. Those who follow the military custom in the present time abuse it through the enormous greed that overcomes them. They should be ashamed to imprison women, children, helpless and old people. And what has been done by the English should be considered especially blameworthy, as carried on while fortune was favorable to them in the kingdom of France, where they didn't spare women or maidens, important, ordinary, or small, when they captured fortresses, but put to ransom all they found there, though it was a great shame for them to take those who could not avenge themselves. The capture of the fortress should have sufficed, and the ladies should have been allowed to go free. But what has happened to these warriors subsequently could and should be an example to other warriors to do otherwise, for thanks be to God they no longer have the power to imprison anyone. For rest assured that what has been wrongly acquired cannot be possessed a long time by those who have taken it or by their heirs.

Now let us consider another question: A blind man is captured by a man-at-arms. Should he be retained in prison?

I tell you that if a blind man has taken it into his head to want to be a man-at-arms and has done so, he deserves worse than another. I can prove this by Holy Scripture, where it tells how Cain killed Abel, his brother, and how a blind man named Lameth took a bow and arrow and went about woods and hedges shooting wild animals; so he struck by chance Cain and killed him. Then God said that Cain's crime should be punished seven times over, but the sin of Lameth should be punished seventy-six times. Thus it appears that taking on a task of which one is not capable is often folly. But if a simple blind person is captured, he deserves pity. If he formerly had his sight and had been a man-at-arms and in the war, so that he gave advice to the English about waging battles or mounting assaults or some other stratagem, he can rightfully be held for ransom.

## XXII.

HERE IS EXAMINED WHETHER HORSES AND CARTS HIRED IN
BORDEAUX FROM ENGLISHMEN, TO CARRY
THE LUGGAGE OF AMBASSADORS EN ROUTE TO THE KING OF
FRANCE, CAN LATER BE TAKEN AWAY FROM
THESE AMBASSADORS. LIKEWISE, WHETHER OR NOT AN ENGLISH
CHURCHMAN CAN BE PUT TO RANSOM IN FRANCE.[22]

Master, I should like to bring up another matter. Let us suppose that the king of Scotland sends his ambassadors to France. They land at Bordeaux or Bayonne, where they hire horses, mules, carts, and other necessary things and then go on to Paris. It happens that on the way they encounter a French captain or some other military man who is well aware that these horses, mules, and carts belong to the English and not to these ambassadors, so he arrests them and says that as these things belong to the enemies of the king, he can properly keep them through right of conquest. Now tell me, Master, if they should rightfully remain with him.

I tell you that by right of written law ambassadors or legates are privileged to go about safely with their belongings. As they are going to the king, it is not for any of his men to prevent them. What is more important is that the ambassador's privileges are so great that if he were under obligation to a French merchant, payment could not be collected for the duration of his assignment, for the law does not permit or compel the representative of a prince or someone from an important place to pay except for what he has taken en route. And even in the event that they were obliged to take horses and carts for themselves or to carry their luggage, as illness or other necessity might overtake them on the way, or perhaps to carry certain gifts for the king, they and their belongings should have

22. *Tree of Battles* IV, xcvi: "WHETHER THE LEGATES OR AMBASSADORS OF ANY KING COMING INTO FRANCE MAY BRING WITH THEM THROUGH THE KINGDOM THE KING'S ENEMIES"; xcvii: "WHETHER A BISHOP OF THE KINGDOM OF ENGLAND CAN LAWFULLY BE IMPRISONED BY A FRENCHMAN."

secure passage both coming and going. Of course it can be debated to some extent in cases where there is no true necessity, as when they might bring with them some Englishmen to provide them with entertainment, and when they might have with them jewelry, horses, or other things belonging to them. For on what authority could they bring into France enemies of the kingdom? This could be reasonably debated.

Further tell me, Master, whether a Frenchman has the right to imprison an English cleric, or an Englishman seize a French cleric, whether he be a priest, or abbot, or monk.

Fair friend, I have already given you many times conclusive answers to that question. We say in accordance with written law that the office of churchmen is separate from warfare, for the service of God, in which they are or should be engaged, makes it unsuitable for them to bear arms or any other harness for worldly battle. It is not for them, for their only office is the absolution of sins and bringing back to the right way those who have gone astray and administering the sacraments. Even to defend themselves they should use only gentleness and benignity. It would indeed be hard for them to do penance for something of which they are or ought to be guiltless. But if you say to me: True enough, but they assist the king of England, in the pursuit of his war, with their rents and revenues, or even with their advice—I reply that this they should not do, for they are not required to. It is not the duty of a churchman to give advice concerning war, but is rather his place to try to bring about peace among Christians. If it should come about that through violence the king seizes their belongings for use in his wars, I say that this cannot be done. Even so, they would not be obliged to pay ransom, nor should they be taken captive and held as enemies anywhere. But, on the other hand, if it should come about that any chaplain or anyone else connected with the Church should become involved, certainly such a man should not be spared if he were captured. He should be seized and treated with rigor, prelate or any other, in the matter of paying a ransom. I would say that such a man should be taken to the pope, who would punish him suitably. But otherwise, to imprison churchmen is quite improper and beyond all right.

## XXIII.

### WHETHER A PRISONER OF WAR WHO IS GUARDED CAN DEPART, ESCAPING PRISON, AND IF HE IS DOING WRONG IN THIS CASE.[23]

Now I will pose another question, which in the case of prisoners of war has a number of precedents. I am supposing that a knight has captured his enemy in battle and has put him in a castle or some other prison. My question is whether this prisoner, if he sees an opportunity, by some trick or by cleverness, to get away, can properly do so according to the law of war. I doubt this for several reasons, one of them that he has given his word, so he cannot leave without perjuring himself, which is something the law does not permit. Another reason is that it is not permitted that one do to another something he would not want to have done to himself, and he would not want his prisoner to do such a thing. So he breaks this law in doing this. Another reason is that he is like a servant and in the power of another until he is free of his ransom, so he does wrong, it would seem, in that he takes something that is not his own, which cannot properly be done.

Now, fair friend, I shall reply concerning another aspect of the matter, which is worth considering well, for it needs to be decided according to the circumstances. I tell you that he who has escaped has not done anything wrong, for he has acted according to the law of nature, which gives everyone the right to be free. Likewise, he gave his word under duress, and a forced promise does not have to be kept, according to law. Other reasons could be mentioned, but the most important, according to the right of arms, that is permitted by all law is of little importance. I tell you that when a man is captured and gives his word to remain in prison, needless to say he cannot break his word to God and the world by going off without his master's agreement. True, there are some reservations you should understand, which is to say that the master should not do him any harm in a proper prison, as is set forth by law, for I agree that if he were to be held so closely and so mistreated that his life and health were threatened, and all this were inhuman and cruel—or if the captor was unwilling to accept a reasonable ransom that had been offered several times—it would be sensible for him to find a way to escape, nor should it in any way be considered improper. Likewise, if the said captor were so cruel

---

23. *Tree of Battles* IV, lv: "IF ONE KNIGHT IS IN THE PRISON OF ANOTHER WHO KEEPS HIM SHUT UP IN A STRONG TOWER, MAY HE, WITHOUT ACTING AGAINST REASON, BREAK PRISON AND GO?"

that he had the habit of killing or torturing his prisoners or making them languish in prison, or subjecting them to other such hardships as are against gentlemanly custom, anyone held by such a man would not be obliged to keep his word to him if there were some way he could escape, for his given word assumes that the captor is lord of the prisoner through military custom, and that the captor should treat him humanely, as is his right, and not treat him like an animal, or worse than a Saracen or Jew, who should not be treated so badly that it gives them reason to despair. For this reason I say to you that the one who first breaks and oversteps the custom deserves to be treated likewise.

True, Master, but if it happens that a gentleman captures another in a proper war, and even though the prisoner swears to his captor to remain in prison, and the captor in question keeps him in a good tower or in a strong prison, I ask you if such a man, on seeing his opportunity, can without doing wrong depart, for some would think so, in view of the fact that the captor does not believe in the oath or in the good faith of the prisoner. And as he does not take it seriously, what promise can the other thus break? For if he does not believe in the first link, but supplies another stronger one from which he expects more, then the prisoner does not take it seriously.

I say yet again that the law is very clear in matters of arms. If the gentleman has sworn to remain in prison, and his captor gives him enough to eat and drink and adequate lodging, and is willing to discuss with him a reasonable ransom when the time comes, and assures him that from the prison he will not suffer death or damage to his body or his health, such a prisoner breaks his word and does wrong, against military custom and to his dishonor, if, despite being well guarded, he escapes. For if he is a gentleman, he should do what is expected of him, which is to say, keep his word to his captor, who could have killed him at the time he captured him if he had wanted to. Supposing that he is kept shut up, his captor does him no wrong, for he has promised to remain in prison loyally without breaking his word. Such a fugitive cannot claim that he did no wrong. For as he put himself in the danger of battle, he should know that prison is not a place of entertainment or of celebration. So he should, when he has been captured or fallen into peril, endure the punishment gently and patiently in the hope of once more achieving a better fortune.

## XXIV.

### HEREIN IS ASKED WHETHER A GENTLEMAN PRISONER OF WAR SHOULD PREFER TO DIE RATHER THAN BREAK HIS OATH AND PROMISE.[24]

I am supposing, Master, that a knight or a man-of-arms is imprisoned by another, either a lord or a town. He is held so rigorously that he is told that if within a certain time he has not paid his ransom, he will be put to death, whereupon he asks, for God's sake and in pity, that they let him go to his own country to arrange his finances, and says that without fail he will return on the day he promises. In short, they let him go on his oath made on the Holy Evangels of God, on which he swears that on pain of death he will not fail to return on the promised day. Then it turns out that it is impossible for him to arrange for his ransom. So the question is whether he should return to be put to death as promised, for it is even written in Roman histories that this is what the noble Roman conquerors formerly did, for they would rather expose themselves to death than break the oath of prison. If such as they, who were pagans and nonbelievers and who swore on their false gods that they yet wished to die rather than forswear their oath, it is believable that Christians swearing on God's holy faith would do better.

Fair friend, you speak truly, and there are even more reasons that might be adduced. But the truth of the matter is that many might excuse the man in such a case, although some doctors insist that a man should prefer to die rather then forswear God's name, which is true in certain cases. But as for an oath that is violent and made by force to save one's life, it is not certain that fidelity thereto is for the best, and I will explain why it should not be held to. I tell you, according to written law, an oath extracted against what is good and useful, and even against acceptable custom, is not proper to keep. Although it is wrong to perjure oneself, it is even worse to carry out such an oath, so the lesser of two evils should be chosen, as when a man has sworn on Holy Scriptures or on the sacred body of Christ that he will kill a man or do some other great wrong. There is no doubt that it would be worse to kill the man or set fire to a house or do some other great evil than to perjure himself, although he has committed a mortal sin as soon as he has so sworn. For things that are

---

24. *Tree of Battles* IV, lvi: "HIS MASTER KEEPS A MAN WHO HAS GIVEN HIS PAROLE SHUT UP IN A VERY STRONG PRISON. IF HE SUCCEEDS IN ESCAPING THENCE AND GOES OFF DOES HE COMMIT AN OFFENCE OR NOT?"

unreasonable to do should not be sworn to. For it is true, and nobody should think the contrary, that according to law no man is obliged to put his body in a position to be killed, or his limbs to be drawn and quartered, any more than he should do this to another. For if he were to kill himself, justice would punish his body shamefully on the gibbet. Likewise, if he cut one of his members, he would be punished by justice just as if he had done it to another. For this reason, I tell you once more that it is not in him or in his power to oblige himself in such a manner, nor should he bind himself by such an oath, for it is null and void. And I tell you further, it is in written law that if one man can protect another from death and does not do so, we say that he has killed him. Therefore he is not doing wrong if he keeps for himself the right that he is obliged to observe for another—which is to say, if he avoids his own death. This is to excuse the extremity of the affair and to beg mercy for what he cannot change about paying the ransom. But nevertheless I am not saying that he is not obliged to arrange matters as soon as he can and make every effort to keep to his obligation and pay his ransom. Likewise, all others are obliged in a similar situation, supposing that they have been imprisoned, to obtain their freedom, though they should not be excused from paying their ransom in cases where they have been properly captured, according to the proper law of arms.

# PART IV

HEREIN BEGINS THE FOURTH PART OF THIS BOOK, WHICH SPEAKS
OF THE LAWS OF ARMS WITH REFERENCE TO
SAFE-CONDUCTS, TREATIES, LETTERS OF MARQUE, AND THEN
OF PRIVATE COMBAT. IN THE FIRST CHAPTER
CHRISTINE PRESENTS THE CASE OF A NOBLEMAN WHO
SENDS TO ANOTHER WHO IS HIS ENEMY,
BE HE KNIGHT, BARON, OR ANYBODY ELSE, A SAFE-CONDUCT
IN WHICH THERE IS MENTION ONLY OF COMING
TO SEE HIM, AND ASKS THE MASTER IF THE NOBLEMAN
CAN RIGHTFULLY ARREST HIM BY DECEIT
AND CAPTURE HIM WHEN HE WANTS TO LEAVE.[1]

At the beginning of the fourth book, dear Master, I want to pass on to another aspect of war, although it is related to what has already been said.
This is to find out about a sort of assurance that is given to those going
and coming between conflicting parties, an assurance known as a safe-
conduct, concerning which I first want to question you. Let us suppose

---

1. *Tree of Battles* IV, lvii: "WHETHER A MAN WHO HAS A SAFE—CONDUCT FOR A JOURNEY MAY BE
MADE PRISONER ON THE JOURNEY."

that a baron is at war with a knight, and that friends on both sides are trying to bring about peace, whereby the baron sends a safe-conduct to the
knight to come to see him, and commands him surely to come with it.
The knight has confidence in it and comes, but when they have spoken
together and he wishes to leave, the baron has him arrested and insists
that he is his prisoner. For, he says, you are at war with me, as everyone
knows, so I can take you according to my advantage, as I find you. The
other replies that he cannot do this, for his own safe-conduct prevents it.
The baron then says that this has nothing to do with it, for the safe-
conduct in question speaks of coming safely, but says nothing of returning; therefore he does no wrong in detaining him. So I ask you if the
baron is within his rights? It would seem so, as it suffices between enemies to observe the letter of what is written. As the knight is so foolish as
to misunderstand, it is not without reason that he should pay for it, for it
is permissible in situations of war, as you yourself have said, for one to use
traps to deceive another; so let him beware.

I tell you, fair friend, that you are mistaken in this matter, for if it were
as you say, then too much trouble would result. For this reason there is a
law that expressly says that nobody should be misled by deceitful or crafty
words, for would you concur with a judgment in which a man was heard
to say: "I sold someone a hundred pounds worth of land, so I indeed delivered to him what I had sold him, for he had from me earth weighing a
hundred pounds"? Likewise in other cases, I tell you, such judgments
would be no more than jokes. Any deceiver who tried to get away with
them would be punished. In our case, to do away with any scruple, nobody should have confidence in such a letter unless it says specifically a
safe coming, a safe stay, and a safe return. As for the other circumstances
involved, the law does not intend that the ill will of a fraudulent deceiver
should take advantage of the naïveté of the man who puts faith in him.
So it should be understood: safe-conduct according to the intention of
the one who gives it means safe arrival, stay, and return, for otherwise it
would not be a safe-conduct, but hidden treachery, which would deserve
great blame; this is the truth. Nevertheless, perhaps in fact some without
rhyme or reason have made use of this or would use it willingly, which is
greatly to their discredit, but not everyone has the power to do all the evil
he would like to.

## II.

### AN INQUIRY WHETHER A KNIGHT OR ANOTHER GENTLEMAN WHO HAS A SAFE-CONDUCT FOR HIMSELF AND TEN PEOPLE COULD RIGHTFULLY TAKE WITH HIM A MAN OF HIGHER ESTATE INSTEAD OF ONE OF THE TEN INTO AN ENEMY LAND. AND WHETHER ONE CAPTAIN WHO COMMANDS A SMALL NUMBER OF MEN-AT-ARMS CAN GIVE A SAFE-CONDUCT TO SOMEONE OF HIGHER RANK THAN HE.[2]

As we have entered into the matter of safe-conducts, please answer another question for me. An English knight has a safe-conduct from the king of France for himself and ten others on horseback to enter France for some business matter. It happens that a great lord or baron of England asks him if he could be one of his ten companions, for he has a great desire to go to France to amuse himself, a request the knight agrees to, so the lord accompanies him. It comes about that when they are nearing Paris, and lodged at an inn, this baron is recognized by a knight from the French king's court. This latter, well accompanied, immediately comes to the baron and tells him to give himself up, for he is the knight's prisoner. To this the English knight escorting the baron replies that he cannot do this, for by virtue of his safe-conduct ten men can accompany him, and this is one of the ten, whom he can choose as he pleases. The French knight replies: "You are only a simple knight, so you cannot bring those greater than yourself on your safe-conduct; for if it were so, you could equally well have brought your king or one of his children. Such a thing is not reasonable, and even the one you are bringing would better bring you than you him, because he is considerably more important than you." The other says: "I am not bringing him on my safe-conduct, but on one from the king of France. So I insist that it be observed according to what it contains." If this question were up for judgment, I ask you, which would be right?

I tell you that it would be the Frenchman, for according to written law such a general safe-conduct should not include a greater person than oneself. For if a man gives to another the right to do certain things, that does not mean that he gives it in general, or that anyone should abuse it.

2. *Tree of Battles* IV, lviii: "WHETHER THE HOLDER OF A SAFE—CONDUCT MAY TAKE WITH HIM A MAN OF HIGHER ESTATE THAN HIMSELF"; lix: "IF A MAN IS TAKEN PRISONER WHILE UNDER THE SAFE-CONDUCT OF ANOTHER IS THE LATTER BOUND TO DELIVER HIM AT HIS OWN EXPENSE?"

Especially in the matter of arms, such a thing would never be permitted, for it might in the end harm the person who grants it.

Now I would ask you something else. I am supposing that an officer of the French army who has been sent by the king to the frontier insists that he has the authority to give safe-conducts throughout Guyenne. On this basis he commands the seneschal of Bordeaux to come to a certain place in French territory, for he would like very much to speak with him. For this purpose he sends him a safe-conduct, whereby the seneschal leaves with this security to come to the place agreed upon. It turns out that on the way the French capture and imprison him. I ask you if the captain is obligated to get him out at his own expense, for it would seem so, in view of the fact that the problem was brought about by his assurance.

I tell you quite the opposite. Do you know why? Because it is commonly said that a man would be considered a fool without cause if no harm should come from his folly. It is quite clear that the marshal should not have believed a captain if it was not certified that the French would observe his safe-conduct. If this was simple, a problem remains, for in this case it should have been known that a captain does not have the right to guarantee the security for more than his own people. Thus if this were not the case, what is the obligation of the captain? In addition, it is not proper for anyone to give someone above himself the right to go about the realm of his lord, not even if he is obligated to protect him. This is worth noting, for obligation beyond power is without value. Such things, as well as all others concerned with the rights of arms, should not be unknown to the marshal or the seneschal, for otherwise they are useless and not worthy of their offices. Thus I conclude for you that although the captain gives the safe-conduct in good faith, it is not worth anything; and he is not obliged to pay the ransom involved. Nevertheless, if he is a gentleman, he is obligated to use his authority to obtain the other's freedom from the king, as this misfortune has come about through his own fault.

### III.

CHRISTINE SAYS TO THE MASTER THAT SHE IS AMAZED, IN VIEW
OF THE LITTLE FAITH THAT EXISTS IN THE WORLD,
THAT ANYONE DARES TO HAVE CONFIDENCE IN SAFE-CONDUCTS.
THEN SHE ASKS WHETHER, IF SOME CHRISTIAN
KING OR PRINCE WERE TO GIVE A SAFE-CONDUCT TO A SARACEN,
OTHER CHRISTIANS BY WHOM HE MIGHT PASS
WOULD TRY TO TAKE HIM CAPTIVE.[3]

Master, it certainly seems to me a great wonder, in view of the slight loyalty that exists in the world today, how a prince, a nobleman, or some
other gentleman, or indeed any man, dares to have confidence in a safe-
conduct to go into a place where his enemies are more powerful and
stronger than he.

Friend, if you are astonished, it is not without cause. A safe-conduct,
according to the traditional institution of military law, or of any law,
should by its nature be a sure thing between parties, even mortal enemies, whom we call capital enemies in our laws. These letters of security
the good, valiant conquerors of the past would not have broken for their
lives; but at present, because of the schemes and devices thought up, by
which one is not ashamed to betray one's word or break an oath among
Christians any more than among Jews or infidels, it is recommended by
some of our masters that one should not lightly trust a safe-conduct, as
the time has come when fraud and ruse are called subtlety and cleverness; so there is great danger. For in fact a man of any estate or condition,
if he wishes to betray, if he has someone in a spot where he is at an advantage, will find a way to get the better of him, or a hundred ways to
have him killed if he wants to, or imprisoned as if it happened by chance,
or to stir up trouble for him; one might even set fire to a house or under
some other guise get the better of him. As it has already been done, there
is no right that comes in time or any that can restore him. Because of
these problems the law says quite rightly that whoever puts himself in his
enemy's power cannot take too many precautions for the security of his
person; for amends after the fact would certainly be useless.

Master, that is pure truth, but in this regard tell me about another

---

3. No reference for the first part. *Tree of Battles* IV, cvi: "WHETHER A CHRISTIAN KING CAN GIVE
SAFE-CONDUCT TO A SARACEN KING."

point of law. Let us suppose that a Christian king has given a safe-conduct to some Saracen. I ask you what sort of Christians should observe this safe-conduct of his, for in regard to what has already been said, it seems to me first of all that the people of the pope or the emperor would have nothing to do with it, as they serve a greater master than the king.

I know what you mean. In truth they are not obliged to observe it, nor are any other Christian kings, according to the intent of the laws, which say that a man cannot mandate or issue an order outside his own jurisdiction. So I tell you truly, because some might doubt that it would be observed even by his own subjects. The reason is that Saracens are generally enemies of all Christianity. This is the truth, and it is also in written law that no Christian should receive any enemy of God's faith. All men are supposed to obey God before their earthly prince, in witness to the law that says everybody is permitted to contradict his lord if it is a question of protecting, sustaining, or granting favors to the enemies of God's faith. So by what right is a subject of this king obliged to observe this safe-conduct? Furthermore, Saracens are not merely at war with one Christian, but with all. The law says that something that affects all must be approved by all, for otherwise it is worthless. But there is another matter to consider, which is that the safe-conduct has been given for a good reason, to discuss and arrange the ransom of some lord, knight, or any other who is a prisoner in their hands, or for any other just and reasonable matter. Do not doubt then that not only the subjects of this king but generally all Christians by whom he must pass should let him go securely for two principal reasons: One is so that among themselves they cannot say that there is so little faith and love among us Christians that we are unwilling to further deliverance to those who have fallen into Saracen hands through Christian faith. The other is that if the Saracens who came here were treated rudely by Christians, supposing they came on business, or an embassy, or for some other just reason, they in turn could take advantage of our Christians. For such a reason they often go among them. So their rights should be observed as we would wish ours to be. But if it should happen that a king or a city should be at war with another, and for vengeance or some other unworthy cause had some powerful Saracen come to his aid on his safe-conduct, in such a case no Christian subject or any other should allow it, nor for this reason should they be considered perjured or less than loyal to their lord, for likewise the law says that if a man is found carrying letters against the public welfare, even without a warrant one can seize and destroy them. Likewise, another law says that every man should cast out from around him all heretics and other such people outside the law.

## IV.

HERE BEGINS A DISCUSSION OF THE MATTER OF TREATIES.
IT ASKS IF EITHER OF TWO WHO ARE AT WAR CAN,
AS LONG AS TREATIES EXIST BETWEEN THEM, TAKE BY ANY
MEANS SOMETHING THAT BELONGS TO THE OTHER.
AND IF ONE OF THE PARTIES BREAKS THE TREATY,
IS THE OTHER OBLIGED TO OBSERVE IT.[4]

Master, it seems to me that another safeguard in war between enemies is called a treaty, which is a sort of peace made for a certain time; so I want to ask you a slight question. I have from time to time heard that certain countries, even England, have sometimes abused the French while there has been a treaty, indicating that there is no wrong if during the term of a treaty one seizes one's advantage by some device to take a castle, or a town, or some prisoner. I ask you if it is true that this can be done without committing any wrong.

To this I answer that in truth anyone who does this infringes on the true intent that treaties represent. So that you may know more about it, I will tell you what our master says on this matter. First of all, this is a royal assurance, which according to ancient law should not be broken under pain of death, as any proper law of king or prince should not be broken. Item, that it contains three principal parts, which is to say, that it protects property, possessions, and other people. Item, the same for men as for other things and, in the third place, that it encourages negotiation and the hope of peace. Thus, as in themselves treaties contain as much in general as in particular, by what right could one party take from the other a prisoner, or anything else? Without a doubt, friend, those who do so, or who claim such can be done without wrong, are evading the law. They are only finding various ways to practice deception. And what is worse, they want to cover falseness with right and legality, when it is clearly against them, for everything seized through confidence in truces should

---

4. *Tree of Battles* IV, ciii: "WHETHER A PLACE CAN BE TAKEN BY ESCALADE IN TIME OF TRUCE"; cvii: "WHETHER IF TWO KINGS HAVE MADE A TRUCE AND ONE OF THEM BREAKS IT THE OTHER OUGHT TO BREAK IT."

be returned and restored with all expenses paid. Do you know what a king or prince, according to law, should do to his own people who have done such harm as to make him out to be untruthful and not faithful to his promise and sworn word? In God's name, he should have their heads cut off. Thus the others would have their example, for this is the intent of the law, and from this he would be praised for being a very just prince, and would be the more respected for it. In this way he would give his enemies greater cause willingly to submit to him, namely those who break agreements, and he could get some of them into his hands; no ransom should spare them from such punishment as would be fitting.

I ask you, Master, if the kings of France and England have sworn to observe a treaty for a certain period, and the king of England in fact breaks it, is the king of France obliged to observe it? It would seem that he should, in view of the fact that if someone does wrong, another person is not obliged to do likewise, but rather every man should continue in fair dealing.

I tell you that as one of the kings, whichever one it may be, and any others in a similar case, has broken his word and has perjured himself, the other is not obliged to keep his word, and in this case he would not also perjure himself. For according to law, he is not obliged to keep his word, and according to written law he is absolved from his oath. What is more, he would commit a mortal sin if he allowed his country to be laid waste and his people to be killed without his defending them.

V.

HERE BEGINS A DISCUSSION OF A SORT OF WAR
KNOWN AS MARQUE (REPRISAL):
THE QUESTION IS IF THIS SORT OF WAR IS JUST.[5]

Master, as I am still enthralled by your wise and just decisions, I want to ask you certain questions and make requests concerning another sort of contention that in some circumstances leads to war, and I don't know if

---

5. *Tree of Battles* IV, lxxx: "WHAT THE KING OUGHT TO DO BEFORE HE GRANTS MARQUE AND AFTER WHAT FASHION IT OUGHT TO BE GRANTED" (letters of marque grant permission for reprisal). See *Tree of Battles*, lxxix, p. 173: "We must consider whether this kind of war is good, just, and due. And on this point you must know that, according to written law, this kind of war is by no means permitted, and the law does not allow its exercise: for on this theory one person suffers loss for another, and receives damage and molestation for the deed of another, which ought not to be, either according to reason or law."

that is right. But princes and lords, for a certain period of time (in ancient chronicles there is no mention of it), have taken to using what is called marque: marque occurs when a man from some kingdom, France or someplace else, who cannot have his due for some injury done him by a powerful foreigner, is given by the king a sort of permission to capture, arrest, and imprison this foreigner, by virtue of certain letters he has obtained, and also to seize the goods of all others coming from the country and place of residence of the one who has committed this wrong. This could be the case until justice and restitution have been made to the one who has filed the request. Thus I should like very much to know if such a thing is right. It is a great wonder that a man from the country of another who has caused the trouble, even though he does not know who this other is and is in no way to blame, should for such a reason, if he finds himself where an injured party exercises power, be imprisoned and have his goods forfeited and be obliged to pay and make restitution for something of which he is innocent.

Dear daughter, you must know that, speaking truly according to ancient written law, that sort of war called marque, by which one man is penalized for another without deserving it, is not just, nor does the law authorize it. This law states that if a merchant of Paris or any other place is obligated to a merchant of Florence, the latter should ask for justice from the former before his judge, and that if he does not receive satisfaction, he may make a claim before the king's justice, which is indeed his right. But it carries no reason or right to say that because a merchant of Paris is under obligation to him, he can imprison another merchant or another citizen of Paris or of any part of the kingdom, or take his goods and arrest him. But here is the possible right for the lords that are to be found in the case, and it is not without cause. Let us suppose that an Italian is obligated to a Frenchman for a large sum of money, and he would like to defraud the one who is his creditor. He goes to live in England, for he knows very well that the Frenchman will not pursue him there. Or in another possible case someone from Genoa might be under financial obligation to a Frenchman. He knows well that because of the ill will that now exists between the king of France and the rulers of Genoa his creditor will not go there to pursue his debt, so he will be of such bad conscience that he does not intend to pay up: what will the Frenchman do then? In God's name, he will turn to his king, as a subject should do with his lord, for help in recovering what is his due. Then the king, assured that the man is telling the truth, will give marque. He will likewise give it if it should happen that a knight, or some other gentleman, complains of having been robbed and insulted in some place where the king does not have suspicion of war, and it shall remain in effect until restitution and amends are made. So this device was invented by the advisors of princes to deal with such tricks. This marque indicates that every person who comes from the city or country or place of the perpetrator of the outrage but is found in the country of the prince who gives the marque should be captured and his goods be put into the hands of the law until the merchant in question is paid or otherwise given satisfaction or sufficient amends are made to the victim. Thus, when the merchants find themselves so badly treated in the foreign country where marque is given against them, they make so many representations to the justice of their own country that the individual or individuals who have brought the problem about are obliged to make restitution. For that reason it was invented and put into practice. So the common proverb serves very well when it says that by one disadvantage sometimes another disadvantage is done away with: for by repairing that grievance, it is possible to deal with all the tricks that are played or can be played on foreigners going on their way. Although this affair may have some appearance of law, I tell you that any king or prince of whom it is requested should not give it lightly, for it is a grievous and burdensome affair. It should rarely be considered for two practical reasons: one, that it is something that might weigh heavily on the conscience; the other, that it might mark the beginning of a war. For this reason, what should a king do when he is requested to give it against some city, country, or lordship? He should first of all question carefully, or have investigated by his representative or some other wise legist or judge, for what reason it is being requested, what is the cause. If the person in question says that when he was in the city of Asti, on his way from Milan, ten thousand francs were taken from him, or something more or less than that sum, and that he cannot have justice for it, but that rather those of the city uphold the theft even though the one who complains has done what their system of justice requires, then the king should write to them and ask them by his letters that they willingly make restitution to his subject for the outrage done him by one or more of their citizens. If it then turns out that nothing comes of this, or that they pay no attention to the king's letters, and in a council it is decided that they should give marque, then, following the custom of temporal lords, it can be given.

## VI.

### MORE ON THE SAME SUBJECT: WHETHER ALL LORDS CAN GIVE REPRISALS, WHETHER THE KING SHOULD DECREE THEM FOR A STRANGER WHO HAS DONE SOMETHING TO A CITIZEN OF HIS, AND WHETHER STUDENT SCHOLARS CAN FOR THAT REASON BE EXCLUDED.[6]

So, Master, if it should come about that the people of Florence, or some place else, should take the goods of a Parisian merchant, how would he effect reprisals against that city? According to the law he should go to demand justice of the sovereign judge of the place, who is the emperor. But if it happens that these subjects are Florentines, doubtless they would not do anything for him. If the merchant should go to plead to their top official, who that year might be a shoemaker or a tailor of that city, and if, according to their custom of being governed by the people, the official carried gold in his belt like a knight, although repairing shoes, I think little would be gained. I say nothing more against Florence than any city governed by common people. What will happen then?

Then, fair friend, just as I have said before, the king will send his letters there, and if they take no notice of them, he will simply decree reprisals against them, as they themselves say they have no sovereign but are themselves lords of Florence.

Master, I ask you if all lords can decree these reprisals.

I reply to you that they cannot, for as you yourself have already said, no lord can judge a war if he is not a sovereign in his own right. As this matter of ordering reprisals, according to its nature and condition, is similar to war, nobody can give them if he is not a sovereign lord, as is the king of France in his kingdom.

Then tell me this: let us suppose that a merchant who is a native of Milan has lived for a long time in Paris, has there his dwelling, his lands, and possessions, for which reason he would be considered a burgher according to custom. I ask you if the king would decree reprisals on behalf

---

6. *Tree of Battles* IV, lxxxi: "AFTER WHAT MANNER MARQUE SHALL BE GRANTED AGAINST A CITY WHICH RECOGNISES NO SOVEREIGN"; lxxxii: "WHETHER ALL KINDS OF LORDS CAN GRANT MARQUE"; lxxxv: "WHETHER THE KING SHOULD GRANT LETTERS OF MARQUE TO A CITIZEN OF MILAN POSSESSING A HOUSE AND EXCHANGE AT PARIS WHO ON HIS WAY TO PARIS HAS BEEN DEPRIVED OF HIS GOODS AND IMPRISONED"; xc: "WHETHER A STUDENT CAN BE IMPRISONED BY WAY OF MARQUE"; xcviii: "WHETHER CLERGY CAN BE IMPRISONED BY WAY OF MARQUE"; xcix: "THAT PILGRIMS CANNOT BE IMPRISONED BY WAY OF MARQUE."

of that man if the situation mentioned should come about, in view of the fact that he does not come from the French nation, but rather from the Empire.

I reply to you that according to law, one who is involved in an improper affair, as a participant, should enjoy the benefits of the protection; so that if the merchant is accustomed to paying taxes and assessments to the king for his merchandise and his property, and as he is a burgher, certainly the king is obligated to support him in all matters just as he would a citizen and a subject. And likewise I tell you that a knight or any other foreign gentleman living for a long time in France and serving the king in his wars receives a benefit from it.

I ask you if a cleric studying in Paris, because of reprisals ordered by the king, would be affected, including possessions.

I reply to you as before that he would not, nor even his father who might have come to see him, as I told you. Nor would it even be possible if the king happened to declare reprisals against some churchmen, as he has no power over them, for these prelates belong to the pope. There are also some others who should be obliged by their superiors to make amends, so the king could not rightfully remedy the situation, except by request. And I tell you also that all pilgrims, wherever they may come from, whether it be in time of war, truce, or reprisals, are under the protection of God and of the saint to whom they are going on pilgrimage, whereby they are privileged above all other people. As they are considered people of the Holy Church, anyone who harms them will be excommunicated by the holy father.

## VII.

### THIS CHAPTER BEGINS TO SPEAK OF JUDICIAL COMBAT. IT ASKS IF IT IS JUST AND RIGHT FOR A MAN TO PROVE BY HIS BODY AGAINST ANOTHER SOMETHING NOT KNOWN AND SECRET.[7]

After these matters, as I am unhappy about previous solutions, dear Master, I should like, in continuing the matter of war, to ask you another question. In my time I have seen it in France, and even before my time it was used in deeds of arms. This is a contest carried out between only two contenders, or sometimes several over a single quarrel, in restricted fields, a conflict that is called single or judicial combat, which one gentleman undertakes against another to prove with the strength of his body some hidden and concealed crime. I ask you if such encounters are just and permitted by law.

Daughter and dear friend, in this matter among others, as nobles who are not clerks may hear this book read to them in order to know what is proper to do, it pleases me to answer you in order that those who love chivalric practices may understand this matter, and so that you who, after me, will write of this matter can speak of it properly. I tell you that among all the other customs of arms, according to divine law, according to human law, according to civil law, and according to ecclesiastical and canon law, giving a wager for such an encounter or accepting it is condemned and disapproved. Among other things that forbid it, the one who gives it as well as the one who accepts it are excommunicated under canon law, and what is more, so are those who witness it. Now you can see what sort of matter it is! That this is true was well demonstrated by Pope Urban V. When a single combat was to take place at Villeneuve-les-Avignon, between two knights who had remained there to fight before

---

7. *Tree of Battles* IV, cxi: "THAT TO GIVE WAGER OF BATTLE IS A THING CONDEMNED"; cxii: "CONCERNING THE CASES IN WHICH IT IS PERMISSIBLE TO GIVE WAGER OF BATTLE."

See Maurice H. Keen, *The Laws of War in the Late Middle Ages* (London: Routledge & Kegan Paul, 1965), 41–42, where it is explained that a "case under the law of arms might . . . be decided by judicial duel. If he thought it to his advantage our knight could throw down his gage of battle and demand his right to prove his case on his opponent's body in the lists. This would be a risky and adventurous step on his part, and it was not one to be lightly resorted to. The Church frowned on duels and they were only permitted in certain circumstances. For a duel to be allowed it had to be shown that the honor of at least one party was at stake, that both parties were entitled by rank to fight one, and that there was not sufficient evidence to judge the case by ordinary process of law . . . Nevertheless duels were fought and frequently."

King John of France, our holy father the pope expressly ordered that as it
was something forbidden, nobody should go to see it, under pain of ex-
communication. If you or someone else should tell me that such a thing
is customary in arms, I should reply that God's law is greater and so
should be more obeyed than a custom of arms. There are many good reasons it is proper that nobody should be permitted to do this, and divine
law states them: this divine law is the law of the Holy Scripture, which we
must obey under pain of mortal sin; it forbids anything by which one
may wish to tempt God. For as judicial combat seeks to discover if God
will help the right cause, so it is like tempting God's will. Or so it seems,
for we say that asking for something against nature, or above nature, is
presumptuous, and so it is displeasing to God to believe that the weak
will vanquish the strong, the old the young, or the ill the healthy on the
strength of having the right, as some have had and have confidence that
they are undertaking such a thing because it is their right; such an act is
tempting God. I tell you that if it happens that they win, it is by chance
and not because they have any right to it. That this is true I shall demonstrate by reason. Has not our Lord allowed many brave men to be wrongfully killed without reason, men whose souls are in glory in paradise,
although He performed no miracle for them? Do they think God would
do more for one poor sinner than He did for these others? So it is true, as
it has often been seen, that the one who was right has lost. A decretal recalls such an instance, how once in the city of Poulent two brothers were
accused of robbery, whereby according to the custom of the city they
were obliged to defend themselves in combat and lost. But soon afterward the one who had committed the robbery was discovered in the city,
so it was definitely known that the two brothers, now dead, were not
guilty. As this has been known to happen on many other occasions, and
because it is not a reasonable thing to do, canon law has disapproved of
such a kind of combat. Also, as the law says, if one wished to prove one's
just cause in such a manner, judges who have been established to administer justice would be useless. It is also poor logic to say: "If I can't prove
what I say, I will fight and prove it with my body, for nobody but God and
I, and the one I challenge, know it." And if anyone were to say to me:
"True, but the evils that are committed secretly cannot be justly punished, because they are not proved," I say to you that truly they are, but
the one who tries to punish a secret fault is trying to usurp the divine
power and wisdom of God, to whom alone belongs the right to punish.
This is confirmed by a decretal that says that if all sins were punished in

this world, God's judgments would not take place. Another reason that condemns this matter is that the law orders judges and judgments to establish right and to plead causes, and that nobody's testimony is believed in his own cause; so the man who tries to prove this with his body is trying to corrupt the law.

Likewise, this is even more reproved by canon law, for that expressly commands that one must obey the pope and his commands, and he has expressly ordered that one should never fight in that way.

So, fair friend, you can indeed know that such combat is forbidden, for which reason, God be thanked, the king of France and his good council took notice of this four years ago, whereby it can no longer be used in his kingdom. May the good Lord give joy, peace, honor, and paradise to those who by virtue of good judgment took up and saw to it that this should be accomplished in his very Christian kingdom of France. All other foolish feats of arms undertaken through youth and for no reason except for the sort of vanity of conquering each other (something displeasing to God) have been set aside. And as this kingdom, the greatest of all Christian kingdoms, has achieved this, may other countries, God willing, follow this example and likewise not allow their noblemen to disobey the Church by endangering their bodies with dishonorable death for no reason, and their souls with eternal damnation. O Lord! what a foolish habit.[8]

### VIII.
### IN WHAT CASES IMPERIAL LAW PRESCRIBES SINGLE COMBAT.[9]

As the restrictions of written law mentioned have not always been observed, and with regard to single combat still are not in all kingdoms, I will speak of the cases of those who have permitted it. That is to say, the emperor Frederick, who was so much opposed to the Holy Church that he drove the pope from his residence, so that the pope took refuge with the king of France. Likewise, another document called Lombard Law speaks of various cases, which will be described later. In the first place, the law of this emperor says that if a man is accused of treason, either car-

8. See also a "Lettre patente du 27 janvier 1406," by which the king had forbidden duels or armed contests in his kingdom, in the *Ordennances des rois de France de la troisième race*, ed. D. F. Secousse et al. (Paris, 1723–1849), IX:105; also S. Solente in "Christine de Pisan," in *Histoire littéraire de la France* (Paris, 1969), XL:64.

9. There is no source for this chapter in the *Tree of Battles*.

ried out or attempted, against his prince or his city, or harmful to public welfare, whatever the case of which the truth cannot be proved, an offer by the person accused to defend himself against his accuser in single combat should be accepted.

Likewise, it is said that if a prisoner of war is held in prison by his adversaries, and during this time peace is made between the two sides, if the guard should kill the prisoner, for which lapse of justice he should lose his head, if he insists that he killed the said prisoner in self-defense, and that he at first treacherously or otherwise had been attacked when only the two of them were present, and that he would like to prove this with his body in single combat, if nobody disputes him, he should be granted permission to do so.

Likewise, in a similar case, let us suppose that the king of France and the king of England have established a truce between them, and that a Frenchman then wounds an Englishman, or vice versa, in which case the law says that by law and justice a greater punishment is due the aggressor than if he had wounded someone else. If the one who has done this wishes to prove by his body that the act has been done in self-defense against the other, who had attacked him first, according to that law he should be heard.

Likewise, if one man accuses another of having wished to kill the king or prince by poisoning or otherwise, and the other man says that it is not true and challenges his accuser, he is obliged to answer him and set a date for an encounter.

IX.

HEREIN IS EXPLAINED IN WHAT CASES LOMBARD LAW
DECREES TRIAL BY COMBAT.[10]

There are other laws called Lombard Laws, in which many different things are especially set forth by masters who established them and who have written concerning certain cases where wager of battle and trial by combat can occur. From these laws have come and arisen all the opinions about giving wagers of battle; so I will recount for you some of these

10. *Tree of Battles* IV, cxii: "CONCERNING THE CASES IN WHICH IT IS PERMISSIBLE TO GIVE WAGER OF BATTLE." With regard to Lombard Law, N.A.R. Wright points out in "The *Tree of Battles* of Honoré Bouvet and the Laws of War," in *War, Literature, and Politics in the Late Middle Ages*, ed. C. T. Allmand (Liverpool: Liverpool University Press, 1976), 26: "The regulation for the conduct of trial by combat that derived from Lombard laws had little relevance to French customs. These had rather been regulated by an *Ordonnace* of Philip IV in 1306."

cases. If a husband accuses his wife of having tried to kill him, either with poison or secretly by another method, of which there exists some suspicion, though the truth cannot be known, or the husband is dead and his relatives accuse the wife of having killed him, Lombard Law insists that the wife in question, if she considers this false, should be heard.

Item, if a man is accused of killing another without there being any proof against him, the law insists that if he makes a wager against the one who accuses him, it must be accepted.

Item, likewise if he has gotten the better of a man in an agreement.

Item, if one man has killed another when they were alone, and wishes to prove by combat that he was defending himself and that it was the other who attacked him, he should be heard.

Item, if a man, after the death of a relative whose inheritance he should have, is accused of having killed him in order to have that inheritance, he can defend himself by combat.

Item, if a man is accused of improper relations with a married woman, in such a case the law says, if the husband or the relatives complain to justice, the man can defend himself by combat.

Item, likewise in the case of a marriageable daughter under her parents' supervision, if they complain of some man who has enjoyed her favors, even if she has given them willingly, the law intends that he should die if he does not defend himself by combat. In case this is so secret that nothing can be proved against him, or if it is evident, there is no avoiding combat if the relatives wish it. As it seems very strange in France and elsewhere that a man should by law die in such a situation, when the woman was consenting, whether she was married or unmarried, it is established for this reason. As is true, it says, that a man is condemned to death for having committed a very small robbery of gold, silver, jewels, or some such thing, in which case he cannot be excused for any need that might have inspired it, so that justice should not spare him unless he is given mercy through pity, why then should someone be spared who has ruined the honor not only of a woman but of a whole family? As the people who established these laws prized honor more than gold or silver, they decided that one deserved death more for having dishonored another, or a whole family, than for having stolen some other possession. For this reason some say that, even so, the law is very generous in that such people are not more severely punished than others, which is to say that they should be made to die a more cruel death than others.

Item, in another case that seems rather unreasonable, the law says that if a man had owned and possessed a heritage in land or a house, even furnished, for a period of thirty years or more, and another should accuse him of having falsely inherited and possessed it, the offer of such a one to prove this by his body in trial by combat should be accepted. Nevertheless, in spite of that law, I tell you that anyone is very foolish to accept such a wager. For the one accused, who is already in possession of the property, could reply to the other: "Good friend, I want nothing to do with your wager. Fight by yourself if you want to, for I won't fight over this matter." There is no law that can oblige him, for the right of possession is maintained by all laws.

Item, if two men should have a quarrel and complain against each other before the law, and both should produce witnesses to support them, either one, if he wishes to contradict the witnesses of the other, proving by combat his own cause, should be granted permission.

Item, if a man demands from another a certain sum of money, or a jewel, or some other possession, that he claims to have lent to his father or mother, and the other denies that it was ever received, a wager of combat may prove his intention.

Item, if a man who has suffered damage from a fire in his dwelling, or barn, or some other thing, wishes to prove by a wager his case against some other man whom he accuses of setting the fire, he should be heard.

Item, if a man complains of his wife that she is not virtuous, supposing that he does it as a ruse to shut her up, get rid of her, or deprive her of her dowry, she can defend herself against him by finding a champion in a wager, and if he refuses, he will never be believed.

Item, if some man loiters about the house of a married man, and the husband insists that the other has been there because of designs on his wife, the other can defend himself by a wager. This folly makes me laugh, thinking that if the one accused is tall and strong, he would do well, if he considers himself innocent, to beat up thoroughly in combat the wicked, jealous husband.

Item, if one man accuses another of having perjured himself, the one accused can take exception.

That the law covers other cases of wagers of combat, I leave aside for brevity as not needing to be mentioned here. It is to be understood that these combats are sometimes fought by the principals involved and sometimes by others when the principals are prevented by a reasonable cause, as would be the case if a man too young should he be accused, or a man too old, or a man who suffered from some affliction or was too weak, and sometimes a woman. All such people are expressly mentioned in the aforesaid Lombard Laws. Even if a serf insisted that his lord had freed him from servitude and he wished to prove it by his body, his master would not be obliged to take part, but should provide a champion.

There is further mention of two clerics of equal standing who are given permission to fight each other. In this matter, I say that it is wrong to allow an ecclesiastical person, saving his grace, to become involved in such an affair, for the canon law they are supposed to obey expressly forbids them all conflict and violent injuries.

And I ask you if, as has been mentioned, a helpless man could put in his place whatever champion would please him.

I reply to you that the champions appointed for others represent them as procurers and advocates of appeal, an office anyone can fulfill for another if he wishes, if authority does not expressly forbid it. So it is with champions, for whoever wants can serve as one if not forbidden by certain circumstances, for a thief or someone who has previously committed a serious crime would not be accepted, nor any man of ill repute. The reason for this is good, for if such a person entered into combat for another and was overcome there, it would be supposed that this was for his own sins, and that for such reason he had lost the conflict.

X.

AS TRIAL BY JUDICIAL COMBAT SHOWS AND REPRESENTS
A CERTAIN FACT AND PROCESS OF APPEAL,
IS IT PROPER FOR THE CONTESTANTS TO TAKE AN OATH
ON ENTERING THE FIELD?[11]

Although a wager of battle, as I have said, is disapproved of by our doctors, nevertheless it is in use in the affairs of noblemen and the pursuit of arms and of chivalry. Thus combats have been judged by kings, princes, and lords according to their right, so the custom has not disappeared everywhere. So it is still useful to speak of it for the instruction of those who may be judges, and likewise those who may undertake these contests, for I insist that only a small part of the nobility, even though many speak of it, really knows what is involved in judging, undertaking, and carrying out such combat. Hence I will tell you.

First of all, you should know, for it is most evident, that these single combats represent in symbol the nature of a judgment, for in a trial there is a judge and one who enters a plea and also a respondent and the wit-

11. *Tree of Battles* IV, cxiv: "WHETHER THE COMBATANTS IN THE LISTS SHOULD TAKE AN OATH AND AS TO THE FORM OF THAT OATH."

nesses, and then the sentence is given. Likewise, in single combat there is the judge, the lord before whom the action takes place, the one who makes the plea and the defendant as two opposing parties, the witnesses, then the blows they exchange and the arms by which each one tries to prove his intention. Afterward comes the victory, achieved by one of the two, representing the definite sentence.

Master, I beg you not to be annoyed if I interrupt you briefly to ask you something, for I have heard it said that around the field the contenders take an oath, etc. Is it a proper thing for them to take an oath? It would seem not, for if it is never necessary to take any oath for a general battle in which two kings and their men take part, why then would it be for two people?

Friend, I answer you that to take an oath is the right of such a battle, and the reason that you give, that it is not done in large battles, in not a good one. Do you know the reason? Because such large general battles are decided on by the deliberation of a great council and carried out by the lords, so an oath is not suitable. But in an individual combat the prince cannot know the truth of the quarrel, and so he wishes to have the oath of those who bear witness with their bodies. Thus Lombard Law calls it the oath of the head, and it is an oath, as you know, that can be in the nature of a false charge that might be given at the beginning of any suit, when the accuser swears that he is making a just demand, and after this the defendant swears that he has a just defense. So it is done in judicial combat. But so that you may understand, there is a subtle way of taking this oath: the accuser swears absolutely against the other concerning something that really is not certain, as if I were to swear on the Holy Bible that you had murdered or had had my father or my brother murdered, though nevertheless it was in no way certain. He has not witnessed it, but has perhaps heard it said or for some reason suspects it. That oath is foolishly taken, for nobody should swear to anything absolutely if he has not seen it or personally known it for certain. For this reason his quarrel can be unfortunate, for he perjures himself if it is not as he says. But for the defense it is another matter, for he cannot fail to know if he is guilty of the deed or not. For this reason his quarrel is better if he knows that he is innocent. But if he knows that he has perjured himself, his cause is worse than that of the one who thinks he is speaking the truth. Thus, in order to be more certain of having a just cause, the accuser should merely swear that he firmly believes that the other has killed his father, or has done him the injury of which he is accusing him. In this way his cause will be better. So he should state before the prince the cause that has moved him, the way it came about, and his position. The prince should then decide from the circumstances if this can be true, for if the crime in question was committed on the previous day near the Bois de Vincennes and the one accused could prove that on that day he had been nowhere near there, the affair would be impossible. So the prince should decide whether the quarrel is suitable before he accepts it, not hearing contenders with frivolous, foolish contentions or opinions and beliefs. For there are so many lacking in good sense that they would like to involve themselves in such affairs for no reason, or very little, but it would seem to them well done because they have little consideration other than pity for themselves. But for their part there is pity that convinces them that they should defend themselves; otherwise the custom of arms would blame or dishonor them in the opinion of the young and foolish.

I ask you, if it should come about that the accuser and the accused wished to fight in private combat, or without the presence of the prince, would the prince permit this?

I would say no, for it is a case he is supposed to know about and judge, where their wish cannot be considered wise, for it is necessary that the lord in question, or the one commissioned to represent him, and also those who guard him, should be present, and each one of them be safe from all the others. No man in the world should speak under pain of being severely punished if it is not by order of the lord, who should be final judge of which one of the combatants is vanquished and which the winner.

## XI.

IF IT SHOULD HAPPEN THAT ONE OF THE COMBATANTS,
WHILE FIGHTING, LOSES ONE OF HIS WEAPONS,
HIS SWORD OR SOMETHING ELSE, BY RIGHT SHOULD IT BE
RESTORED TO HIM? WHICH OF THE TWO SHOULD
FIRST ATTACK THE OTHER? LIKEWISE, IF THE KING SHOULD
PARDON THE LOSER, CAN THE OTHER DEMAND
RECOMPENSE FOR HIS EXPENSES, AND IF IT IS FOUND THAT A
MAN IS WRONGFULLY ACCUSED AND
CHALLENGED TO COMBAT, WHAT SHOULD BE DONE TO THE
ONE WHO ACCUSED HIM?[12]

I ask, Master, if it happens between two combatants in the lists that one breaks the other's sword, or throws it out of the enclosure, as they must oppose each other as strongly as they can, and the other has no ax, dagger, hammer, or any other weapon to defend himself, can he reasonably be given a new means of defense? For, as you have said, the offensive and the defensive arms are like the two sides of testimony in a trial, so it would seem that arms should be returned or restored if needed. For if certain witnesses I have produced in order to prove my case should fail me because of death or some other reason, I could produce others to support my cause. Therefore why, if that combatant has not been able to prove his case by that sword, or some other weapon of his, should he not have another?

Fair friend, to tell the truth, it is reasonable that there might be need for particular consideration and for the judge to decide such a matter, for it is one thing if the sword has been dropped by chance, and another if it has been taken by his adversary. If the sword broke by chance through the blows he himself was giving with it and in no way through the efforts of his adversary, and should he have no other weapon to defend himself, thereby losing everything, some masters say that without fail he would be wronged if he were not given another weapon. But it would be unlikely that a man would enter combat without being provided with more than

---

12. *Tree of Battles* IV, cxvii: "WHETHER THE CHAMPION WHO BREAKS HIS SWORD IN SINGLE COM-
BAT SHOULD RECEIVE ANOTHER"; cxviii: "IF NEITHER OF THE CHAMPIONS IS CONQUERED IN THE LISTS
ON THE FIRST DAY MUST THEY CONTINUE ON THE MORROW?" cxix: "WHICH OF THE TWO CHAMPIONS
MUST STRIKE FIRST?" cxx: "IF THE KING PARDON ONE OF THE COMBATANTS BEFORE HE IS VANQUISHED
IN THE FIELD IS THE LATTER OBLIGED TO PAY COSTS?" cxxi: "AS TO THE PUNISHMENT OF THE MAN WHO
CONFESSES HIS OFFENCE IN TRIAL BY BATTLE."

one weapon, or that he would lose them all. Thus he can make use of another when one fails him.

Now, Sire, if it should come about that on the first day the judge cannot decide which one is defeated, are they obliged to return the next day?

I say that this is certainly so, if it is in their power, as they have undertaken to fight to the death, unless another condition has been agreed upon. Thus they cannot be absolved or freed until one is vanquished. There is of course the restriction that the prince may command otherwise, or they themselves may come to an agreement by order of the prince. Otherwise it is impossible once they have entered the lists. But the prince should always be merciful and show concern for these two men who are in peril of soul, body, and honor.

Tell me further, Master, and explain to me which of the two should strike first when they are in the lists. For I have not forgotten what you have told me about this combat's being partially in the nature of a trial by law, where it would be evident that the accuser should strike first. For through what I know of trials (as I have experienced them and paid for it), the one who initiates makes his demand, and then the accused replies. Therefore, in this case, if the one who is accused should strike first, would he not become the accuser and not the defendant?

Friend, however reasonable these points are, nevertheless in this case it is necessary to follow another direction not covered by the legal procedure carried out by words. Here the fact is that a man in mortal danger should not wait for the first blow, for it could be so great and heavy that it would then be too late for him to defend himself. Has this not been started when a wager was first given to call the other to combat? And if in a trial the initiator gives his demand first, it is only by word, involving much discussion or a little in writing. So it is not such a perilous demand for justice as would be a blow from an ax or lance. As the contenders are in an enclosed space and there is the cry "Do your duty," does not each know what he has to do? Because of this I say to you that according to all reason in such a case, whether by bargain, trap, trick, force, expertise, or anything else, as they are there, the one accused can strike first, if he has the chance and the skill, and in any case take advantage of the situation as best he is able. But the truth is that he must first wait for the other to leave his place, take a step or two, or appear to come toward him.

Item, one more question. I assume that the king, who sees two contenders fight in this fashion, takes pity on the one he observes to be on the point of defeat, so he has his constable cry: "Stop!" When the better fighter asks the king to do him justice and give him his due, the king replies: "I award you the honor of the combat, but I pardon the other because it pleases me to do so." This first person asks to be reimbursed for his expenses. Should this be done? It would seem not, because the king has not condemned him, nor has he confessed to the cause of the conflict.

I tell you that if the first were entirely victorious, the other, even though the king pardoned him, as is in his power, could not blame the one who rightfully made the demand. But if "Stop" was said before he was either attacked or overcome, he is not guilty, for although he has had the worst of the contest, he has not confessed the deed that would give the rightful victory to the other. That is to say that the other could have made him confess and have had some hope of striking a blow that would kill him, as has sometimes been seen when the underdog has struck with a dagger or sword the one who expected to kill him. In the matter of combat, however it may appear, it cannot be judged until the end.

Good, kind Master, if on certain occasions it was learned that someone had wrongfully accused another, of murder or some other criminal case, what should be done to the accuser?

Without fail, our masters would then decide what to do, or they should decree a penalty equal to the one that would have been given to the other if he had been proved guilty.

XII.

THE QUESTION WHETHER A MAN PUNISHED BY JUDICIAL<br>COMBAT FOR ANY MISDEED CAN BE<br>ACCUSED BY THE LAW FOR THAT SAME REASON.[13]

Once more I ask you: A man calls another to trial by combat to prove with his body that the other has perjured himself, and it turns out that he proves it, and then they punish the other according to the case. But after this it turns out that the second man is involved with the law for the same reason. Should this man be judged more than once for the same cause?

---

13. *Tree of Battles* IV, cxxii: "CAN THE MAN WHO HAS BEEN VANQUISHED IN THE TRIAL BY BATTLE BE AFTERWARDS ACCUSED AT LAW?" cxxiii: "IS THE KNIGHT WHO APPEALS ANOTHER ALLOWED TO REPENT AND WITHDRAW FROM THE COMBAT?"

It does not seem to me that it is just or that God would wish it, or that Holy Scripture permits one to be condemned twice for one sin.

Fair friend, I will reply to you in this way: although the accusations you mention were good enough and there were even enough others for the man accused, we are now in a court of written law, by which law cases requiring punishment should be known and judged; but as a wager to combat is not approved by any written law, it is not sufficient for such cases. Supposing that in such a way he has been corrected, it is still not punishment, for justice has not examined it, and in the view of the law it represents no more justice than if a father had punished his child for some misdemeanor he has committed. That would not be sufficient to prevent justice from punishing him. So I will explain to you the truth of these two problems. You may indeed know that if the combat between the accuser and the accused had been so long delayed that the affair had come to the attention of the law, I tell you that, in spite of the undertaking of this combat, justice could punish if the matter were proved. But if you ask me if, after the punishment had taken place, he could still have the combat, I would say not, for by what law can there be defense for what has already been convicted? But if the prince, or the one appointed to supervise the combat, had already punished the delinquent, or if he had adjourned the combat or pardoned the misdeed, by oath or otherwise, that should suffice, for without fail the authority of princes is so great that if they have given their approval to the customary judicial combat and punished those arraigned in that way, it should be sufficient for them to be punished only one time, for princes or lords would not permit their sentences to be revoked.

Master, if it does not annoy you that I pursue this matter so far, tell me a little more about this situation. A knight accuses another, challenging him to combat, and then repents. Can he do away with the challenge as he pleases and expect nothing more to be said of it? It would seem that he could truly give it up, as if one man accuses another, or speaks ill of him because of heat or anger, he might indeed repent of it, if he wishes, and give it up, as it does not seem sensible to cause more pain than he should if he proceeded and was obliged to prove what he had said against the other. Why should it not be so in such a case?

To this I reply that if a gentleman calls another in a wager, in the absence of his lord, or a constable or marshal or some other judge, and he afterward repents because he may have been badly informed, or angry or somewhat depressed, perhaps by wine, this affair can easily be put aside in a manner satisfactory to the other, without pursuing the matter. Furthermore nobody should be too acrimonious about this, as it is a very dangerous thing, whatever may be one's right, in view of the fact that the other experiences considerable shame, to repent and lose interest in the encounter, because through this foolish move he has certainly shown that he was not very wise. It is a great shame and also a sign of poor judgment to make such claims that later one has to renounce. Nevertheless, it is indeed better to repent of a folly before one acts on it by entering into combat over a mistaken quarrel, nor is it wrong to repent of such a mistake. It is, rather, sinful and foolish to undertake it and carry it out. But in the case where the words have gone so far as the prince or his constable or marshal or someone suitable to receive them, he has made his wager, and he cannot withdraw it without the consent of the prince and the agreement of his opponent, who could then reasonably ask for recompense. For with reference to what I have already said, the judicial combat represents an appeal; this wager is a sort of demand for justice, after which the one who makes it is obliged to follow with the appeal, if the two sides cannot come to an agreement. But it is indeed true that the prince should be generous in pardoning those accusers who repent and wish to withdraw, for God and the Scriptures wish it to be so.

## XIII.

### THINGS A KING OR PRINCE SHOULD CONSIDER BEFORE HE JUDGES A JUDICIAL DUEL, AND HOW THOSE WHO ARE TO ENGAGE IN SUCH COMBAT SHOULD BE ADVISED.[14]

Judicial combats, of which you have spoken to me, kind Master, are now in use in many countries and have been for such a long time that all have put up with them through long habit, in spite of the restrictions of decretals and canon law, and they have become like law. But it seems to me that it is important for princes to judge them and decide on the circumstances required for such combats. There is no doubt that the lords want and intend that everyone should have his rights, and for that reason they permit such combats to take place, so that obscure and hidden cases can be resolved.

Dear friend, what you say is certainly true. This is in agreement with

---

14. *Tree of Battles* IV, cxxx: "CERTAIN DOCTRINES OF THE NATURE AND CONDITION OF BATTLE IN THE LISTS AND TRIAL BY BATTLE." (six rules).

what you say about the judging of such combat being very dangerous and subtle, so it pleases me for the indoctrination and instruction of noblemen (for which purpose you are writing this book) to mention here and explain some rules that should be observed in this manner. The first rule is this, that no worldly prince, no matter how prudent and wise he may be, whatever good counsel of wise knights and other secular persons he may have, should judge a judicial combat without regard for wise legists, for in all cases that might arise, their opinions would be better than any others, for this is what their study of law teaches them. So it is for them to say whether a case is good or bad to carry out, if it is to be disapproved and condemned or approved and permitted, or if one case is privileged over another. It is true that such people, as experts, know how to determine better than others what civil law permits; for these advocates are protectors and directors of human lineage. There is still another reason why it belongs to them to determine these matters before others, which is that knights and other secular gentlemen are more easily moved to judge by arms than clerks are. This comes from an agreement they have among themselves that a man is dishonored if he does not immediately accept the wager of the one who makes it, an opinion without regard for reason. As for this, saving their grace, the one who makes or accepts a wager of little merit, or for a foolish or stupid reason, should be less honored than one who refuses it, for certainly it is not dishonor, but rather the contrary, to refuse a foolish undertaking, especially when one considers what precious possessions are body and soul. The one accused could say: "My friend, if you wish combat, fight by yourself, for as for me, I don't want any part of your folly."

The second rule the prince should observe is that should a gentleman accept the challenge of another, even if he might by chance be against him maliciously, or from temper, or some favor, or having a vain, exaggerated idea of wanting to overcome the other, thinking he is worth more, or for some other unreasonable motive, the prince or his lieutenant in such cases would be well advised to hear and consider carefully the way the appellant speaks and note it well, for there are some who try to color the truth by loose talk and are so foolish they think they could deceive God; but all this falls on their heads. Along with this, the prince should consider well the cause that moves him, and for what he is trying to blame the other: if it is as he says, if it is because of some debt, the prince or his representative should inquire why recompense for this debt is due him, in what country, in what place it was incurred, if he has a letter or some other evidence, or if it was concluded so secretly that nobody knows anything about it, if there is no description nor any seal. If it turns out that there is little evidence or proof, or any details by which a judgment of right would be possible, he should not accept the case, for nobody could rightfully claim that such a combat should take place.

Item, the third rule is that the prince should make the accuser set forth the cause of his complaint against the other, and that the accused should also be heard, with his advisor present from the best legists. The complaint should be examined and analyzed whether the accuser has just cause or not. After that, if it is found that the motive is inspired by pride, presumption, or foolishness, as if to say: "I want to prove by my body against his, in combat to the death, my superiority in order to gain honor, or for the love of my lady, or to prove that she is more beautiful than his lady," or such nonsense as this, the matter should immediately be thrown out and not heard, and there should be no more said about it. And I say further that for certain words, however harmful they may be, if they have been spoken in anger or heat, through suspicion or depression, so that the one against whom they have been said wishes to fight, there should be no judicial combat unless the one who has spoken them wishes to maintain that it was the other who said them to him. In a case where this should come about, an effort should be made to calm both of them without their coming to blows, which should never be undertaken, permitted, or judged if there is not a very serious reason, but rather they should be forbidden and turned aside insofar as possible. But if it turns out that the case is serious and weighty, involving such as treason, murder, violence, arson, or some other such matter that the accuser cannot prove or demonstrate except by his body, and the defendant cannot sufficiently show that there is no guilt, that he has not done any such thing, or that it was not as the other has said, then, with the attention and consent of the whole council, the prince should judge the combat as the law of the case requires. That is, as soon as it is judged, although both are so proud that they, having confidence in the strength of their bodies, pay no attention to God or His help, then some wise gentleman should be appointed to call their attention to the great peril in which they have placed their bodies and souls and to advise them to put themselves in a good state with wise confessors. They should thus call God to their cause, for they will have need of Him, and so they should be advised, each one by himself, wisely and well, being told that this is a serious matter in which they would be obliged to die or be dishonored. They should take note that they should not repent too late, and should also be loyally advised not to leave to the last the matter in which they need to be well counseled, even in the maneuvers in arms that are useful in such cases, in both assault and defense. For this purpose, which is to say, to counsel both one and the other, they should be provided with gentlemanly knights, expert and wise in this art and science.

## XIV.

### IF A JUDICIAL COMBAT CAN PROPERLY BE FOUGHT ON A FEAST DAY, AND IF IT IS ACCEPTABLE IN LAW FOR A MAN IN ARMS TO SAVE HIMSELF. IF CLERICS CAN OR SHOULD TAKE PART IN SUCH COMBAT OR IN ARMS.[15]

Master, now tell me if combat, be it general or individual, can take place on a feast day, for it would appear not, in view of the fact that such holidays are decreed to serve God. It is scarcely service to God to take part in individual combat.

Without a doubt, friend, on this matter you will find in the Old Testament that God permitted the Children of Israel on any day that they were attacked to defend themselves; and so they went out to give battle. For this reason I say to you that through necessity one can fight on a holy day, in case one is attacked. Nevertheless, to set aside such a day for combat is not proper, even though today there are Christians of so little faith, who hold God and His saints in such little reverence, that they are scarcely true men-at-arms. But they see their profit in riding, scaling, or skirmishing as much on Easter or Good Friday as any other time, which should not be done if great necessity does not require it or unless great common profit may come of it.

I ask you, Master, whether we believe that a man-at-arms could save himself while exercising this office. This could be very doubtful, in view of the wrongs one is necessarily obliged to commit, and also because whoever dies while desiring to injure his neighbor is not following a good path. So it seems to me that such is the desire of the men-at-arms who go to war against their enemies, whom God wishes them to love; if they then die, how can they be saved?

---

15. *Tree of Battles* IV, l: "WHETHER IT IS LAWFUL TO GIVE BATTLE ON A FEAST DAY"; lii: "IF A KNIGHT HAPPEN TO DIE IN BATTLE DO WE SAY THAT HIS SOUL IS SAVED?" xxxv: "WHETHER PRIESTS OR CLERKS SHOULD ENGAGE IN WAR VOLUNTARILY."

Daughter, I reply to you in this matter with three conclusions: the first, that without doing what is ordered by decree, the knight or man-at-arms who dies in battle with the infidels for the fulfillment of the Christian faith, if he is repentant of his sins, goes like a martyr straight to Heaven; the second, that if a man-at-arms dies in a just battle to protect what is right, for the proper defense of the country or for public welfare, or to guard the freedom and good customs of the place, his soul is not endangered unless by some other sin, but rather has great merit, and perhaps the case and the conflict are such that he goes directly to Paradise. It is determined that he dies well who exposes his life to defend justice, the rights of his prince, his country and its people. But the third is different, which is to say that if a man dies in a battle that is against his conscience, that is, if he thought the cause was wrong, to take away and usurp the rights of others that did not belong to him, but which he could seize, or take possession of—certainly if such a one does not have time for great repentance—we cannot assume that he is on his way to salvation. So all those involved should take care, for they place body and soul in great peril if they allow themselves to uphold false causes. In this matter foreign soldiers should take especial care, for it is not to the credit of those who are not involved in the contention, but who are merely paid wages and can loot. Such people do even worse, and those are even less to be excused who, rightly or wrongly, are in danger of losing their possessions and lands through their sovereign lord, for they owe him their support, even if they know that he is in the wrong. They should undertake to discourage him and turn him aside from war.

I beg of you, tell me if clerics can or should, without being in error, go into battle.

I tell you that indeed our doctors raise many questions about this. According to them, these can take up defensive, but not offensive, arms, which is to say, in cases of defense but not of aggression. Others say that it is not proper for them to leave their usual places for any such reason, but is only permissible for them to defend the city, fortress, or manor where they find themselves, on the walls or at the windows, with stones and such weapons as they have, but without metal darts. Others say that they may use any weapons for their defense, and even without waiting to be attacked, for sometimes to save one's body it is necessary to go on the offensive and not wait to be attacked, for one can wait to the point that it is too late to resist the attack. Another opinion insists that on the order of the pope, who rules over all the clergy, a cleric can do either the one or the other. Others say that bishops and other ecclesiastical authorities who rule lands and administer justice, such as those appointed to certain places by the king of France, are expected to go to war with their lord if he wishes it, and especially the prelates who are peers of France, who can indeed say to men-at-arms whom they capture and imprison that they do not kill, for this would be improper. But unless someone should strike them, in no way is it suitable for them to strike others or to fight, for there is no bishop or any other prelate who cannot properly defend himself in case he is attacked first, even if he kills someone. But to say that churchmen should be armed to fight in battle is not proper, even if they are present.

## XV.
### CONCERNING COATS OF ARMS: IF ANYONE CAN TAKE THE ARMS HE WISHES.[16]

Master, certainly I see and recognize how great your knowledge is in solving problems and drawing proper conclusions. And truly, all the questions that cannot be ascribed to the importunity of my ignorance in raising various points, and what you have already told me about the rights of arms should be sufficient without bothering you further, would you please say another word to inform me about certain matters that depend on what has already been said concerning rights of coats of arms? After these questions, if they do not bother you too much, I will stop and conclude my book. Will you tell about the matter of coats of arms, banners and pennants that lords and gentlemen are accustomed to carry and have painted on their belongings, whether anyone can take them and carry them at his pleasure.

Dear friend, concerning these arms, which were first of all invented by the nobility so that in battle each nobleman could be recognized by his arms and his sign, I will reply to you. You should know that generally speaking, with regard to these arms, there are three distinctions. Certain ones were created and decreed in ancient times for a position of dignity, and not at all for individuals or their families, such as the eagle, designated for imperial dignity, to be worn by anyone who is an emperor. Likewise, there are other arms that stand for some office, as we would say of

16. *Tree of Battles* IV, cxxiv: "CONCERNING COATS OF ARMS AND PENNONS IN GENERAL"; cxxv: "CONCERNING THE ARMS OF ALL GENTLEMEN IN PARTICULAR."

the Capitoliers of Toulouse, who during their term of office bear certain arms designated for this office. As do the counsels of Montpellier; if assemblies of arms occur in that city, they bear the arms of their office, and if others should assume them, they would be taken away and would not be permitted. Also other places have their own arms.

Item, the second distinction in arms is the one that comes through the family succession of kings, dukes, counts, and other noblemen: the fleur de lys for the House of France, the leopard for England, and so for other kings. It is the same with less important lords, such as the ermine for the duke of Brittany, the silver cross for the count of Savoy, and so with other noblemen, be they dukes, counts, marquises, or others, wherever they may be from. Nobody should take the arms of these in particular. You can see that in this way one always recognizes the head of a lordship because he bears the basic arms while others of the house mark various differences, and so it is with other barons and all gentlemen. I assure you that it is proper and reasonable that nobody should copy anything from the coats of arms of such gentlemen, or bear anything like them, if it is not to show that in ancient times they had the same ancestor, or that some lord had given a band, quarter, or some part of his arms to him or his predecessors, for in this way he could bear them without lineage or anything else to prevent it. Some knights, barons, or other gentlemen have been given the arms they bear in the distant past, or the details in them by certain princes or great lords, so they should not be assumed by anyone else. But indeed, if a stranger should appear, who has the same coat of arms as those of some gentlemen in France, or elsewhere, and whose ancestors had likewise borne them in the past, it would harm nobody, and nothing could properly be demanded of him.

Item, the third difference concerns arms that everyday are assumed at pleasure, as it sometimes happens that Fortune at her pleasure raises men to higher estate. Sometimes the outstanding qualities of people in arms, learning, wisdom, or counsel, or with some other faculty, have allowed men to distinguish themselves, so that it is not a bad idea to create nobles through virtue. So these, when they see themselves risen in estate, take arms at will, choosing some device that pleases them—sometimes based on their surname, as a Pierre Maillart might take knots, or Jean de la Pie take magpies, and so on—and so in various ways any device that pleases them. Their descendants will always bear them, and in that way are arms decided upon and adopted in the first place.

## XVI.

### IN WHAT WAY A GENTLEMAN CAN CHALLENGE THE COAT OF ARMS OF ANOTHER AND IN WHAT WAY NOT.[17]

Now tell me this so that I may understand it: let us suppose that my father had taken for his arms a hind *gules* with three stars above it, or some other such thing; another man, in no way related to my father, had taken the same. Can both bear them without a problem?

I reply to you concerning this dispute that the authorities have made laws dealing with this question of a man or a family that has taken new arms, and has borne them publicly, after which another man of the town, or even of the country he comes from, has wished to take them and has done so. This is not right, for they should belong to the first one, nor should the lord of the place permit it if complaint is made to him, for such arms are and were invented to distinguish between people. But here there would be no distinction, but rather confusion, and it is for a prince and his courts not to allow one subject to shame another or wrong him. Doing such a thing, that is, taking arms that another has already adopted, would seem to be a matter of disdain caused by spite or malice in order to start a quarrel or trouble between them.

But now explain to me another difficulty that can arise: A gentleman from Germany comes to Paris to see the king and his court, where he finds another gentleman who bears the arms of his family. The German wishes to challenge this, but the Frenchman replies that he has not adopted them but that his family has borne them for a long time. The German says that his family is more ancient, so that they should be his. What is more, as the Frenchman contradicts and resists this, he replies that he will enter into a judicial combat about this dispute, and in fact makes a challenge before the king. I ask you if he has a proper complaint, and if according to the law of arms the king should judge the combat.

In good faith, friend, if such a combat were judged, it would not confer any right, and the reason is quite obvious. What harm or dishonor can come to the German if a Frenchman, who is not from his country or under the same lord or territory, bears arms similar to his? As his are also

17. *Tree of Battles* IV, cxxvi: "CONCERNING THE ARMS OF ALL GENTLEMEN, BOTH BARONS AND OTHERS"; cxxvii: "IS A GERMAN WHO FINDS A FRENCHMAN BEARING HIS ARMS FREE TO OFFER HIM WAGER OF BATTLE?" cxxviii: "THOSE WHO WEAR THE ARMS OF ANOTHER IN ORDER TO COMMIT A FRAUD MUST BE PUNISHED."

ancient, why should he challenge them or disturb their long possession? Certainly it is not a question of judging a combat or other right save that each one should retain his own rights. I do not say that the German would not have the right to challenge a knight or man-at-arms from France, or anywhere else, some man of ill repute, a great vagabond and pillager, should such a one, with intent to deceive, take the arms of the German knight in order to set fires in Burgundy or pilfer in Lorraine, and rob every man he meets on the way. Indeed the German's quarrel would be good and just. But a combat would not need to be judged against the evil man, but rather he should be hanged, for it would not be right for the German to risk his life against one who was so obviously a disreputable criminal. For this deception of taking the arms of someone else, one could be punished in several ways: if a soldier without any distinction of family, from Germany or elsewhere, who came to France to be hired by the king for his wars, was wearing the arms of some ancient family of his country that had the reputation of providing very good warriors, which arms he had taken in order to be more honored and have better pay and more distinction, certainly he would be punished, or should be, if this became known and the family raised objections. Likewise, anyone who counterfeited the signature of a clerk, or a merchant who counterfeited the trademark of another, should be punished. Otherwise, endless frauds would be committed.

## XVII.

### OF ARMS AND BANNERS AND OF THE MOST NOBLE COLORS OF COATS OF ARMS.[18]

As we have entered into this matter and you have reminded me of the banners and coats of arms of great noblemen, I will speak to you of the colors that are considered the most exalted and the richest, for there is a difference in nobility corresponding to what they represent according to their nature. Thus the masters of the laws of arms consider the color gold the richest. The reason is that gold by its nature is bright and shining and so comforting that doctors give it as a sovereign comfort to a man sickened unto death. Along with this it represents the sun, a very noble light, for the law says that nothing is more noble than light. The Scriptures say that for his excellence the just and saintly person shines like gold and the

---

18. *Tree of Battles* IV, cxxix: "OF THE COLOURS OF COATS OF ARMS."

sun. Because the properties of gold are compared in several respects to the sun, ancient laws ordered that no man but a prince should bear it. So gold is the most noble color.

Item, the second color is purple, which we call vermilion or red. It represents fire. Fire is by its nature the most shining after the sun and the most noble of all the four elements. For this nobility the laws ordered that nobody except princes should bear this vermilion, which signifies loftiness.

Item, the third noble color is azure, which by its figure represents air, which after fire is the most noble of the elements, for in its nature it is subtle and penetrating and capable of receiving luminous influences.

Item, the fourth color is white, in arms is silver, which color is the most noble of those that follow, for it is nearest to luminous bodies, and so signifies purity and innocence. The Scriptures say that the clothing in which Jesus Christ appeared to the apostles was white as snow. This color white stands for water, which is the most noble after air.

Item, the fifth color is black, called in coats of arms sable. It represents the earth and signifies grief, for it is farther from light than the others. For this reason it was established that as a sign of grief black clothing should be worn by the bereaved. As it is the lowest and most humble color, it was decreed that the religious should wear it.

Through these six colors are distinguished all coats of arms and banners by various devices borne by nobility since very ancient times.

So ends the fourth and last part of this book.

HERE ENDS THE BOOK OF THE DEEDS OF ARMS AND CHIVALRY.

# Index